choosing
the right
fish
for your
aquarium

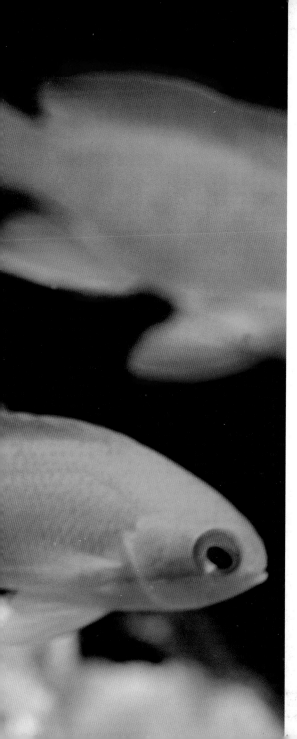

hamlyn

choosing
the right
fish
for your
aquarium

Jeremy Gay

First published in Great Britain in 2006 by
Hamlyn, a division of Octopus Publishing Group Ltd
2–4 Heron Quays, London E14 4JP

Distributed in the United States and Canada by
Sterling Publishing Co., Inc.
387 Park Avenue South,
New York, NY 10016–8810

ISBN-13: 978-0-600-61219-3
ISBN-10: 0-600-61219-8

A CIP catalogue record for this book is available
from the British Library

Printed and bound in China

10 9 8 7 6 5 4 3 2 1

Contents

Introduction

Fishkeeping is a tremendously absorbing and relaxing hobby. The calming effect an aquarium produces on the space and people around it has long been recognized, and scientific investigations have shown that simply watching fish can help to lower blood pressure and act as an antidote to the stresses of modern life. However, choosing the right fish – and looking after them properly – is not always straightforward.

Aimed at novice and experienced fishkeepers alike, this book provides an in-depth guide to the arts of purchasing and keeping aquarium fish. There is a vast choice of livestock available to the fishkeeper, but many species have exacting needs. If these are not properly met, there is a chance that the fish will not thrive in your aquarium. The detailed accounts of the different sizes and special requirements of fish that are given in this book will enable you to make informed choices and ensure that you succeed with any type of fish. Even if the idea of having to care for fish seems like a chore at first, a few trips to an aquatic store will soon make developing an aquarium an appealing prospect and tempt you to delve further into fishkeeping and all its associated delights.

In this book all the most popular fish are listed, together with some rarer and more unusual finds. The range of species should inspire even the most experienced fishkeepers to try something new, while those fresh to the hobby will have no trouble in picking out the fish that are best for beginners. The profiles are packed with information on everything to do with each species, including tips on their care and breeding.

The size that any species will reach is an essential consideration when choosing fish for an aquarium, and average adult sizes are quoted for all species listed in the book, including size differences between the sexes. The minimum size of tank necessary to keep each species is always recommended, and fish that grow excessively large come with a warning as they will outgrow all but the largest private aquariums and may be unsuitable for life in captivity. Species compatibility is also a major consideration as the aim is to enable all your fish to live together in harmony. The profiles suggest which species can be mixed together and which should be kept apart, and give a description of the general behavioural patterns of each fish together with advice on special needs.

Maps of the origins of the fish species are included in order to give you an extra insight into their natural habitats. You can refer to these maps, as well as the listings of countries of origin, if you want to create a biotope aquarium that mimics a particular environment. Also provided are descriptions of the habitats and practical suggestions for decor, to enable you to tailor the aquarium to the needs of the fish that will inhabit it.

This book was written by a fishkeeper for fishkeepers, with the aim of sharing the knowledge that will enable anybody, whatever their level of exerience, to enjoy a wonderful pastime and become the owner of a colourful tank full of life and movement. A thriving aquarium is within reach of everyone. Happy fishkeeping!

For a successful aquarium, the fish must live together in harmony.

Choosing fish

One of the hardest decisions that you will have to make is about the type of fish you would like to keep. Fish differ in levels of difficulty, and in their demands on your time and budget. Take these factors into consideration when you are choosing your fish, as you should avoid committing yourself to a style of fishkeeping that doesn't suit you. If in any doubt, tropical fish-keeping is a great area to start with as it includes both fish that are easy to keep and those that are more challenging.

Freshwater fish

Most of the fish kept today come from the warmer, tropical zones of the world. The tropical fish most often seen originate from South America, Africa and Southeast Asia, but they can come from anywhere that has a constant water temperature of 20–30°C (68–86°F). Their main habitats include mountain streams, rainforest streams, rivers, lakes and estuaries, and some species, such as killifish (see pages 178–85), even inhabit semi-permanent ponds that dry up in summer.

The coldwater fish that we keep originate from the temperate zones of the world, including Europe, North America and China.

The vast majority of fish available to aquarists is farmed commercially in Southeast Asia and the Far East, where favourable outdoor temperatures mean that hundreds of fish species can be bred outdoors in ponds.

Marine fish

The marine fish we keep occur naturally near to the coral reefs of the world, including those in the Red Sea and the western Atlantic, western and southern Pacific and the Indo-Pacific Oceans. Coral reefs occur only in areas where conditions such as sunlight, currents and water depth combine with temperature and the appropriate

Top: Killifish naturally inhabit semi-permanent pools that dry up in the summer.
Bottom: Clownfish are popular marine fish. They occur in and around coral reefs.

nutrients. The huge diversity of tropical marine species means that coral reefs produce such a wide range of foods for the fish that they have become extremely specialized, and some fish cannot survive without their preferred conditions.

Tropical fish tanks are suitable for people of all skill levels and will hold a number of different species.

Choices

Before you buy fish for your first aquarium, you must make a series of choices:

• What sort of fish do you wish to keep?
• How large a tank can you accommodate?
• Where will your tank be positioned?

Some types of fish – marine fish, for example – will make greater demands on your time and your budget, and the need to ensure the welfare of the fish will mean that you cannot cut corners. Keeping tropical and cold-water fish can be easier and less expensive, but some tropical freshwater species need extra care as well.

You can choose from the old favourite species or among new, exciting species and varieties, and they will all make different demands on you in terms of skill and time.

The key to successful fishkeeping is to enjoy it – it is, after all, a hobby and not your work – so the time and effort involved should never be seen as a chore. Fish-keeping should be, above all, relaxing, and as long as you are armed with the proper information you will be able to succeed. There has never been a better or more rewarding time to keep fish, as technology and our understanding of each species' requirements have never been better.

The perfect species is out there for you to keep, and your experience and knowledge will continue to grow throughout your fishkeeping life.

Biotopes

An aquarium biotope is a copy of a natural environment. It should contain species of fish and plants that live together in nature, and the decor in the tank should look similar to, and use the same materials as, the wild. Natural decor will make the scene look authentic and to scale, and can also be used to hide equipment such as heaters and filters. A well-furnished aquarium will show the fish off to their best.

An example of a biotope that is replicated frequently in aquariums is that of the Amazon River system. This is an environment where warm, soft acidic waters flow through areas of rainforest, collecting driftwood and leaves as they go. The leaves and wood stain the water the colour of tea, and not many plants grow in it because it is too acidic and devoid of nutrients. The river bottom is mainly made up of fine sand with lots of sunken wood.

The re-creation of biotopes in aquariums is a popular pastime and one that takes a certain amount of skill and research by the fishkeeper. There is no doubt that fish do better in conditions that are similar to those of their natural environment, and if you keep fish that use camouflage, such as some catfish, you will be able to observe just what that camouflage is for and how they use it. Experienced aquarists tend to steer towards biotope aquascaping and away from the garish, multi-coloured decor that they may have once chosen.

Imitating nature

The first step towards replicating nature in the aquarium is to find a suitably sized tank. The advantage of Amazonian biotopes is that there is a wide choice of small and larger species, so even a small tank can be made into a biotope. Second, the equipment must include a heater-thermostat, a filter and appropriate lighting. A power filter is perfect because it also provides flow in the water to replicate a river current.

The base of the tank should be covered with fine sand, and the tank should be decorated simply with

This natural-looking tropical aquarium looks great but is not biotope-correct. Most Amazonian rivers don't contain plants.

added to the filled tank, and the water temperature should be set to about 26°C (79°F), an average Amazonian temperature. And there you have it: an aquarium set up to replicate a natural aquatic environment, and one that suits the needs of the fish that would naturally live there.

There are lots of different biotopes, each one uniquely different, that can be replicated, including Lake Malawi, mangrove swamps, mountain streams, weedy backwaters and so on. A themed tank doesn't even have to represent a far-off location, but can be made to resemble the rivers near where you live. All you have to do is research the natural habitat of the fish species you want to keep.

Marine biotopes can be created by choosing fish and corals from the same region.

copious amounts of bogwood, which will look natural and will stain the water brown. The water used should be purified so that it is soft and contains no minerals, like that of the Amazon itself. No plants should be

Keeping captive fish

The benefits to the fish species kept in a biotope are that the water conditions and available decor could be crucial to their conditioning and even breeding. You might also be able to observe more natural behaviour. Biotopes will certainly appeal to the purists among you who want the best for their fish and to make their captive lives as comfortable and appealing as possible.

Biotopes

Fish for an Amazon Biotope

Cardinal Tetra (page 74)
Hockeystick Pencilfish (page 85)
Marbled Hatchetfish (page 83)
Midget Sucker Catfish (page 170)
Panda Corydoras (page 162)
Ram (page 147)
Rummy-nosed Tetra (page 67)

Fish for an Asian Biotope

Coolie Loach (page 91)
Dwarf Gourami (page 125)
Glass Catfish (page 177)
Harlequin (page 106)
Rosy Barb (page 93)
Rosy-line Shark (page 105)
Siamese Algae Eater (page 100)

Fish for a West African Biotope

Congo Tetra (page 76)
Jewel Cichlid (page 143)
Kribensis (page 152)
Leopard-spotted Climbing Perch (page 120)
Peter's Elephant-nose (page 191)
Upside-down Catfish (page 173)

Fish health

Like any other animal, fish can become ill. Some ailments are terminal, but others can be survived with some intervention on the part of the aquarist. Fish are rarely taken to the vet and instead are treated by the owner with a variety of medications available from aquatic stores. Useful tools that owners should invest in include testing kits and a quarantine tank for newly purchased or sick fish.

Keeping your fish healthy and disease-free should be a top priority, and there are a number of ways to achieve this. The most important is to avoid placing stress on the fish, which is often a key factor in the outbreak of disease. After poor water quality, disease is the second biggest killer of fish, and diseases can, in most cases, be directly linked to water quality.

Stress

Stress can be caused in a number of ways, including inadequate water quality, a sudden change in temperature, loud noise and vibration, bullying and transportation. The effect of stress, no matter how it has been caused, is to make the fish feel tired and under the weather. Just like humans, when fish are fatigued they are more susceptible to illness because their immune systems are compromised.

To avoid stress we must provide the right environment for our fish, which includes optimum water conditions with the right parameters of temperature, pH and hardness, an aquarium of adequate size, and the right decor to make them feel at home. Suitable tank mates will also help to keep stress levels low.

The raised scales on this fish indicate dropsy. This may have been caused by poor water quality.

Disease

If they have a lowered immune system fish can catch disease – there is some truth in the saying that a happy, healthy fish rarely becomes ill. Disease can take the form of a parasitic infection, such as whitespot, or a bacterial infection. Fish can also catch secondary bacterial infections and fungal infections if they already have a parasitic infection.

If your fish start to look ill and there are visible symptoms, such as white spots or fungus, it is a good idea to get a definite diagnosis from your usual aquatic store, because different ailments need different treatments. If the fish are clearly not well but have no definite symptoms – clamped fins or loss of appetite, for example – use a testing kit to check the water quality because it is often the case that if the water is improved the fish will get better.

Hospital tank

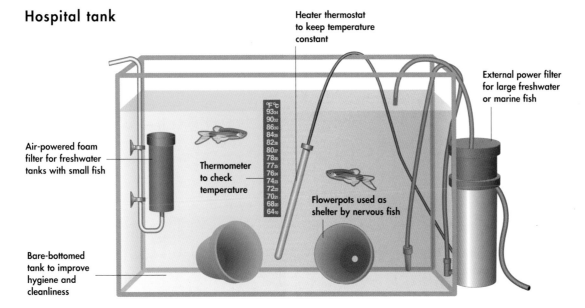

Heater thermostat to keep temperature constant

External power filter for large freshwater or marine fish

Air-powered foam filter for freshwater tanks with small fish

Thermometer to check temperature

°F °C
93 34
90 32
86 30
84 29
82 28
80 27
78 26
77 25
76 24
74 23
72 22
70 21
68 20
64 18

Flowerpots used as shelter by nervous fish

Bare-bottomed tank to improve hygiene and cleanliness

Fish health

Treatment

If disease is diagnosed, the fish must be treated quickly and effectively because most sick fish won't survive for more than a few days. All treatments will make reference to the volume of water in the aquarium, and you will have to add a quantity of medication according to tank size. Always remove any chemical media and turn off ultraviolet sterilizers if you have them, because these will render medications less effective.

Test the water before using medication because the fish will not get better if the water quality remains poor.

TIP

If any fish in the main tank is ill the whole tank should be treated, even if the other fish seem fine.

Quarantine

Once the main tank has been treated you can remove the affected fish to a hospital tank if you have one. Even if this is simply a bare tank with a mature filter, it will enable you to keep a closer eye on the fish. You will also find it easier to medicate and change the water, because spare aquariums are generally fairly small, 60 cm (24 in) long or less.

Newly acquired fish also should preferably be placed in a quarantine tank before they are put into the main tank, so that they can be isolated if they are harbouring any disease and so that the fish in the main aquarium will remain unaffected (see pages 26–7).

Fish that have been medicated should have shown no symptoms of disease for about two weeks before they are added to the main aquarium. Some aquatic stores quarantine their fish before offering them for sale, to ensure that they are disease-free, feeding properly and getting used to the aquarium. A store that quarantines fish before selling them is worth revisiting.

Water quality

We need to be able to manage the quality of the water our fish live in to keep them healthy. In the wild, bodies of water such as lakes, rivers and oceans are naturally pure and free of pollutants. Fish have evolved to suit their natural environment and will tolerate little else. Aquarium water should, therefore, be clean, well oxygenated and free of pollutants. The three main killers of fish in aquariums (ammonia, nitrite and nitrate) are pollutants generated by the production of waste; these will kill the fish if they are not dealt with and the water made safe by a filter.

Testing water

Water is tested to monitor its levels of ammonia, nitrite and nitrate, as well as to establish its pH and whether it is hard or soft. The pH and hardness of water vary in different parts of the world, and fish have evolved to suit a particular type of water. A high pH can make ammonia more toxic.

Testing the water reveals if the bacteria in the filters are working properly and whether it is safe to add fish. Testing nitrate levels can tell us if ammonia and nitrite are being converted by the bacteria, and will also give an indication as to whether the water should be changed, because nitrate levels should be kept low in this way. Water tests can also help determine why fish have become unhealthy.

Test the pH and choose fish that are appropriate for your water parameters.

The nitrogen cycle

When you keep fish you will find the biology lessons you had at school suddenly become useful. There is a phenomenon known as the nitrogen cycle, which is the method by which nature deals with fish waste. Fish produce toxic ammonia and CO_2 when they breathe and defecate. *Nitrosomonas* bacteria, which are present in water, consume these harmful bacteria and convert them into nitrites. In turn, the nitrites are converted by

TIP

Nine times out of ten failing water conditions are to blame for sick fish. Test the water with a kit, available from aquatic stores.

How the nitrogen cycle benefits fish and plants

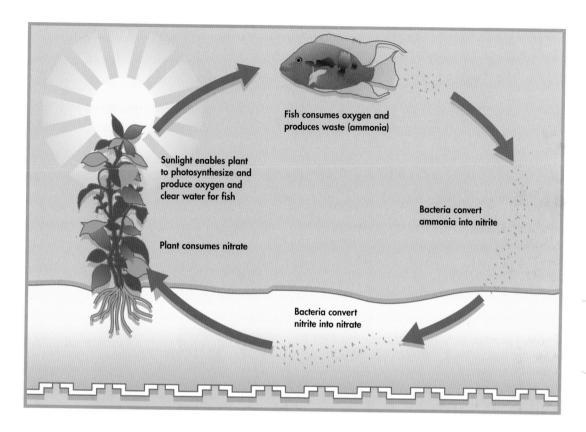

Fish consumes oxygen and produces waste (ammonia)

Sunlight enables plant to photosynthesize and produce oxygen and clear water for fish

Bacteria convert ammonia into nitrite

Plant consumes nitrate

Bacteria convert nitrite into nitrate

Water quality

another form of bacteria, *Nitrobacter*, into nitrates. Finally, live plants consume nitrates and CO_2 as they photosynthesize and produce oxygen for the fish, and the whole process starts again.

The nitrogen cycle also works to break down waste in aquariums. However, tanks are overstocked in comparison to natural waters, and many plants would be needed in proportion to the number of fish for the cycle to work unaided. Nature therefore requires a helping hand in the form of water changes, which will assist the invisible workings of the nitrogen cycle.

Maintaining water quality

In order to maintain good water quality, you should:
- Buy a good filter that contains media which will be colonized with bacteria and break down waste.
- Stock the tank slowly with fish, allowing the bacteria levels to catch up each time new fish are added.
- Do not overstock the tank, because the filter will not hold sufficient bacteria.
- Change part of the water regularly to flush away any excess nitrates.

Filtration

The filter is the life-support system of any aquarium. It breaks down the poisonous waste produced by the fish and can provide oxygen and water flow as well as physically clearing the water of debris. There are several types of filter, all with their own merits and drawbacks. Finding the right filter for your aquarium is vital for the success of the system and long-term health of your fish.

Types of filter

There are two main types of filter, air-powered models and power filters, and these can be further divided into external and internal systems.

Air-powered filters

Air-powered filters are powered by an air pump, which sits outside the aquarium. The pump pushes air down a narrow tube and into the aquarium, where it is connected to the filter. Air rises up a wider plastic tube, to the surface of the water, and as it does so water is pulled up the tube together with the air bubbles. An air-powered filter places media in front of the water that enters the unit, thereby filtering the water by physically trapping any particles in it. The particles are trapped by a sponge in a sponge filter or by gravel in an under-gravel filter. The gravel or sponge will also become colonized with bacteria, which will help to break down the waste that is trapped.

Power filters

Also known as canister filters, power filters are powered by electric water pumps. They generate more suction than air-powered filters so are more suitable for larger tanks and larger fish.

External power filter

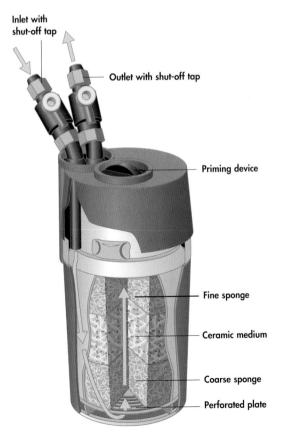

Inlet with shut-off tap

Outlet with shut-off tap

Priming device

Fine sponge

Ceramic medium

Coarse sponge

Perforated plate

Internal power filters are held inside the aquarium with rubber suckers, and are normally placed discreetly in a rear corner. They are usually available only with a sponge as medium, but it, too, will be colonized with bacteria over time.

Multi-stage internal filters may contain more types of media and additional – and larger – aeration devices, known as venturi devices, which blow air bubbles into the water.

External power filters are placed in a cabinet under the aquarium and are connected to the tank via two PVC hoses, an inlet hose and an outlet hose. They are powerful, pressurized units, which contain several types of media for the best all-round filtration. External power filters are more expensive than internal filters but are the best choice for larger aquariums, and although they are placed outside the tank they are quiet and rarely leak.

TIP

Without biological filtration to break down fish waste we would be unable to keep the range and number of fish we do today. To master the use of bacteria to break down waste is to master water quality, and that is a major part of being a successful aquarist.

Types of filtration

Aquarium water can be filtered in three different ways: mechanical, chemical and biological.

Mechanical filtration is the simplest system. It traps particles of waste as water flows through it. Examples of mechanical media that may be used are sponges and filter wool.

Chemical media absorb contaminants from the water, including dyes and medications. The most common chemical medium is carbon.

Biological filtration uses friendly bacteria to consume the ammonia produced by fish. The bacteria convert ammonia into nitrites and, finally, nitrates, which are less toxic to fish.

Top: Peat fibre can be used to alter conditions in the tank and to simulate Amazonian conditions. It is a chemical medium.
Bottom: Filter wool is a basic mechanical filter. It is cheap and should be thrown away when dirty.

Aquarium maintenance

Maintenance is an essential part of fishkeeping, and involves cleaning the tank to improve its appearance as well as changing the water to help keep the fish healthy and nuisance algae at bay. Tank maintenance will involve daily, weekly and monthly tasks. Some are essential, while others are for purely aesthetic purposes, but all aquariums need maintaining, and some types need more care than others.

Algae wiping

This task should be carried out at least weekly, and it is done chiefly to enhance the tank's appearance. Algae will grow on all the surfaces inside the aquarium, and when it grows on the front glass it will obscure the view of the fish.

Algae can be removed simply by scraping it off with an abrasive pad or an aquarium scraper containing a metal blade. Clean all inside surfaces of the tank at the same time. If left to build up, algae can become much more difficult to remove and wiping it off will be more of a chore. At this stage, use a scraper with a metal blade. If algae grows very quickly in the tank, ask yourself whether conditions should be changed. Excessive lighting and high phosphate levels could be to blame and these problems can be addressed easily.

TIP
Excessive algal growth in aquariums is a major reason why people give up fishkeeping. Removing algae regularly will leave your tank looking clean and your enthusiasm for your fish and fishkeeping undiminished.

Water changing

Changing the water is even more essential than algae wiping because it dilutes the build-up of pollutants, and if the water is not changed the health of the fish will be jeopardized.

The main reason for changing water is to lower levels of nitrates, which are produced by filter bacteria as they break down more harmful substances. If you have high nitrate levels, more algae will grow and newly added fish may be shocked and even die.

The best water to use is purified water, which does not contain much nitrate, phosphate or chlorine. The best purified water to use is reverse osmosis (RO) water, which is available from specialist aquatic stores. If you use tapwater, test the levels of nitrate in it first to make sure that they are low. If the tests show that the nitrate in the tapwater is higher than 20 parts per million, using it may increase levels of nitrate in the main tank.

As a rule, about 25 per cent of aquarium water should be changed every two weeks, and tests should show that nitrate levels are being controlled or lowered by that regime. If they are not, larger and more frequent water changes may be necessary.

When you are changing water use a siphon hose to suck it up and discharge it into a bucket. The bucket of old water can be poured down a drain. Always make sure that the new water you are going to add is at the

Use a siphon hose to remove aquarium water from the tank. This siphon hose is attached to a gravel-cleaning device.

same temperature as that in the main tank, and if you are using tapwater you must also use a treatment to remove chlorine and chloramines. To heat water place a heater-thermostat into a bucket of water for some time or add some water from a kettle.

Warning!
Water that is added too suddenly or too cold may cause an outbreak of whitespot in the aquarium.

Maintaining the filter

Filter media will need to be cleaned once a month or they may become blocked. Sponges should be cleaned in old tank water to remove dirt while keeping their bacteria intact. Ceramic media should also just be rinsed in old tank water and returned.

Chemical media, such as carbon, should be removed and replaced every four weeks, as they become saturated and may leach chemicals back into the water. The filter body should be cleaned and filter inlets freed of any debris. The impeller inside power filters should also be removed and cleaned periodically; as a dirty impeller may stop spinning and prevent the filter from working.

FAQ

Should I change all the water and strip down the tank periodically?

No. This will remove any good bacteria that are in the gravel and on the surfaces of the decor. If you strip down the filter and clean it under the tap you will sterilize it and lose all good bacteria, which is bad for the system and may lead to fish deaths.

Compatibility

As much as we would like them to, not all fish species will mix and live happily together in the same tank. Apart from the fact that fish from different areas need different types of water, even fish from the same natural habitat will not necessarily mix, as one species might be a predator and one species prey, or one might be territorial and hate the sight of its own kind. Fish that will mix with anything are called community fish; fish that won't mix with anything are called non-community fish.

Community and non-community fish

Community fish are well-behaved species that are not aggressive and can be combined with other species, even smaller ones, without eating them.

Non-community fish can be given that title for a number of reasons. They might grow too large for most aquariums, or they could be aggressive towards other fish. Some are territorial or very predatory. Some fish may be all of the above and will not cohabit with any other fish, meaning that they must be kept on their own for their entire lives.

Fancy goldfish should be kept together in a coldwater community aquarium.

Species aquariums

A species aquarium is one that is set up to contain just one species of fish, either in a group or as individual fish. The term can be used to describe a type of display aquarium or a tank that contains a group of piranhas, which cannot be mixed with other species but can be mixed with their own kind. It can also be used as a term to describe tanks for non-community fish that must be kept on their own.

Reef and non-reef

Marine fishkeeping also has community fish, such as clownfish (*Amphiprion* spp.), which can be mixed with most other fish, and non-community fish, such as lionfish (*Pterois* spp.), which will eat small fish.

There is another factor to take into account with marine fish and that is whether they can be mixed with corals and invertebrates in a reef tank. Most of the tropical marine fish kept in aquariums naturally inhabit coral reefs, but some fish from this environment actually feed off the reef itself. Take the clownfish again: it is a community fish that is also safe to keep with most types of invertebrates, including corals, so it can be termed reef friendly or reef safe. The lionfish is safe to keep with corals but will eat shrimps and other mobile invertebrates, so it is not reef safe and is non-reef compatible.

Freshwater fish

The following lists of community and non-community tropical freshwater fish have been compiled to include species from each of the fish families, to demonstrate the diversity of each group.

Community fish

Dwarf Gourami (page 125)
Florida Flag Fish (page 184)
Guppy (page 55)
Neon Tetra (page 75)
Panda Corydoras (page 162)
Platy (page 60)
Ram (page 147)
Rosy Barb (page 93)
Rummy-nose Tetra (page 67)
Threadfin Rainbowfish (page 114)
Twig Catfish (page 166)
Zebra Danio (page 99)

Non-community fish

Cigar Shark (page 104)
Edward's Mbuna (page 153)
Green Spotted Pufferfish (page 200)
Leopard-spotted Climbing Perch (page 120)
Oscar (page 139)
Pike-top Minnow (page 53)
Red Snakehead (page 188)
Red-bellied Piranha (page 78)
Red-tailed Catfish (page 175)
Silver Arowana (page 192)

Marine fish

As with tropical freshwater fish, marine fish can be divided into those that will mix with all other fish and those that will not. Examples of popular community and non-community species are listed below.

Community fish

Bangaii Cardinal (page 209)
Chalk Bass (page 249)
Common Clownfish (page 238)
Coral Beauty (page 235)
Firefish (page 230)
Green Chromis (page 239)
Lyretail Anthias (page 248)
Mandarin (page 212)
Neon Goby (page 222)
Royal Gramma (page 224)
Yellow Tang (page 207)

Non-community fish

Domino Damselfish (page 240)
Frogfish (page 208)
Leaf Fish (page 246)
Long-snout Seahorse (page 252)
Panther Grouper (page 247)
Picasso Triggerfish (page 210)
Porcupine Pufferfish (page 219)
Snowflake Moray Eel (page 231)
Volitans Lionfish (page 245)

Compatibility

How many fish?

If you have too many fish in your aquarium, the health of all of them will be in jeopardy because of the extra demand on oxygen and filter bacteria, and the spread of disease. The number of fish you will be able to keep successfully depends on the type of fish you choose: tropical, coldwater or marine. Tropical freshwater fish can be stocked at the greatest fish to tank space ratio, and marine fish need the most room. Coldwater fish are somewhere in between, requiring space to grow but remaining reasonably hardy.

Freshwater and coldwater fish

Tropical freshwater and coldwater fish need to be stocked in different ratios, even if similarly sized fish are placed in the same size tanks. This is because different fish have different oxygen requirements. Cold water holds more dissolved oxygen than warm water does, and the inhabitants of tropical waters have adapted to this, as have coldwater fish such as goldfish.

The water temperature also affects a fish's metabolism. A fish's bodily processes increase when it is warmer, including its breathing rate, so a coldwater fish placed in warm water will have an increased breathing rate, increasing the amount of oxygen it will need.

Tropical freshwater fish can be stocked in a tank at the ratio of 2.5 cm (1 in) of fish to every 30 sq cm (12 sq in) of tank surface area. According to that equation, a tank 60 cm (24 in) long by 30 cm (12 in) wide will have a surface area of 1,800 sq cm (288 sq in) – that is, length x width = surface area. When divided by 30 cm (12 in) the tank will hold 60 cm (24 in) of fish, which equates to 15–20 small fish when fully grown. Tail length does not count: fish length should be calculated from the tip of the nose to the base of the tail. This is known as the standard length.

To calculate how many coldwater fish the same aquarium will hold, take the same surface area and divide it by 60 cm (24 in). As the coldwater stocking ratio is 2.5 cm (1 in) of fish per 60 sq cm (24 sq in) of surface area, the result is that the tank can hold 30 cm (12 in) of fish – 1,800 ÷ 60 = 30 cm (288 ÷ 24 = 12 in). With an average size of 8 cm (3 in) for sub-adult goldfish, the same aquarium will hold only four goldfish safely, without being overstocked.

These equations are only guidelines and need to be used rationally. For instance, if the 60-cm (24-in) tropical aquarium will hold 60 cm (24 in) of tropical fish, that certainly does not mean two 30-cm (12-in) Oscars, or 60 1-cm (½-in) lone Neon tetras. Use the equation to give you a rough idea. It is always better to understock. Allow for growth of all the species that you keep and use the average adult size stated in the profiles. Modern fishkeeping methods do allow for occasional overstocking but filtration, water changes and feeding must also be increased.

TIP

Fancy goldfish have heavy, rounded bodies with a much larger mass than standard goldfish. Take this into account when you are stocking and feeding the fish and choosing a filtration system.

Marine fish

Marine fish are the most sensitive type of fish, and stocking levels should be lower than for coldwater and freshwater tropical fish. Marine stocking levels are calculated not by fish length per surface area but by volume, as most marine tanks have a high water turnover and lots of filtration, which means that there is more dissolved oxygen than would normally diffuse through still water.

In fish-only aquariums the stocking ratio is 2.5 cm (1 in) of fish per 9 litres (2 gallons) of water. For reef aquariums containing sensitive invertebrates the ratio is a tiny 2.5 cm (1 in) of fish per 18 litres (4 gallons) of water. This means that a 60-cm (24-in) tank, which holds about 68 litres (15 gallons), will accommodate only 18 cm (7 in) of fish as a fish-only tank and less than 10 cm (4 in) of fish as a reef tank. This equates to just one clownfish (*Amphiprion* sp.) in a reef aquarium of that size and demonstrates just why marine aquariums need to be large.

Recently Nano reefs have become popular. They consist of marine tanks of less than 45 litres (10 gallons) in capacity. Although suitable for small invertebrates, they are less stable than larger tanks and can suffer from high temperatures and rapidly changing water parameters. It is not advisable to add marine fish to these aquariums.

FAQ

How many invertebrates can be accommodated in a marine aquarium?

Compared with fish, invertebrates produce very little waste, and crabs and shrimps actually clean the tank. Invertebrates are therefore not counted when it comes to fish stocking and, within reason, you can have as many as you want.

Calculating cubic volume

An aquarium of 60 x 38 x 30 cm (24 x 15 x 12 in), showing a cube (30 x 30 x 30 cm/12 x 12 x 12 in) within it.

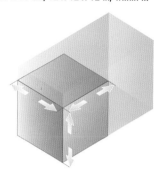

Calculating surface area

The surface area of the aquarium is calculated by multiplying the length by the width.

Calculating volume

The volume of the aquarium is calculated by multiplying the surface area by the height.

How many fish?

Buying fish

When you have set up your tank and it has had time to mature (develop beneficial bacteria), the fun finally begins and you can buy your first fish. Buying fish should not be rushed, and you should draw up a list of species that you most want to keep and that are best suited to your tank before you even walk into the aquatic store. Once inside the store you will be surrounded by hundreds of colourful and tempting fish. You may well be able to keep the majority of them, but not all the fish you will see are suitable for new tanks and only a few can be bought in one go.

New tanks

If your tank is newly set up your choice of suitable first fish is quite a narrow one. Take this book as a reference and ask the assistant lots of questions, too.

Explain that your tank is newly set up and that you would like to keep your first fish. Note down the results of your water tests for the assistant to look at or take a sample of the tank water for the assistant to test to make sure that everything is all right. If it is, take your time and don't make any impulse buys.

If you really don't want to keep the recommended species but are desperately interested in looking after the miscellaneous fish that are sometimes described as 'oddballs' (pages 186–93), it is still a good idea to buy some small, hardy fish to put in a new tank. You can use these to generate waste to mature the tank, instead of putting one big fish in an immature tank and then experiencing problems. The retailer may agree to take the small fish back in a few weeks in part exchange for the bigger purchase. Alternatively, you will just have to be patient and mature the tank with no fish for four weeks instead of one week, letting beneficial bacteria build up over that period.

A tank must be matured properly if it is to support a number of fish.

Before you buy

Before you even walk into the aquatic store you should run through a checklist of your aquarium's parameters to make sure that it is ready to take fish. You should always check the following before making any purchases:
- The filter and heater are plugged in and are functioning normally.
- The temperature of the water is correct for the species you have chosen.
- The pH and hardness are correct for the species you have chosen.

- Ammonia and nitrite levels are both reading zero.
- Nitrates are at acceptably low levels.
- The aquarium is suitably mature.

When it comes to the fish you will be purchasing, check that you are aware of the following facts about them:

- How large they grow.
- What they eat.
- If they are compatible with each other.
- If they are compatible with other fish.

What to look for

To the untrained eye all fish in a retailer's tanks may look fine, but the experienced aquarist will be looking for signs of poor health and illness. Look for the following:

- The fins and eyes of all fish should be intact and all scales should be present.
- There should be no sores or fungus on the bodies.
- Tiny white spots could be a sign of whitespot, a potentially fatal disease.
- The fish should swim easily and freely, not with clamped fins nor at an angle.

Make sure, too, that fish are not hanging just below the surface or sitting motionless on the bottom, unless they

Acclimatize newly purchased fish by adding some aquarium water to the polythene bag.

Ten questions to ask when buying a fish

1   How long have the fish been in the shop?
2   Have they been quarantined?
3   Are they wild caught or tank bred?
4   Are they suitable for a new tank?
5   How long will they be able to survive comfortably in a polythene bag?
6   What are they being fed?
7   Will they accept other foods?
8   Will they be compatible with the other fish on your list?
9   How much are they?
10 Is there a discount for buying a small group?

are adapted to live like that – as is the case with the surface-dwelling Marbled Hatchetfish (*Carnegiella strigata strigata*; page 83) and the shy and sedate Golden Nugget Plec (*Baryancistrus* sp.; page 165), which should be on the bottom and should not be bought if it is at the surface.

Acclimatizing fish

Once they are in the polythene bag your fish should be taken home as quickly as possible.

When you get home, turn off the aquarium lights and float the unopened bag on the surface for about 20 minutes to equalize the temperature in the bag with that of the main tank. Next, cut off the knot and roll down the sides of the bag until it floats on the surface. Introduce some aquarium water, a little at a time, over the next few minutes then catch the fish in a small net and place them in the tank. Discard the bag water and watch the fish closely over the next few days.

Quarantine

All new fish should be quarantined in a separate tank when you get them home. Retailers do all they can to ensure that only healthy fish leave the store, but, like humans, fish can carry a number of potential ailments that their immune systems cannot always hold at bay. In times of stress – such as when the fish are shipped over long distances, or when they are overcrowded, underfed or subjected to the wrong water conditions – fish can become tired, and that is when illness can strike.

Why quarantine?

New fish should be quarantined so that they do not spread any infection to the fish already in the aquarium. If this is the first fish that you have purchased, the main tank can serve as the quarantine tank, but bear in mind that it will not, for several reasons, be as effective as a special tank if a fish becomes ill and you need to use medications. In the first place, medications can be made less effective by an efficient filter, and a chemical filter will intefere most strongly with the treatment. Bright light can also render medications less effective.

The quarantine tank

The tank itself can be simple, and it doesn't matter if it is old and scratched as long as it holds water. The purpose of a quarantine tank is, above everything else, to be functional, so it does not have to be particularly aesthetically pleasing.

The filtration can be quite basic, too. You will need an air-powered sponge filter for tropical and coldwater tanks and a power filter for marine tanks. Before you add any fish the filters should be matured by the use of a bacterial culture; alternatively, simply place the filter in another, mature tank for a few weeks so that it naturally gains bacteria.

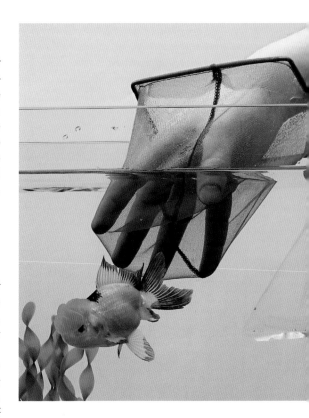

You may not be able to see it, but a new fish may be carrying a disease. Quarantine new purchases to avoid infecting your other fish.

A heater-thermostat should be placed in tropical and marine quarantine tanks, with the temperature set to the optimum for the species you wish to hold there. The bottom of the tank should be bare as the lifecycle of some parasites involves a larval stage in gravel; removing the substrate will allow you to watch the tank bottom and prevent such development. Lighting should be subdued because the clean, bare tank may make the fish nervous; ill fish will do better in dimmer lighting conditions as lowered stress may aid recovery.

TIP

Filters containing chemical media, such as carbon, should not be used in a quarantine tank, as they would soak up any medications, rendering them ineffective.

Water conditions

The water conditions should be optimum for the species that will be held in the tank, but there are two other factors to consider.

First, remember that your new purchase may have been in quite different water conditions. If it all possible, begin by matching your water conditions to those in the fish bag and then bring them into line with the optimum for the fish over a few days. Second, if the water conditions in your main tank are different from those in the quarantine tank, the conditions in the quarantine tank should be matched, again over a few days, to those in the main tank. This will involve less stress to your fish than would large water changes or changing the parameters of the water in the main tank.

This cichlid has developed an ulcer on its side. Effective quarantine will prevent other fish from being infected.

Fish profiles

The purpose of profiling species size and requirements is to give you, the fishkeeper, an insight into what you are about to purchase and into whether a particular fish will be suitable for your tank. As you will discover, fish species are incredibly varied in size, water requirements, behaviour and feeding, and many species will not mix. Each of the fish illustrated in this book has been profiled to provide a useful reference for its captive care.

Aquatic stores

Your local aquatic store will be your point of purchase for livestock. A good store will keep hundreds of species for coldwater, tropical and marine aquariums. The profiles list all the popular species in the three categories, of which the tropical species are the most numerous.

Size

The adult size given in each profile will highlight the fact that nearly all fish available in stores are juveniles and may be much smaller than their eventual mature size. As well as the potential size of the fish, the profiles also include the size of tank that is necessary to keep them in the long term. The adult size of fish may vary, and the size listed can be considered an average. The tank sizes given are the minimum in which the species should be kept.

Ease of keeping

Each species profile includes an indication of the ease of keeping of that particular fish, which may be easy, moderate or difficult.

An easy-to-keep species can almost certainly be recommended for fishkeepers of all levels of experience. Fish described as moderate should be able to be kept healthy and happy by most fishkeepers apart from complete novices. Difficult species should be avoided by all but experienced aquarists, and some of these may raise ethical questions about whether they should be offered for sale at all.

Species compatibility

As we have already seen (pages 20–21), not all fish can be kept with other fish or even with other members of the same species. The compatibility levels indicated in the profiles are given as low, moderate and high for each species. High compatibility fish are excellent community fish, which can be mixed with members of their own species and sex in the same tank and not cause problems. They can also be mixed with fish of all other species and size, again without causing any problems.

Low compatibility may mean that the species cannot be combined with any other species or, in some cases, even with members of their own species.

Moderate compatibility indicates that the fish can be kept with most species in most circumstances, but if they possess antisocial characteristics – fin nipping, for example – this is described and advice included on dealing with it.

Jargon buster

Most terms associated with fishkeeping are self-explanatory, but some technical terms are defined below for convenience.

Andropodium A modified anal fin that is used by the male fish in reproduction.

Aquascape An arrangement of aquatic decoration inside an aquarium.

Biotope A tank set up to contain fish and decoration that naturally occur together in the wild.

Brackish Water that contains some marine salt but is not as salty as seawater. Brackish water occurs naturally where freshwater rivers meet the sea.

Caudal fin A fish's tail fin.

Copepod Minute planktonic or parasitic crustacean.

Dither fish Plain, shoaling fish that are used to attract the attention of over-attentive male cichlids. This lessens the harassment of female cichlids in the same tank.

Dorsal fin The fin on a fish's back that is nearest to the head.

Flank The side of a fish's body.

Gonopodium A modified anal fin found on male livebearing fish. It is used to deliver sperm and inseminate the female fish.

Hard water Water that is high in dissolved minerals causing it to have a high pH reading and high hardness.

Live rock Rock for marine aquariums in which minute invertebrate and plant organisms live.

Nuchal hump The swelling that occurs on the foreheads of mature male cichlids.

Oddball A term sometimes given to strange-looking fish that are chosen for their habits or behaviour rather than for their good looks. Oddballs are often non-community fish because they may be predatory.

Pelagic Living in the deep or open sea.

Protein skimmer A device included in a marine tank to remove waste products from the water.

Quarantine A period of isolation in a spare tank undergone by newly purchased fish. Quarantine may help to reveal any signs of disease that could be spread to the fish in the main tank.

Soft water Water that is low in dissolved minerals and that has a low pH and low hardness.

Substrate The material, such as sand and gravel, used to cover the base of the tank.

Fish profiles

Coldwater fish

The best known and most popular of coldwater fish are goldfish, which have been kept for centuries in aquariums or ponds – and sometimes even bowls – for ornamental purposes. They were first kept for pleasure in the Far East. The red coloration was bred for first, followed by variations on fin type and body shape to create the fancy goldfish varieties that are widely available today.

Goldfish varieties

Collectively known as fancies, the short-bodied, twin-tail varieties of goldfish are popular fish for unheated tanks. They have not been genetically modified in a modern sense. Instead, the technique of line-breeding was developed to enhance a certain characteristic that one in a thousand youngsters might show. Breeders then had to find another fish with the same characteristic and then mate the two together, so that the subsequent off-spring showed the desired characteristic. Unfortunately, a certain amount of inbreeding has taken place to develop some traits, and, hundreds of generations on, fancy goldfish are much weaker than their relative, the Common Goldfish.

Fancy goldfish are slow swimmers, and they tire easily because of their long, flowing fins. They also tend to suffer from buoyancy problems, because the swim bladder can be disfigured by the bent spine. Care must be taken to keep fancies only with other fancies and to decorate the aquarium to suit their needs, by providing open water and space for these fish to be able to turn around. They can become stuck between obstacles and exhaust themselves trying to get out.

There are about ten named varieties of fancy goldfish, and breeders work hard to produce the perfect specimen. Show-quality fancies can be very expensive, and the best may never even leave the fish farm, having pride of place in the breeder's own display tank. They are long lived – 20 years or more – and can grow large. Small tanks and bowls will stunt their growth and be detrimental to their long-term health, so be prepared to upgrade the tank size as they grow, and you will watch them prosper.

Problems with the swim bladder can cause fancies difficulties while they are swimming, and occasionally fish turn upside down. It is saddening to see and the fish can become distressed by its ordeal. Lowering the level of water or increasing the temperature sometimes helps.

Temperate species such as minnows can be kept in unheated aquariums instead of goldfish.

Koi Carp grow far too large for most aquariums and are better off in a pond.

FAQ

Can I keep goldfish in a bowl?

Although goldfish used to be kept in bowls, this practice now always ends in the premature death of the fish. Goldfish aren't as hardy as they once were, and tapwater contains more chemicals. Bowls will not take filters because of their shape, and fish should not be kept in their own waste. Keep your goldfish in a suitable filtered aquarium.

Other species

The White Cloud Mountain Minnow (*Tanichthys albonubes*; page 43) is a tiny fish that is best kept away from the mouths of goldfish. It is a pleasant species and can come well within budget if you are setting up a simple, unheated aquarium for small children. They may also breed.

The Borneo Sucker (*Gastromyzon borneensis*; page 44) is a more demanding species, which needs a well-oxygenated, mature aquarium and the right foods. The Weather Loach (*Misgurnus anguillicaudatus*; page 45) is a hardy, gregarious species that can be mixed with single-tail goldfish.

Koi Carp (*Cyprinus carpio*; page 42) carry a size warning: although they are well-behaved and colourful fish, they can grow to 1.2 m (4 ft) and are wholly unsuitable for most aquariums.

Common Goldfish

hardy • colourful • active • easy to keep

SCIENTIFIC NAME: *Carassius auratus* • FAMILY: Cyprinidae • ORIGIN: China • NATURAL HABITAT: Ponds and slow-moving rivers • AVERAGE ADULT SIZE: • 30 cm (12 in) • COLOURS: Red, orange, yellow, brown, black

SEXUAL DIFFERENCES: Females have fuller bodies; males develop tubercles at spawning time • REPRODUCTION: Egg-scatterer • BREEDING POTENTIAL: Moderate • TANK LEVEL: Middle • FOOD: Dry, frozen and live foods

PLANT FRIENDLY: No • SPECIAL NEEDS: Swimming space • EASE OF KEEPING: Easy

Coldwater fish

Aquarium needs

MINIMUM TANK SIZE: 90 cm (36 in)

TEMPERATURE: 4–20°C (39–68°F)

PH: 7–8

WATER HARDNESS: Neutral to hard and alkaline

COMPATIBILITY WITH OTHER FISH: Good

The Common Goldfish is the first fish to be kept by millions of people around the world, but it has been abused over the years, even being kept in small bowls.

To keep this fish healthy, set up as large a tank as possible and install a power filter to clean and aerate the water. The substrate should be small, rounded pea gravel, which the fish can take into its mouth without getting stuck.

When you are buying look for fish that have short fins and are well built. They should be orange, red or yellow; any black is usually juvenile coloration, which will disappear as they mature.

Goldfish will eat live plants, so use artificial plants as decoration or omit them from the aquarium altogether. Other decoration should consist of natural products, such as rocks and bogwood, or ornaments, such as bridges and castles. They do not use the aquarium decor for retreats or breeding sites, so just make sure that anything that is included in the tank is not so sharp that the fish injure themselves while they are swimming about.

These hardy fish are fine at room temperature and can survive outside in a pond, even in icy conditions.

Shubunkin

hardy • colourful • active • easy to keep

SCIENTIFIC NAME: *Carassius auratus* var. • FAMILY: Cyprinidae • ORIGIN: China • NATURAL HABITAT: Ponds and slow-moving rivers • AVERAGE ADULT SIZE: 30 cm (12 in) • COLOURS: Blue, red and white with black and gold spots • SEXUAL DIFFERENCES: Females have fuller bodies; males develop tubercles on their pectoral fins and heads at spawning time • REPRODUCTION: Egg-scatterer • BREEDING POTENTIAL: Moderate • TANK LEVEL: Middle FOOD: Dry, frozen and live foods • PLANT FRIENDLY: No • SPECIAL NEEDS: Swimming space • EASE OF KEEPING: Easy

Aquarium needs

MINIMUM TANK SIZE: 90 cm (36 in)
TEMPERATURE: 4–20°C (39–68°F)
PH: 7–8
WATER HARDNESS: Neutral to hard and alkaline
COMPATIBILITY WITH OTHER FISH: Good

Shubunkins are nacreous (mother-of-pearl) or calico (matt) forms of goldfish. The pattern is made up of black and gold spots on a blue, red and white body. They can be partially or fully scaled, with a long or short tail. The standard long-tailed Shubunkin is known as a Bristol Shubunkin; the short-tailed, stockier fish is a London Shubunkin. A fish with a narrow caudal fin is an American Shubunkin. Nearly all Shubunkins available in aquatic stores are calico Comets and not true Shubunkins. These are available only through national societies.

Shubunkins can be kept in the same way as Common Goldfish and mixed with them in indoor aquariums or outdoor ponds. They are long lived and can attain a length of 30 cm (12 in), so if they do grow larger than about 15 cm (6 in), a larger tank will be necessary to keep them in the long term.

They eat live plants, so don't add these to the aquarium. Offer a variety of foods, including sticks, pellets and frozen foods. The water should be well filtered with a proportion changed regularly.

Coldwater fish

Comet

hardy • active • colourful • easy to keep

SCIENTIFIC NAME: *Carassius auratus* var. • FAMILY: Cyprinidae • ORIGIN: China • NATURAL HABITAT: Ponds and slow-moving rivers • AVERAGE ADULT SIZE: 30 cm (12 in) • COLOURS: Red, orange, white, red and white
SEXUAL DIFFERENCES: Females have fuller bodies; males develop breeding tubercles on their heads and pectoral fins at spawning time • REPRODUCTION: Egg-scatterer • BREEDING POTENTIAL: Moderate • TANK LEVEL: Middle
FOOD: Dry, frozen and live foods • PLANT FRIENDLY: No • SPECIAL NEEDS: Swimming space • EASE OF KEEPING: Easy

Aquarium needs

MINIMUM TANK SIZE: 90 cm (36 in)
TEMPERATURE: 4–20°C (39–68°F)
PH: 7–8
WATER HARDNESS: Neutral to hard and alkaline
COMPATIBILITY WITH OTHER FISH: Good

Comets are goldfish with long, pointed tails. If the tails are very long and hanging downwards they are called veil tails. Comets account for the bulk of world goldfish sales and are frequently sold as Common Goldfish. Their bodies are more slender than those of Common Goldfish and are seen in red and orange forms as well as a red and white form, the Sarasa Comet – a popular pond fish.

All forms should be treated like Common Goldfish. Provide them with spacious accommodation and well-filtered, well-maintained water. Offer a variety of foods – healthy fish will readily accept all foods several times a day.

They will eat live plants, which should not be included in the aquarium but can be used to catch the sticky eggs if the fish spawn. When they are sexually mature, female Comets, like other goldfish varieties, develop fuller bodies and can look lop-sided when viewed from above. Males develop white spots (tubercles) on the gill covers and forehead and white ridges on the pectoral fins.

Small Comets deserve good water quality and plenty of space to swim, like adults, and they should not be kept in bowls.

Black Telescope Eye

poor swimmer • unusual looking • sensitive • popular

SCIENTIFIC NAME: *Carassius auratus* var. • FAMILY: Cyprinidae • ORIGIN: China • NATURAL HABITAT: Ponds and slow-moving rivers; this variety would not survive in the wild • AVERAGE ADULT SIZE: 15 cm (6 in) • COLOURS: Black, bronze, red, calico • SEXUAL DIFFERENCES: Females have fuller bodies; males develop tubercles on their heads and ridges on their pectoral fins at spawning time • REPRODUCTION: Egg-scatterer • BREEDING POTENTIAL: Moderate • TANK LEVEL: Middle • FOOD: Dry, frozen and live foods • PLANT FRIENDLY: No • SPECIAL NEEDS: No sharp objects • EASE OF KEEPING: Moderate

Aquarium needs

MINIMUM TANK SIZE: 60 cm (24 in)
TEMPERATURE: 10–20°C (50–68°F)
PH: 7–8
WATER HARDNESS: Neutral to hard and alkaline
COMPATIBILITY WITH OTHER FISH: Moderate

Black Telescope Eyes are fancy goldfish that have been bred to have protruding eyes. They have recently become available in red and calico forms, and there are fan tail or veil tail forms. There is also a variety with even larger eyes, called Dragon Eye. The black coloration should be matt black on a nice specimen, and not shiny. Older fish can turn a bronze colour from the belly region upwards and can develop eye problems, including cataracts.

Their breeding has made them sensitive, and their fat bodies make them slow swimmers. They require well-filtered, well-maintained and well-aerated water, and they should be mixed only with other fancy goldfish that have a similar body shape and swimming action. This way, no individual will be out-competed at feeding time by faster-swimming fish.

Tank decoration should be rounded so as not to cause damage, and live plants, which will be eaten, should be omitted. Large fish become deep bodied, and they need a varied diet to maintain their coloration and condition. Pellet foods should replace flake as they grow.

Newly purchased fish should be checked for signs of fish louse and treated if necessary.

Oranda

deep bodied • unusual looking • cute • sensitive

SCIENTIFIC NAME: *Carassius auratus* var. • FAMILY: Cyprinidae • ORIGIN: China • NATURAL HABITAT: Ponds and slow-moving rivers; this variety would not survive in the wild • AVERAGE ADULT SIZE: 15 cm (6 in) • COLOURS: Red, black, brown, blue, red and white, orange, calico • SEXUAL DIFFERENCES: Females have fuller bodies; males develop tubercles on their heads and ridges on their pectoral fins at spawning time • REPRODUCTION: Egg-scatterer • BREEDING POTENTIAL: Moderate • TANK LEVEL: Middle • FOOD: Dry, frozen and live foods PLANT FRIENDLY: No • SPECIAL NEEDS: Swimming space; no sharp objects • EASE OF KEEPING: Moderate

Coldwater fish

Aquarium needs

MINIMUM TANK SIZE: 60 cm (24 in)
TEMPERATURE: 10–20°C (50–68°F)
PH: 7–8
WATER HARDNESS: Neutral to hard and alkaline
COMPATIBILITY WITH OTHER FISH: Moderate

Orandas are deep-bodied fancy goldfish that have been bred to develop a fleshy growth or 'hood' as they mature. The hood should be large and well spread over the head without obscuring the eyes. The best, show-quality Orandas are worth a lot of money because it takes years of selective breeding to develop a good specimen. The largest fish now often exceed their previous recorded maximum growth.

They have fan tails and are slow swimmers. There are several colour strains available, including red, red and white, calico, chocolate, blue and black. A red-cap form has a red hood on a white body.

The water must be well filtered and aerated. Decoration should be kept to a minimum so that the fish do not collide with it. The substrate should consist of fine, rounded gravel.

Offer a range of foods to obtain the best condition, including the specially formulated fancy goldfish foods available from stores.

Orandas should be mixed only with other fancy goldfish to avoid being out-competed. They are not hardy enough to be kept outdoors.

Ryukin

deep bodied • colourful • popular • sensitive

SCIENTIFIC NAME: *Carassius auratus* var. • FAMILY: Cyprinidae • OTHER NAME: Fan Tail • ORIGIN: China
NATURAL HABITAT: Ponds and slow-moving rivers; this variety would not survive in the wild • AVERAGE ADULT SIZE:
15 cm (6 in) • COLOURS: Red, white, orange, calico, red and white • SEXUAL DIFFERENCES: Females have fuller
bodies; males develop tubercles on their heads and ridges on their pectoral fins at spawning time
REPRODUCTION: Egg-scatterer • BREEDING POTENTIAL: Moderate • TANK LEVEL: Middle • FOOD: Dry, frozen and live
foods • PLANT FRIENDLY: No • SPECIAL NEEDS: Swimming space • EASE OF KEEPING: Moderate

Aquarium needs

MINIMUM TANK SIZE: 60 cm (24 in)
TEMPERATURE: 10–20°C (50–68°F)
PH: 7–8
WATER HARDNESS: Neutral to hard and alkaline
COMPATIBILITY WITH OTHER FISH: Moderate

Ryukin have the deepest bodies of all fancy goldfish strains. The very deep body can cause buoyancy problems and affect the fish's swimming behaviour, as the swim bladder inside the fish can become bent against the spine. The only way to remedy this is to provide excellent water conditions and a wide range of foods, including more frozen than dry foods, which are full of air and can make the problem worse.

On the plus side, a good Ryukin is a wonderful fish, and large specimens have real presence in a tank. They can be distinguished from Orandas because they have a more angled face and mature fish do not have hoods.

They are best kept with other fancy goldfish in a sparsely decorated tank with plenty of aeration. Frequent water changes should be carried out, and the fish should be well fed. They are available in red, red and white and calico varieties. Female fish are fuller in the body; males develop tubercles on the gill cover and forehead and ridges on the pectoral fins at spawning time.

Coldwater fish

Ranchu

deep bodied • cute • short tailed • sensitive

SCIENTIFIC NAME: *Carassius auratus* var. • FAMILY: Cyprinidae • OTHER NAME: Lionhead • ORIGIN: China
NATURAL HABITAT: Ponds and slow-moving rivers; this variety would not survive in the wild • AVERAGE ADULT SIZE:
15 cm (6 in) • COLOURS: Black, green, red, gold, orange, calico • SEXUAL DIFFERENCES: Females have fuller
bodies; males develop tubercles on their heads and ridges on their pectoral fins at spawning time
REPRODUCTION: Egg-scatterer • BREEDING POTENTIAL: Moderate • TANK LEVEL: Middle • FOOD: Dry, frozen and live
foods • PLANT FRIENDLY: No • SPECIAL NEEDS: Swimming space • EASE OF KEEPING: Moderate

Aquarium needs

MINIMUM TANK SIZE: 60 cm (24 in)
TEMPERATURE: 10–20°C (50–68°F)
PH: 7–8
WATER HARDNESS: Neutral to hard and alkaline
COMPATIBILITY WITH OTHER FISH: Moderate

Ranchus are similar to Orandas in that they develop a fleshy growth on their heads. They have been bred not to have a dorsal fin and have shorter bodies and tails than Orandas. Their shape makes them poor swimmers, and they should be kept only with other fancy goldfish or other Ranchus. Some Ranchus are also susceptible to swim-bladder problems; as a rule, the shorter and fatter the body is, the more susceptible to swim-bladder problems the fish will be.

They are available in a range of colours, including black, green, red, gold, orange and calico. Show-standard Ranchus have a rounded back and short twin tail.

The aquarium should be free of obstructions and contain well-filtered and well-aerated water. A proportion of the tank water should be changed frequently. You can give the fish specially developed pellet foods that sink. These allow the Ranchus to feed from the bottom and so to avoid taking in air, which could help both their buoyancy and their swimming.

Pearlscale

deep bodied • poor swimmer • cute • sensitive

SCIENTIFIC NAME: *Carassius auratus* var. • FAMILY: Cyprinidae • ORIGIN: China • NATURAL HABITAT: Ponds and slow-moving rivers; this variety would not survive in the wild • AVERAGE ADULT SIZE: 15 cm (6 in) • COLOURS: Red, red and white, orange, brown, calico • SEXUAL DIFFERENCES: Females have fuller bodies; males develop tubercles on their heads and ridges on their pectoral fins at spawning time • REPRODUCTION: Egg-scatterer BREEDING POTENTIAL: Moderate • TANK LEVEL: Middle • FOOD: Dry, frozen and live foods • PLANT FRIENDLY: No SPECIAL NEEDS: Other slow fish; swimming space • EASE OF KEEPING: Moderate

Aquarium needs

MINIMUM TANK SIZE: 60 cm (24 in)
TEMPERATURE: 10–20°C (50–68°F)
PH: 7–8
WATER HARDNESS: Neutral to hard and alkaline
COMPATIBILITY WITH OTHER FISH: Low

The Pearlscale is a newer variety of fancy goldfish, and the fish are not at all hardy. It has taken many years of line-breeding to produce the 'pearlscale' effect and the almost spherical body shape, but the breeding has had adverse consequences. These fish are poor swimmers and they can be susceptible to buoyancy problems. In extreme cases fish cannot swim at all and just sit on the bottom of the tank; other fish, however, are perfectly all right.

When choosing Pearlscales in an aquatic store, select the fish that are active and swimming well as these will be the least likely to develop the above problems. There is a Crown Pearlscale. Mature specimens have a hood on their heads.

The tank set-up should be simple and sympathetic to the needs of the fish. Water quality should be good, but filter flow not too powerful. Decor should be minimal to provide maximum swimming space.

Sinking foods are a good idea to stop the fish from gulping too much air and becoming stuck at the surface. Don't keep them with single-tail goldfish, which will harass them.

Bubble Eye

bizarre looking • poor swimmer • fragile • sensitive

SCIENTIFIC NAME: *Carassius auratus* var. • FAMILY: Cyprinidae • ORIGIN: China • NATURAL HABITAT: Ponds and slow-moving rivers; this variety would not survive in the wild • AVERAGE ADULT SIZE: 10 cm (4 in) • COLOURS: Orange, red, white, calico, black • SEXUAL DIFFERENCES: Females have fuller bodies; males develop tubercles on their heads and ridges on their pectoral fins at spawning time • REPRODUCTION: Egg-scatterer • BREEDING POTENTIAL: Low • TANK LEVEL: Middle • FOOD: Floating foods • PLANT FRIENDLY: No • SPECIAL NEEDS: Bubble Eye-friendly tanks and tank mates; floating foods • EASE OF KEEPING: Difficult

Coldwater fish

Aquarium needs

MINIMUM TANK SIZE: 60 cm (24 in)
TEMPERATURE: 10–20°C (50–68°F)
PH: 7–8
WATER HARDNESS: Neutral to hard and alkaline
COMPATIBILITY WITH OTHER FISH: Low

Bubble Eyes produce extreme reactions in people who view them for the first time. Those who love them think they are endearing, while people who hate them think that breeding fish like this is tantamount to animal cruelty.

The bubble eyes are actually fluid-filled sacks, and they mean that the fish can only look up, although some can also see a little in front. The sacks are delicate and can be punctured. Burst sacks can become infected.

The fish are not able to find food very well, and they lack a dorsal fin, so are also poor swimmers. Their tank should be virtually bare to avoid collisions. Filtration should be good, but the filter flow should be slow so that the fish can rest. They are best kept on their own or with Celestials.

Celestial

bizarre looking • poor swimmer • fragile • sensitive

SCIENTIFIC NAME: *Carassius auratus* var. • FAMILY: Cyprinidae • OTHER NAME: Stargazer • ORIGIN: China
NATURAL HABITAT: Ponds and slow-moving rivers; this variety would not survive in the wild • AVERAGE ADULT SIZE:
10 cm (4 in) • COLOURS: Orange, red, black • SEXUAL DIFFERENCES: Females have fuller bodies; males develop
tubercles on their heads and ridges on their pectoral fins at spawning time • REPRODUCTION: Egg-scatterer
BREEDING POTENTIAL: Low • TANK LEVEL: Middle • FOOD: Floating foods • PLANT FRIENDLY: No • SPECIAL NEEDS:
Gentle tank mates; floating foods • EASE OF KEEPING: Difficult

Aquarium needs

MINIMUM TANK SIZE: 60 cm (24 in)
TEMPERATURE: 10–20°C (50–68°F)
PH: 7–8
WATER HARDNESS: Neutral to hard and alkaline
COMPATIBILITY WITH OTHER FISH: Low

It is said that Celestials were developed in ancient China so that they could gaze at emperors as they walked by. This is testament to the fact that the variety is not a new one, and that man has been modifying goldfish for centuries. The Celestial itself appears to be a tele- scope-eye type of fish that has been developed with upward-looking eyes. It lacks a dorsal fin, a trait it shares with Bubble Eyes and Ranchus. It has a twin tail and is usually sold in an orange form, although other colours, such as red and black, may be available.

Like Bubble Eyes, Celestials are sensitive fish because they are poor swimmers and may struggle to find and swim to food if there are other more successful varieties in the same tank. The aquarium should be sparsely decorated with no sharp objects. Water quality should be good with a gentle flow of water.

The best way to display this fish may be to put it to its original purpose and keep it in an indoor pond, so that it can be viewed from above. As with the Bubble Eye, its breeding causes contro- versy among aquarists.

Koi Carp

large • majestic • greedy • expensive

SCIENTIFIC NAME: *Cyprinus carpio* • FAMILY: Cyprinidae • ORIGIN: China and Japan (Niigata) • NATURAL HABITAT: Slow-moving rivers, lakes and ponds • AVERAGE ADULT SIZE: 60 cm (24 in) • COLOURS: Red, white, black, yellow, gold, blue and combinations of all colours • SEXUAL DIFFERENCES: Females are larger with fuller bodies REPRODUCTION: Egg-scatterer • BREEDING POTENTIAL: Moderate • TANK LEVEL: Middle • FOOD: Pellets, food sticks and frozen foods • PLANT FRIENDLY: No • SPECIAL NEEDS: Huge aquarium; excellent filtration • EASE OF KEEPING: Moderate

Coldwater fish

Aquarium needs

MINIMUM TANK SIZE: 2.4 m (8 ft)
TEMPERATURE: 10–20°C (50–68°F)
PH: 7–8
WATER HARDNESS: Neutral to hard and alkaline
COMPATIBILITY WITH OTHER FISH: Moderate

Koi Carp are large, colourful coldwater fish usually associated with outdoor ponds. However, they do find their way into the indoor coldwater sections of aquatic stores and may be purchased by new fishkeepers who are unaware of their eventual size and requirements. The maximum recorded size of these fish is 1.2 m (4 ft) long, but 60 cm (24 in) long is a more realistic average adult size. This still means that they require a large expanse of water, and they are at the very limit of suitability for aquariums, which are really inappropriate in the long term.

They are greedy, fast-growing fish with tremendous appetites. Although they are peaceful, they are quite active and boisterous when it comes to finding food. They like nothing better than mouthing the gravel for tasty

morsels, and they have barbels at the corners of their mouths to help them feel around in poor visibility.

Plenty of water changes and oversized filtration are necessary for the fish to thrive. Large Koi may eat small fish just because they are so greedy. They are certainly not suitable for most coldwater aquariums.

Koi Carp come in lots of named colour varieties. The best are worth a lot of money and are much sought after by collectors.

Warning!

This species grows large.

White Cloud Mountain Minnow

small • hardy • easy to keep • tolerant

SCIENTIFIC NAME: *Tanichthys albonubes* • FAMILY: Cyprinidae • ORIGIN: China • NATURAL HABITAT: Cool, fast-flowing mountain streams • AVERAGE ADULT SIZE: 4 cm (1½ in) • COLOURS: Brown with an iridescent, horizontal stripe and red tail • SEXUAL DIFFERENCES: Females are larger; males are slimmer and more colourful REPRODUCTION: Egg-scatterer • BREEDING POTENTIAL: High • TANK LEVEL: Middle • FOOD: Flake, frozen and live foods • PLANT FRIENDLY: Yes • SPECIAL NEEDS: Shoals of six or more individuals • EASE OF KEEPING: Easy

Aquarium needs

MINIMUM TANK SIZE: 45 cm (18 in)
TEMPERATURE: 15–24°C (59–75°F)
PH: 7–8
WATER HARDNESS: Around neutral; slightly acid to slightly alkaline is acceptable
COMPATIBILITY WITH OTHER FISH: Good

White Cloud Mountain Minnows are small fish said to originate in streams on the White Cloud Mountain in China. Their name, *Tanichthys*, means 'Tan's fish' and refers to the young boy who is believed to have discovered them.

They acclimatize well to aquariums and can be kept in unheated tanks indoors. They tolerate a range of temperatures, but prefer conditions within the extremes noted.

They will tolerate a simple tank set-up and are suitable fish for beginners. Put them in a tank 45 cm (18 in) or more long, decorated with gravel, rocks and live plants. Use an air-powered filter or a power filter. Add some live plants, including feathery leaved species, because White Cloud Mountain Minnows are egg-scatterers and the plants may catch the adhesive eggs. The water quality should be good, but these are hardy fish and could be added to a new tank after it has been running for just one week. Feed them little and often on a varied diet of small foods. Do not combine them with large goldfish, which may eat them.

Coldwater fish

Borneo Sucker

small • unusual looking • peaceful • interesting

SCIENTIFIC NAME: *Gastromyzon borneensis* • FAMILY: Balitoridae • OTHER NAMES • Hill Stream Loach, Hong Kong Plec • ORIGIN: China • NATURAL HABITAT: Cool, fast-flowing mountain streams • AVERAGE ADULT SIZE: 10 cm (4 in) COLOURS: Beige, brown, silver, green • SEXUAL DIFFERENCES: Unknown • REPRODUCTION: Unknown • BREEDING POTENTIAL: Moderate • TANK LEVEL: Bottom • FOOD: Aufwuch, algae • PLANT FRIENDLY: No • SPECIAL NEEDS: Well-aerated water; the right food • EASE OF KEEPING: Moderate

Coldwater fish

Aquarium needs

MINIMUM TANK SIZE: 60 cm (24 in)
TEMPERATURE: 15–25°C (59–77°F)
PH: 7
WATER HARDNESS: Neutral to slightly hard and alkaline
COMPATIBILITY WITH OTHER FISH: Moderate

Several other *Gastromyzon* arrive mixed in with *G. borneensis* in fish shipments, including *G. punctulatus* and *G. ctenocephalus*. These fish all look similar and can be kept in the same way. *Gastromyzon* spp. are attractively patterned.

Their natural habitat comprises fast-flowing, shallow streams with lots of boulders that have a good supply of well-oxygenated, cool water flowing over them. These conditions encourage algal growth, and with the algae develops an associated food web of organisms. The tiny invertebrates that live within algae are known as aufwuch. Borneo Suckers eat aufwuch, and their bodies are adapted to cling to the rocks and not be swept away while they feed.

The temperate climate they live in allows them to be kept in coldwater aquariums, and they are often offered as coldwater algae eaters. In fact, they do not tend to eat algae when kept in a tank. They are much happier with more water flow than a goldfish would prefer, so are best kept with other stream-dwelling temperate fish, such as White Cloud Mountain Minnows.

Weather Loach

long • unusual looking • tolerant • bottom dwelling

SCIENTIFIC NAME: *Misgurnus anguillicaudatus* • FAMILY: Cobitidae • OTHER NAME: Japanese Weatherfish
ORIGIN: Northern Asia, including China and Japan • NATURAL HABITAT: Ponds, lakes, rivers and stagnant bodies
of freshwater • AVERAGE ADULT SIZE: 20 cm (8 in) • COLOURS: Beige, brown, grey, gold; a yellow form is
available but may be a hybrid of different species • SEXUAL DIFFERENCES: Females are larger and have fuller
bodies • REPRODUCTION: Egg-scatterer • BREEDING POTENTIAL: Low • TANK LEVEL: Bottom • FOOD: Sinking tablet
and frozen foods • PLANT FRIENDLY: Yes • SPECIAL NEEDS: A substrate for burrowing • EASE OF KEEPING: Easy

Aquarium needs

MINIMUM TANK SIZE: 90 cm (36 in)
TEMPERATURE: 10–22°C (50–72°F)
PH: 7–8
WATER HARDNESS: Neutral to moderately hard and alkaline
COMPATIBILITY WITH OTHER FISH: Moderate

Weather Loaches are one of the few bottom-feeding non-goldfish varieties available to fishkeepers with coldwater aquariums. The choice for tropical aquariums is vast, but aquarists are really limited when it comes to coldwater species. The Weather Loach's common name derives from the fact that it becomes more active before it rains, rising to the surface of the water.

It is an active, eel-like fish, and a gold variety is available. Some people think it ugly, but it has its advantages in that it will eat uneaten goldfish food and burrow through the substrate, keeping it fresh. It can safely be kept with goldfish.

The tank should be fairly large, and the bottom should be covered with fine sand or pea gravel to a depth of 5 cm (2 in) or more. Authentic-looking decor is best, with bogwood and smooth stones placed to provide shelter. Live plants can be used, but ferns are best tied to pieces

of wood because the fish's burrowing activity sometimes uproots them.

These fish are easy to keep, and eat any foods. Newly imported fish can be susceptible to infection.

Coldwater fish

Livebearing fish

The fish in this group are popular with fishkeepers because of their hardiness and because of the wide range of colours they display. The 'big four' – Guppies, Mollies, Swordtails and Platies – account for a large part of the ornamental fish industry, and they are bred in their millions to supply keepers of tropical fish all over the world. The fact that they give birth to quite large, live young has meant that line-breeding can occur easily and quickly, and over just a few generations it is possible for new colour strains or fin types to be developed.

Survivors

Livebearing fish come mainly from Central and South America, where they can be found taking advantage of the abundant mosquito larvae and green algae that live in the sunlit water.

With the exception of the Pike-top Minnow (*Belonesox belizanus*; page 53), livebearing fish are small, prey fish that are low down in the food chain. (The Pike-top Minnow is itself a predator and is higher in the food chain.) Giving birth to live young enables them to reproduce quickly, because the time dedicated to spawning and hatching tiny fry is absent from their lifecycles. Each species can also survive in a range of water types and temperatures to capitalize on the food that is available. The ease, therefore, with which they can reproduce and the way in which they can adapt to different water conditions have made livebearing fish perfect survivors in both the wild and in aquariums.

Endler's Livebearers are pretty little fish and suitable for small tanks.

> **TIP**
>
> **Mollies prefer to be kept in slightly saline water, which will help to keep them healthy and disease-free.**

Aquarium keeping

If they could choose, most livebearers would prefer to be kept in hard, alkaline water rather than in the soft, acidic water that characins prefer. Most are small, community fish, which can be safely kept with nearly all smaller species of fish and all live plants. Indeed, plants can provide a refuge for newborn fry, which adult fish may try to eat. Gravid (pregnant) females should be removed and placed in another aquarium to give birth. Alternatively, smaller livebearers, such as

Predatory livebearers, Pike-top Minnows eat small fish.

Guppies or Endler's, can be placed in a plastic or net breeding trap just before giving birth. The females should be removed straight afterwards, but the fry can initially be kept in the trap, away from hungry mouths.

Other species

The other livebearing species profiled in this section are not as widely kept as the 'big four', and they can even be considered collectable. Total sales of all other livebearing species do not account for even 1 per cent of sales of any one of the main four types, largely because the other species are available only in their wild forms and are drabber in comparison. They are, however, interesting and undemanding to keep. Endler's Livebearer (*Poecilia* sp. 'Endler'; page 58) and the Butterfly

FAQ

Will I be able to sell all the offspring to the aquatic store and make money from breeding?

Generally, no. This is because stores get given baby fish all the time and they are worth nothing commercially, unlike the colourful adults. Some stores might re-home them for you or perhaps offer you some fish food in exchange, but don't expect to make money from them.

Goodeid (*Ameca splendens*; page 49) are endangered or even extinct in the wild, so there is an additional reason to consider keeping them and breeding from them: you can pass them on to other fishkeepers and keep the strains alive.

Four-eyed Fish

unusual looking • active • difficult • brackish

SCIENTIFIC NAME: *Anableps anableps* • FAMILY: Anablepidae • ORIGIN: Northern South America and Central America • NATURAL HABITAT: Rivers and estuaries in freshwater and tidal saltwater • AVERAGE ADULT SIZE: 30 cm (12 in) • COLOURS: Silver, black, white • SEXUAL DIFFERENCES: Males have a gonopodium • REPRODUCTION: Livebearer • BREEDING POTENTIAL: Low • TANK LEVEL: Top • FOOD: Insects, frozen and live foods • PLANT FRIENDLY: Yes • SPECIAL NEEDS: Saltwater; a half-filled tank • EASE OF KEEPING: Difficult

Aquarium needs

MINIMUM TANK SIZE: 1.5 m (5 ft)
TEMPERATURE: 24–28°C (75–82°F)
PH: 7.5–8.2
WATER HARDNESS: Hard and alkaline
COMPATIBILITY WITH OTHER FISH: Low

The Four-eyed Fish is sometimes categorized as an estuarine fish that needs brackish-water conditions. It is, however, a livebearer, which has a gonopodium that can move either left or right, and compatible right and left females must be found for successful breeding.

The four eyes are capable of seeing below and above the surface, and this active fish can hop and jump over vegetation and branches that rest on the surface of the water.

These fish are so specialized that they may quickly decline if kept by any but dedicated experts. Those who do take on the challenge should set up a long, wide, shallow tank with soft sand and bogwood. It should be half-filled with brackish water containing marine salt and tested with a hydrometer for a salinity of 1.010. The fish will take only meaty foods, and they are prone to bacterial infection.

Despite these drawbacks, Four-eyed Fish become available to aquarists from time to time. They rarely breed in captivity.

Warning!

This species is not for beginners.

Butterfly Goodeid

hardy • plant eater • unusual looking • collectable

SCIENTIFIC NAME: *Ameca splendens* • FAMILY: Goodeidae • ORIGIN: Mexico • NATURAL HABITAT: Highland streams and rivers; this species is approaching extinction in the wild • AVERAGE ADULT SIZE: 13 cm (5 in) • COLOURS: Grey and silver with dark, yellow-edged fins • SEXUAL DIFFERENCES: Females are larger; males are more colourful • REPRODUCTION: Livebearer • BREEDING POTENTIAL: Moderate • TANK LEVEL: Middle • FOOD: Herbivore flake, frozen and live foods • PLANT FRIENDLY: No • SPECIAL NEEDS: Vegetable diet • EASE OF KEEPING: Moderate

Aquarium needs

MINIMUM TANK SIZE: 90 cm (36 in)
TEMPERATURE: 25–30°C (77–86°F)
PH: 7–7.5
WATER HARDNESS: Soft and acidic to hard and alkaline
COMPATIBILITY WITH OTHER FISH: Moderate

This species is one of the larger goodeids, and it can be easily included in a community of large, tough fish like cichlids. They should not, however, be kept in aquariums that contain long-finned fish.

Butterfly Goodeids are livebearing fish but have a fin called an andropodium, a modified anal fin that is not quite as developed as that of Poeciliid livebearers. The female grows quite a bit larger than the male and gives birth to huge fry. Male fish develop stronger coloration including a black tail with a yellow edge. The females are mainly spotted.

Their liking for plant matter means that they are good at eating any nuisance duckweed that appears on the surface of the tank water.

Goodeids are on the whole poorly represented in fishkeeping. This may be due to restricted collection sites, the fish's temperament or the lack of coloration in many species. Their natural habitat is under threat, and they are nearing extinction in the wild, but the future of the species is secure as there are many aquarium populations around the world, and the species is commercially bred in eastern Europe.

Livebearing fish

Red-tailed Goodeid

colourful • tolerant • active • hardy

SCIENTIFIC NAME: *Xenotoca eiseni* • FAMILY: Goodeidae • ORIGIN: Mexico, Central America • NATURAL HABITAT: Rivers, lakes and streams • AVERAGE ADULT SIZE: 8 cm (3 in) • COLOURS: Light-coloured body with blue patch around the dorsal fin and a red tail • SEXUAL DIFFERENCES: Females have deeper bodies; males are more colourful • REPRODUCTION: Livebearer • BREEDING POTENTIAL: Moderate • TANK LEVEL: All levels • FOOD: Flake, frozen and live foods • PLANT FRIENDLY: Yes • SPECIAL NEEDS: None • EASE OF KEEPING: Moderate

Livebearing fish

Aquarium needs

MINIMUM TANK SIZE: 75 cm (30 in)

TEMPERATURE: 15–30°C (59–86°F)

PH: 7–8

WATER HARDNESS: Soft and acidic to hard and alkaline

COMPATIBILITY WITH OTHER FISH: Moderate

The Red-tailed Goodeid is rarely stocked in aquarium shops, and when they are juvenile specimens are often overlooked. However, these fish have plenty of appeal. They are colourful, developing the typical red tail as they mature,

along with a pronounced arched back and deep body. They are also tolerant when it comes to water hardness and temperature, and they can even be placed outside in ponds in summer, to condition the fish with extra space and lots of live foods. In addition, they can be mixed with a range of other fish, including quite robust Central American cichlids, such as the Convict Cichlid (*Cryptoheros nigrofasciatus*; page 141) and the Firemouth Cichlid (*Thorichthys meeki*; page 156).

They are stockier than most livebearing Poeciliid species and are largely ignored by other fish. They may, however, nip the fins of other fish so should not be stocked with more frail fish, such as Guppies.

To get the best from the species, make sure there are more females than males and supply a varied diet because they are omnivorous.

The males are smaller than the females, but more colourful. The humpback and best coloration develop over a matter of years rather than months, so make them a long-term investment.

Celebes Halfbeak

unusual looking • predatory • quiet • top swimmer

SCIENTIFIC NAME: *Nomorhampus liemi liemi* • FAMILY: Hemirhampidae • ORIGIN: Sulawesi, Borneo
NATURAL HABITAT: Streams and rivers • AVERAGE ADULT SIZE: 8 cm (3 in) • COLOURS: Grey body with black and sometimes pink fins • SEXUAL DIFFERENCES: Females are larger; males have an andropodium • REPRODUCTION: Livebearer • BREEDING POTENTIAL: Low • TANK LEVEL: Top • FOOD: Frozen and live foods • PLANT FRIENDLY: Yes
SPECIAL NEEDS: Plant cover to help prevent them from damaging their chins on the aquarium walls • EASE OF KEEPING: Moderate

Aquarium needs

MINIMUM TANK SIZE: 75 cm (30 in)
TEMPERATURE: 24–26°C (75–79°F)
PH: 6.5–7
WATER HARDNESS: Soft and acidic to hard and alkaline
COMPATIBILITY WITH OTHER FISH: Medium

This strange-looking fish has a distinctive, extended lower jaw that it cannot move. Mature males develop black on the fins and lower jaws; females do not. Make sure that females outnumber males at a rate of about three to one because male fish can become boisterous with females and with each other. Females grow slightly larger than males and give birth to live young, but they are rarely bred in captivity.

They should be offered meatier foods in the aquarium, including *Mysis* shrimp, mosquito larvae and insects. Their predatory nature means that small fry may be eaten.

Take care with the fish because they may damage their chins when being transported or if they become frightened by sudden or unexpected movements outside the tank.

This species is often kept in hard water with the addition of salt, but it originates in fresh mountain streams and does best at a relatively low pH of about 6.5. The fish are not regularly seen in shops, although bred commercially in eastern Europe.

Halfbeaks, and their close relatives the needlefish, are interesting fish, but they are poorly represented in fishkeeping because of their special needs.

Warning!
This species is not for beginners.

Livebearing fish

Knife-edged Livebearer

hardy • jumper • collectable • active

SCIENTIFIC NAME: *Alfaro cultratus* • FAMILY: Poeciliidae • OTHER NAME: Knife Livebearer • ORIGIN: Costa Rica, Nicaragua, Panama • NATURAL HABITAT: Streams, rivers and ditches • AVERAGE ADULT SIZE: 8 cm (3 in) COLOURS: Yellow with iridescent flanks • SEXUAL DIFFERENCES: Females are larger; males have a gonopodium REPRODUCTION: Livebearer • BREEDING POTENTIAL: Moderate • TANK LEVEL: Top to middle • FOOD: Flake, frozen and live foods • PLANT FRIENDLY: Yes • SPECIAL NEEDS: A tight-fitting cover on the aquarium • EASE OF KEEPING: Moderate

Livebearing fish

Aquarium needs

MINIMUM TANK SIZE: 75 cm (30 in)
TEMPERATURE: 24–28°C (75–82°F)
PH: 7–7.5
WATER HARDNESS: Soft and acidic to hard and alkaline
COMPATIBILITY WITH OTHER FISH: Moderate

The Knife-edged Livebearer is typical of the many livebearing fish species that have been overlooked in favour of the line-bred colour varieties of Platies and Guppies.

Although similar in shape to a Platy (*Xiphophorus maculatus*; page 60), the Knife-edged Livebearer is truer to its wild roots as it is quite quarrelsome among its own species, and males should always be outnumbered by several females to reduce their levels of aggression. Heavy planting with feathery plants can also help.

The gonopodium is large and prominent on male fish, which also have a flash of colour on the flanks.

Females can grow to 8 cm (3 in) long, and they give birth to up to 30 young.

The fish dart towards food items quickly, and they prefer small live and frozen food items, like mosquito larvae. They naturally occur in shallow streams and can jump easily when kept in the aquarium.

This is a freshwater species, and fish do not need the addition of any salt to the tank to thrive. They are best kept in an aquarium on their own so that they can be fully appreciated; they could well be outshone in the average busy community tank.

Pike-top Minnow

predatory • top swimmer • peaceful • quiet

SCIENTIFIC NAME: *Belonesox belizanus* • FAMILY: Poeciliidae • ORIGIN: Costa Rica, Mexico, Nicaragua
NATURAL HABITAT: Slow-moving waters, including ponds and ditches with vegetation • AVERAGE ADULT SIZE:
Females: 20 cm (8 in); males are smaller • COLOURS: Grey to olive green • SEXUAL DIFFERENCES: Males develop
a gonopodium • REPRODUCTION: Livebearer • BREEDING POTENTIAL: Moderate • TANK LEVEL: Top • FOOD: Frozen
and live foods • PLANT FRIENDLY: Yes • SPECIAL NEEDS: Overhanging vegetation at the surface to provide refuge
EASE OF KEEPING: Easy

Aquarium needs

MINIMUM TANK SIZE: 90 cm (36 in)
TEMPERATURE: 25–30°C (77–86°F)
PH: 7–8
WATER HARDNESS: Neutral to hard and alkaline
COMPATIBILITY WITH OTHER FISH: Don't mix with fish small enough to be eaten, such as Neon Tetras

The Pike-top Minnow is one of the largest livebearing species available. It is the livebearing equivalent of a predatory fish and it is more than capable of swallowing any small fish that dwell in the same aquarium. Although the Pike-top Minnow is predatory, it is quite peaceful and should not be mixed with boisterous fish, like large cichlids, or fish that will swallow its lunch before it does.

The gonopodium does not develop until the fish are 8 cm (3 in) long, so don't be put off if a group of young fish appear to be all females. It doesn't breed prolifically in captivity like most livebearers.

In the wild the species may well exclusively eat live fish and insects found on the water surface, but it can certainly be trained to take foods in captivity.

Livebearing fish

Humpbacked Limia

active • hardy • unusual looking • cute

SCIENTIFIC NAME: *Limia nigrofasciata* • FAMILY: Poeciliidae • ORIGIN: Haiti • NATURAL HABITAT: Slow-moving, vegetated waters • AVERAGE ADULT SIZE: 8 cm (3 in) • COLOURS: Olive green, grey • SEXUAL DIFFERENCES: Males develop a humped back and a gonopodium • REPRODUCTION: Livebearer • BREEDING POTENTIAL: Moderate TANK LEVEL: Middle • FOOD: Flake, frozen and live foods • PLANT FRIENDLY: Yes • SPECIAL NEEDS: Females should outnumber males if kept in the same tank • EASE OF KEEPING: Easy

Livebearing fish

Aquarium needs
MINIMUM TANK SIZE: 75 cm (30 in)
TEMPERATURE: 24–28°C (75–82°F)
PH: 7–8
WATER HARDNESS: Hard and alkaline
COMPATIBILITY WITH OTHER FISH: Moderate

At first sight Humpbacked Limia can appear rather odd and not very interesting, but they have character and the potential to turn into good-looking fish. They look a little different to, and display more vigour than, other domesticated varieties of livebearer.

As they mature, male fish develop the characteristic humpback and an iridescent sheen all over their bodies. Males have a very thick tail and a larger dorsal fin than females. The females have a typical Poeciliid shape, with a narrower profile than mature males, although the belly expands when they are pregnant. Females also grow slightly larger. The males use their large dorsal fins to show off to females, who they try to round up and mate with. This is quite an active species.

The species originates in Haiti in the Caribbean and can tolerate salt in the water. The fish prefer hard, alkaline water in the aquarium.

Plant the tank densely if you wish to breed these fish, because the parents will try to eat the fry.

Guppy

prolific • active • colourful • easy to keep

SCIENTIFIC NAME: *Poecilia reticulata* • FAMILY: Poeciliidae • OTHER NAME Millions Fish • ORIGIN: Central America
NATURAL HABITAT: Ditches, ponds, streams and canals • AVERAGE ADULT SIZE: Male: 3 cm (1¼ in); female: 6 cm
(2½ in) • COLOURS: A wide range • SEXUAL DIFFERENCES: Males are smaller and more colourful with a
gonopodium; females have deeper bodies • REPRODUCTION: Livebearer • BREEDING POTENTIAL: High • TANK
LEVEL: Top • FOOD: Flake, frozen and live foods • PLANT FRIENDLY: Yes • SPECIAL NEEDS: Females should
outnumber males; fish farmed in Far East benefit from aquarium salt • EASE OF KEEPING: Easy

Aquarium needs

MINIMUM TANK SIZE: 45 cm (18 in)
TEMPERATURE: 20–28°C (68–82°F)
PH: 7–8
WATER HARDNESS: Slightly acid to slightly alkaline, but adaptable
COMPATIBILITY WITH OTHER FISH: Don't keep with fish that may nip their tails

The Guppy, which used to be classified in the genus *Lebistes*, is one of the most popular of all freshwater tropical fish, and it is often kept and bred by beginners.

There are many colour variations and tail patterns available in male fish, and females are also now being bred to be more colourful. In fact, the true wild form is rarely seen in captivity.

Have Guppies at a ratio of one male to two females to avoid bullying; alternatively, keep a group of males only. Don't put them in the same aquarium as large or boisterous fish. If you hope to breed from your fish, buy from different sources to avoid inbreeding.

Feed the fish little and often, and ideally offer frozen or live mosquito larvae to keep them in their best condition. Because it eats mosquito larvae the species has been introduced to canals and ditches in tropical regions around the world, to help stop the spread of mosquito-borne malaria.

Modern varieites of Guppies are less hardy than wild populations.

Black Molly

peaceful • hardy • prolific • algae eater

SCIENTIFIC NAME: *Poecilia sphenops* • FAMILY: Poecillidae • ORIGIN: Mexico and throughout Central America
NATURAL HABITAT: Lakes, streams and rivers; also estuarine environments • AVERAGE ADULT SIZE: 6 cm (2½ in)
COLOURS: The natural form is green; aquarium varieties are black, yellow, silver • SEXUAL DIFFERENCES: Females
are larger and have fuller bodies; males have a gonopodium • REPRODUCTION: Livebearer • BREEDING POTENTIAL:
High • TANK LEVEL: Top • FOOD: Filamentous algae; dry, frozen and live foods • PLANT FRIENDLY: Yes • SPECIAL NEEDS:
Hard water with the addition of aquarium salt • EASE OF KEEPING: Easy

Livebearing fish

Aquarium needs

MINIMUM TANK SIZE: 60 cm (24 in)
TEMPERATURE: 20–28°C (68–82°F)
PH: 7.5–8
WATER HARDNESS: Neutral to hard and alkaline
COMPATIBILITY WITH OTHER FISH: Keep with other salt-loving fish

The true Black Molly is an excellent community fish, which grazes on algae that grows on surfaces in the aquarium. It also breeds frequently. To keep them at their best, have two females to every male fish in the tank to avoid harassment. The fry are born quite large and may well sur-vive in the main aquarium, taking small flake particles straight away. Greenstuffs make up a large part of the species' diet, so offer vegetable and herbivore flakes when feeding.

There are several colour morphs available, and these include speck-led and lyretail varieties.

Black Mollies can also be acclima-tized to marine tanks. Indeed, when they are kept in tanks without salt in the water or with a low pH, Black Mollies are prone to 'shimmying' (rocking backwards and forwards) in the water, and they become sus-ceptible to bacterial infection.

Sailfin Molly

peaceful • active • colourful • prolific

SCIENTIFIC NAME: *Poecilia velifera* • FAMILY: Poeciliidae • ORIGIN: Mexico • NATURAL HABITAT: Streams, lakes, rivers, estuaries and saltwater lagoons • AVERAGE ADULT SIZE: 15 cm (6 in) • COLOURS: green, gold, black, silver, red • SEXUAL DIFFERENCES: Females are larger; males have a gonopodium • REPRODUCTION: Livebearer
BREEDING POTENTIAL: High • TANK LEVEL: Top • FOOD: Herbivore flake, frozen and live foods • PLANT FRIENDLY: Yes
SPECIAL NEEDS: Females must outnumber males by at least two to one • EASE OF KEEPING: Easy

Aquarium needs

MINIMUM TANK SIZE: 90 cm (36 in)
TEMPERATURE: 24–28°C (75–82°F)
PH: 7.5–8.2
WATER HARDNESS: Hard and alkaline
COMPATIBILITY WITH OTHER FISH: Good

The Sailfin Mollies seen in shops may well be modern hybrids of *P. velifera*, *P. latipinna* and even *P. sphenops*.

Aquarium-kept fish grow quite large, but they rarely attain their maximum adult size in the aquarium. Breeders place them in long troughs to encourage growth and the development of a large dorsal fin in males. Breeding in the aquarium may well actually produce successively smaller adults.

They are active fish; males pursue females around the tank and show off with vigour. There are many coloured forms available, including gold, black, silver, red, marbled and even the natural green of the original wild fish.

Offer a diet containing vegetable matter because they are herbivores, and keep them in hard water with some aquarium salt added. Failure to do so may make the fish susceptible to bacterial infections. They may graze on filamentous algae.

Livebearing fish

Endler's Livebearer

tiny • endearing • active • interesting

SCIENTIFIC NAME: *Poecilia* sp. 'Endler' • FAMILY: Poeciliidae • ORIGIN: Venezuela • NATURAL HABITAT: Ponds and ditches • AVERAGE ADULT SIZE: 2.5 cm (1 in) • COLOURS: Males are multicoloured; females are plain grey SEXUAL DIFFERENCES: Males are much smaller and have a gonopodium • REPRODUCTION: Livebearer • BREEDING POTENTIAL: High • TANK LEVEL: Middle to top • FOOD: Small amounts of flake, frozen and live foods • PLANT FRIENDLY: Yes • SPECIAL NEEDS: Gentle filtration; no large companions that may eat them • EASE OF KEEPING: Easy

Livebearing fish

Aquarium needs

MINIMUM TANK SIZE: 30 cm (12 in)
TEMPERATURE: 24°C (75°F)
PH: 7–8
WATER HARDNESS: Slightly acid to slightly alkaline, soft to hard
COMPATIBILITY WITH OTHER FISH: Don't stock with large fish or with Guppies, with which they may hybridize

Endler's Livebearer is named after John Endler, one of the people who discovered them. At first sight they look very much like a wild form of Guppy, with males having iridescent markings while the females are plain. The fish is, in fact, a distinct species and should not be allowed to hybridize with other species.

One of the most important concerns when keeping the species is their diminutive size, and you must take care to provide a tank in which they will be safe from predation by larger fish and from the suction of a power filter.

The best way to keep them may well be in a small, mature tank with gentle, air-powered filtration and heavy planting to provide cover for the fry. They make great first fish and their antics can be educational, so a small tank set up just for them would be ideal on a table top in a child's bedroom.

Swordtail

hardy • unusual looking • easy to keep • prolific

SCIENTIFIC NAME: *Xiphophorus helleri* • FAMILY: Poeciliidae • ORIGIN: Honduras, Mexico • NATURAL HABITAT: Rivers, ponds and canals with dense vegetation • AVERAGE ADULT SIZE: 10 cm (4 in) • COLOURS: Green, black, red, yellow, orange • SEXUAL DIFFERENCES: Males have the swordtail and gonopodium; females are larger and have fuller bodies • REPRODUCTION: Livebearer • BREEDING POTENTIAL: High • TANK LEVEL: Middle to top • FOOD: Flake, frozen and live foods • PLANT FRIENDLY: Yes • SPECIAL NEEDS: Females should outnumber males • EASE OF KEEPING: Easy

Aquarium needs

MINIMUM TANK SIZE: 75 cm (30 in)

TEMPERATURE: 24–28°C (75–82°F)

PH: 7.5–8

WATER HARDNESS: Neutral to hard and alkaline

COMPATIBILITY WITH OTHER FISH: Can be mixed with most fish

Swordtails are so called because of the tail extension exhibited by mature male fish. Females look similar to Platies and do not have any fin extensions.

The species is easy to look after and suitable for beginners. Fish will breed readily in the aquarium, with females giving birth to live young. Buy fish from different sources to avoid inbreeding. Males can be troublesome if they are not surrounded by a sufficient number of females, but their aggression can usually be controlled or dissipated if they are housed in a large, long aquarium.

Many colour and fin variants are available, including fish with lyre-shaped tails, and many of the new forms do not greatly resemble the original green of the wild fish.

To obtain long swords on male fish make sure they have plenty of swimming space and a varied diet, including vegetable matter and mosquito larvae.

Platy

peaceful • colourful • hardy • easy to keep

SCIENTIFIC NAME: *Xiphophorus maculatus* • FAMILY: Poeciliidae • ORIGIN: Belize, Guatemala, Mexico • NATURAL HABITAT: Slow-moving streams and rivers, canals and ditches • AVERAGE ADULT SIZE: 5 cm (2 in) • COLOURS: Green, red, yellow, blue, silver, black, orange • SEXUAL DIFFERENCES: Females are larger and have fuller bodies; males have a gonopodium • REPRODUCTION: Livebearer • BREEDING POTENTIAL: High • TANK LEVEL: Middle to top • FOOD: Flake, frozen and live foods • PLANT FRIENDLY: Yes • SPECIAL NEEDS: Keep in groups; males should outnumber females • EASE OF KEEPING: Easy

Aquarium needs

MINIMUM TANK SIZE: 60 cm (24 in)
TEMPERATURE: 20–28°C (68–82°F)
PH: 7.5–8
WATER HARDNESS: Neutral to hard and alkaline
COMPATIBILITY WITH OTHER FISH: Platies are compatible with all fish that aren't too boisterous

Platies make excellent community fish and are recommended for all types of tropical aquarium. Their general ease of keeping and hardiness makes them the perfect introductory fish for new aquariums and for those kept by beginners. They are tolerant of less than perfect water and of the odd mistake.

These fish are both inexpensive and readily available, and many colour and fin variants, including high fin forms, are now offered for sale. Breeding these fish is so easy that many female fish are already pregnant when they are purchased, and they will give birth to live young within days of being introduced to the new tank.

Ideally, keep Platies at a ratio of two females to one male, and provide some areas of heavy planting or a breeding trap if you want the fry to survive.

Variegated Platy

tolerant • hardy • prolific • easy to keep

SCIENTIFIC NAME: *Xiphophorus variatus* • FAMILY: Poeciliidae • OTHER NAME Variatus Platy • ORIGIN: Mexico
NATURAL HABITAT: Slow-moving, vegetated waters • AVERAGE ADULT SIZE: 5 cm (2 in) • COLOURS: Green, red,
yellow, orange, black • SEXUAL DIFFERENCES: Males have a gonopodium • REPRODUCTION: Livebearer • BREEDING
POTENTIAL: High • TANK LEVEL: All levels • FOOD: Herbivore flake, frozen and live foods • PLANT FRIENDLY: Yes
SPECIAL NEEDS: Males should outnumber females • EASE OF KEEPING: Easy

Aquarium needs

MINIMUM TANK SIZE: 60 cm (24 in)
TEMPERATURE: 15–28°C (59–82°F)
PH: 7–8
WATER HARDNESS: Hard and alkaline
COMPATIBILITY WITH OTHER FISH: High

The Variegated Platy was thought by some to be a hybrid between the Swordtail and the Platy, but it is in fact a species in its own right. This is a popular aquarium fish, available in nearly as many colours as Swordtails and Platies. The body is slenderer than that of a Platy, and most colour forms show a degree of black speckling on the body, but otherwise the fish could be mistaken for ordinary Platies.

What makes this species special is its tolerance of cooler water conditions, meaning that it is suitable for temperate and cooler water aquariums. It is also very hardy and breeds prolifically.

To enable the fish to remain in peak condition, keep them in hard water at a temperature well within the range indicated. They should also be fed with plenty of herbivore flake, along with occasional treats of mosquito larvae.

Their general hardiness makes these fish very suitable for beginners to tropical and coldwater fishkeeping. They are not too demanding of space and will be happy in a tank only 60 cm (24 in) long.

Livebearing fish

Characins

The fish in this large group of families are found in South and Central America and in Africa. They are all tropical species, and measure from a few centimetres (inches) long to just under 1m (3 ft). Their diets range from almost entirely herbivorous to carnivorous, and they have taken full advantage of every available feeding niche. The characins include one of the most popular tropical fish species in the world, the Neon Tetra (*Paracheirodon innesi*; page 75), which has perhaps been more responsible than any other species for people deciding to keep fish.

Tetras

Tetras are generally small, shoaling species, and they are perfect for the tropical aquarium. Most are under 5 cm (2 in) in length, even when adult, and a medium-sized aquarium will easily accommodate a shoal of six or more individuals.

With few exceptions they come from soft, acidic water, such as rainforest streams and rivers, and have adapted to take a range of small foods, either from the surface or in midwater. They are generally well behaved, but some species, such as the Serpae Tetra (*Hyphessobrycon callistus*; page 69), may nip the fins of long-finned fish.

Tetras can be safely kept with live plants and will appreciate the extra cover that the vegetation provides. The tank set-up should consist of mature water in a tank decorated with bogwood and a layer of fine sand on the bottom.

One to watch, the Serpae Tetra may nip the fins of long-finned fish.

Other characins

Other small characins, including the Hockeystick Pencilfish (*Nannobrycon eques*; page 85) and the Marbled Hatchetfish (*Carnegiella strigata strigata*; page 83), are undemanding fish, which behave like tetras and can be kept with them. Larger characins, such as the Striped Anostomus (*Anostomus anostomus*; page 64), Banded Leporinus (*Leporinus affinis*; page 65) and Six-barred Distichodus (*Distichodus sexfasciatus*; page 81), are more aggressive both with each other and with other species, and they need large aquariums with robust tank mates, such as cichlids. They are also plant eaters.

The Banded Leporinus, Six-barred Distichodus, Flagtail Prochilodus (*Semaprochilodus taeniurus*; page 86), Red Pacu (*Piaractus brachypomus*; page 77), Red-bellied Piranha (*Pygocentrus nattereri*; page 78) and

The Cardinal Tetra is a small, shoaling fish and a popular choice for community tanks.

Wolf Fish (*Hoplias malabaricus*; page 82) all carry size warnings because they will reach a length of 30 cm (12 in) or more when they are adult. They will require large aquariums with powerful filters and, as they are long lived, will also need a similarly long-term commitment from their owner. The first four species are vegetarian and should be offered a diet that includes household vegetable matter, such as squashed peas, blanched lettuce leaves and cucumber. They may even eat fruit and nuts if these are provided.

Predators

The Red-bellied Piranha and Wolf Fish are altogether different fish, crossing over into the 'oddball' category, because their mouths are full of sharp teeth and they are not to everyone's taste. Although both will eat live fish if given the opportunity, they should always be offered dead bait foods instead. Both species are best kept alone, the Red-bellied Piranha in a large shoal and the Wolf Fish as the only fish in the tank. They are equipped to deliver a nasty bite to any hand that strays too close, and should not be kept where there are young children close by.

TIP

Because tetras won't take food from the bottom, a scavenging catfish, such as a corydoras, which will pick up any uneaten food, would be a useful addition to the tank.

Striped Anostomus

unusual looking • bold • hardy • active

SCIENTIFIC NAME: *Anostomus anostomus* • FAMILY: Anostomidae • ORIGIN: Brazil, Colombia, Guyana, Venezuela (Amazon and Orinoco river basins) • NATURAL HABITAT: Rivers, streams and flooded forest areas • AVERAGE ADULT SIZE: 18 cm (7 in) • COLOURS: Dark brown horizontal stripes on a yellow body; a red base to the fins
SEXUAL DIFFERENCES: Females may develop fuller bodies and become slightly larger • REPRODUCTION: Egg-scatterer
BREEDING POTENTIAL: Low • TANK LEVEL: Middle • FOOD: Herbivore flake, frozen and live foods • PLANT FRIENDLY:
No • SPECIAL NEEDS: A large tank; suitable tank mates • EASE OF KEEPING: Moderate

Characins

Aquarium needs

MINIMUM TANK SIZE: 1.2 m (4 ft)
TEMPERATURE: 24–28°C (75–82°F)
PH: 6–7
WATER HARDNESS: Soft and acidic to hard and alkaline
COMPATIBILITY WITH OTHER FISH: Moderate

Anostomus are often described as headstanders, and the fish do swim at inverted angles to feed from the bottom. They are tough, medium-sized characins, which are capable of looking after themselves, even among big fish, and at times can be more troublesome than some cichlids.

The Striped Anostomus is a very attractive fish, which displays well in a large tank decorated with bogwood and no live plants. Space is a key factor in keeping the fish out of mischief, as is choosing tank mates that won't be intimidated or nibbled.

Offer vegetable flake to suit their herbivorous nature. They may graze some filamentous algae, too.

The fish prefer soft water in a mature tank without similar-looking fish. Groups of the same species can be kept, but it is best to introduce them all at the same time. In the wild they shoal loosely and can be found in rivers and large ponds. They inhabit mostly sandy areas with leaf litter that provides plant matter and invertebrate life to nibble on.

They rarely breed in captivity and are mostly caught in the wild, where they are very successful fish.

Banded Leporinus

large • unusual looking • bold • antisocial

SCIENTIFIC NAME: *Leporinus affinis* • FAMILY: Anostomidae • ORIGIN: Brazil, Colombia, Peru, Venezuela (River Negro) • NATURAL HABITAT: Blackwater rivers that flood seasonally, trapping some water in lakes and ponds
AVERAGE ADULT SIZE: 30 cm (12 in) • COLOURS: Black vertical bars on a yellow body and clear, colourless fins
SEXUAL DIFFERENCES: Unknown • REPRODUCTION: Egg-scatterer • BREEDING POTENTIAL: Low • TANK LEVEL: Middle
FOOD: Herbivore flake, frozen and live foods • PLANT FRIENDLY: No • SPECIAL NEEDS: A large tank; suitable tank mates • EASE OF KEEPING: Moderate

Aquarium needs

MINIMUM TANK SIZE: 1.5 m (5 ft)
TEMPERATURE: 24–28°C (75–82°F)
PH: 6–7
WATER HARDNESS: Soft and acidic to neutral
COMPATIBILITY WITH OTHER FISH: Low

The Banded Leporinus is one of nature's true survivors, and the species is widespread in a variety of habitats all over South America. They occur naturally in rivers and flooded areas, where fish up to 10 cm (4 in) long shoal. Larger fish become more territorial and aggressive towards each other and towards other fish.

If you are tempted to keep this fish, bear in mind its eventual large size. Choose tank mates with care as some adults can overcome even large cichlids that they don't get on with. Don't combine it with similarly shaped fish. A single specimen is the best long-term option.

Decorate the tank with rocks and bogwood to break up the space and create territories. Keeping the fish well fed may help to overcome any tendencies to nip fins. Include vegetable matter in their diet.

The vivid markings of the Banded Leporinus earn it a place in large display aquariums containing robust species. However, most domestic tanks are simply too small for it, and it cannot be considered a community fish.

Warning!

This species grows large.

Characins

Black Widow Tetra

hardy • shoaling • unusual looking • easy to keep

SCIENTIFIC NAME: *Gymnocorymbus ternetzi* • FAMILY: Characidae • ORIGIN: Bolivia, Paraguay (Guaporé and Paraguay Rivers) • NATURAL HABITAT: Streams and river tributaries • AVERAGE ADULT SIZE: 5 cm (2 in) • COLOURS: Black anal and dorsal fins with a black rear half to the body, which fades to grey with age • SEXUAL DIFFERENCES: Females are larger and have fuller bodies • REPRODUCTION: Egg-scatterer • BREEDING POTENTIAL: Low • TANK LEVEL: Middle • FOOD: All foods including flake, frozen and live foods • PLANT FRIENDLY: Yes SPECIAL NEEDS: A shoal of six or more • EASE OF KEEPING: Easy

Characins

Aquarium needs

MINIMUM TANK SIZE: 75 cm (30 in)
TEMPERATURE: 22–28°C (72–82°F)
PH: 6–7
WATER HARDNESS: Soft and acidic to hard and alkaline
COMPATIBILITY WITH OTHER FISH: Moderate

These inexpensive and readily available fish have been popular for a long time and have shown themselves to be hardy and long lived. Some aquarists become dis-appointed when the fish grow and lose their juvenile black coloration, ending up mostly silver. Bear in mind, too, that they regularly attain their maximum adult size in the aquarium.

Keep a group of Black Widow Tetras with other larger tetras, barbs and catfish and avoid long-finned fish because they may nip their fins. Keeping them in a group may help to minimize antisocial behaviour, but keeping just two or three fish

together can lead to their becoming territorial, and such a small number will not swim together.

They are easy to keep and feed and can be considered a good first fish for an aquarium. They are not as fussy about water conditions as other tetras and are happy at most tropical temperatures and pH levels.

They are usually only bred by commercial breeders, but female fish can be easily identified by their larger, fuller bodies. Line-bred variants are available, including Long-fin Black Widow Tetras and Gold Widow Tetras.

Rummy-nose Tetra

elegant • peaceful • colourful • shoaling

SCIENTIFIC NAME: *Hemigrammus bleheri* • FAMILY: Characidae • ORIGIN: Brazil, Colombia (River Negro)
NATURAL HABITAT: Blackwater streams and rivers • AVERAGE ADULT SIZE: 5 cm (2 in) • COLOURS: Opaque body
with a bright red patch on the face and eyes and a black and white striped tail • SEXUAL DIFFERENCES: Males
are slimmer • REPRODUCTION: Egg-scatterer • BREEDING POTENTIAL: Low • TANK LEVEL: Middle • FOOD: Flake,
frozen and live foods • PLANT FRIENDLY: Yes • SPECIAL NEEDS: A shoal of six or more • EASE OF KEEPING:
Moderate

Aquarium needs

MINIMUM TANK SIZE: 60 cm (24 in)
TEMPERATURE: 23–28°C (73–82°F)
PH: 6–7
WATER HARDNESS: Soft and acidic to neutral
COMPATIBILITY WITH OTHER FISH: Moderate

Three species are known as Rummy-nose Tetras: *Hemigrammus bleheri*, *H. rhodostomus* and *Petitella georgiae*. *H. bleheri* (illustrated) tends to be the most popular species, and mature specimens develop red coloration all over the top of the head and past the gill cover.

These tetras are peaceful and look good in shoals. They are also just over the average size, which makes them safe with adult Angelfish (*Pterophyllum scalare*; page 154), which are partial to eating fish the size of Neon Tetras. They can be kept in community aquariums together with other peaceful, smaller fish, and planted aquariums suit them well. The water should be soft and acidic.

Like other tetra species, they will not eat food from the bottom, so scavenging species like corydoras catfish are recommended to clear up beneath them.

They rarely breed in community aquariums, and commercial stocks consist of wild-caught fish and fish bred by professional breeders in the Far East and eastern Europe. Commercially bred specimens are hardier than their wild counterparts, but they may need to be quarantined and medicated before being added to the main tank.

Characins

Glowlight Tetra

subtle • small • shoaling • peaceful

SCIENTIFIC NAME: *Hemigrammus erythrozonus* • FAMILY: Characidae • ORIGIN: Guyana • NATURAL HABITAT: Tributaries, streams, rivers and permanent lakes with clear and blackwater • AVERAGE ADULT SIZE: 4 cm (1½ in) COLOURS: Opaque body with a gold sheen and red, neon stripe from the eye through to the tail • SEXUAL DIFFERENCES: Females grow larger and develop fuller bodies • REPRODUCTION: Egg-scatterer • BREEDING POTENTIAL: Low • TANK LEVEL: Middle • FOOD: Small foods, including flake, frozen and live foods • PLANT FRIENDLY: Yes SPECIAL NEEDS: A shoal of six or more • EASE OF KEEPING: Moderate

Characins

Aquarium needs

MINIMUM TANK SIZE: 45 cm (18 in)
TEMPERATURE: 24–28°C (75–82°F)
PH: 6–7
WATER HARDNESS: Soft and acidic to neutral
COMPATIBILITY WITH OTHER FISH: Moderate

Glowlight Tetras are endearing fish that are suitable for smaller, quiet tanks. The red neon stripe shows up well in water that is poorly lit or stained by bogwood. Plant the tank to provide cover and possible spawning sites, but the species is rarely bred by accident in the community tank. As the females mature, they achieve a larger size and deeper bodies than the males.

Offer a variety of foods little and often and keep these fish in soft water with a low pH. Mature the

tank for a minimum of six weeks before adding the fish to make sure that there is no nitrite or ammonia present, which could prove fatal.

They can be kept with other peaceful, similarly sized tetra species together with small, bottom-scavenging catfish, such as corydoras. Don't combine them with any large fish that may eat them. Keep to South American tank mates, which will prefer similar water conditions. A biotope tank, with wood, leaves, fine-leaved plants and a sandy bottom, suits Glowlight Tetras very well.

Serpae Tetra

shoaling • colourful • active • striking

SCIENTIFIC NAME: *Hyphessobrycon callistus* • FAMILY: Characidae • ORIGIN: South America (Amazon and Paraguay River basins) • NATURAL HABITAT: Still waters containing vegetation • AVERAGE ADULT SIZE: 4 cm (1½ in) COLOURS: Rich red body with a black dorsal fin and black patch above the pectoral fin • SEXUAL DIFFERENCES: Females become larger and develop fuller bodies; males are more colourful • REPRODUCTION: Egg-scatterer BREEDING POTENTIAL: Low • TANK LEVEL: Middle • FOOD: All small foods including flake, frozen and live foods PLANT FRIENDLY: Yes • SPECIAL NEEDS: A shoal of six or more • EASE OF KEEPING: Moderate

Aquarium needs

MINIMUM TANK SIZE: 60 cm (24 in)
TEMPERATURE: 24–28°C (75–82°F)
PH: 6–7
WATER HARDNESS: Soft and acidic to neutral
COMPATIBILITY WITH OTHER FISH: Moderate

The Serpae Tetra is probably the reddest tetra available and is a popular fish for that reason. Its main disadvantage is that it may nip the fins of long-finned fish, such as Angelfish, Guppies and Siamese Fighting Fish. Ironically, it is itself available in a long-finned variety, but these fish look pale compared with the natural form.

Have Serpae Tetras in large groups so that they will keep themselves occupied, thus minimizing fin-nipping. Feed them little and often with a variety of foods, including *Daphnia* and mosquito larvae. Optimum conditions can be provided by keeping them in a well-planted, mature tank with soft water. If they are held in the correct conditions the species should rarely cause problems and will complement most tanks.

Other tetra species will make the best tank mates, but you can also include some catfish to clean up the bottom of the tank.

Like many other tetras, Serpae Tetras rarely breed in the aquarium, but they are commercially bred in the Far East.

Characins

Bleeding Heart Tetra

graceful • cute • peaceful • shoaling

SCIENTIFIC NAME: *Hyphessobrycon erythrostigma* • FAMILY: Characidae • ORIGIN: Peru (upper Amazon River basin) • NATURAL HABITAT: Streams and rivers • AVERAGE ADULT SIZE: 8 cm (3 in) • COLOURS: Subtle orange body with a red patch (the bleeding heart) and a black dorsal fin on males • SEXUAL DIFFERENCES: Males are larger and have a more elaborate dorsal fin • REPRODUCTION: Egg-scatterer • BREEDING POTENTIAL: Low • TANK LEVEL: Middle • FOOD: All smaller foods, including dry, frozen and live foods • PLANT FRIENDLY: Yes • SPECIAL NEEDS: Space to swim; shoals for security • EASE OF KEEPING: Moderate

Characins

Aquarium needs

MINIMUM TANK SIZE: 1.2 m (4 ft)

TEMPERATURE: 24–28°C (75–82°F)

PH: 6–7

WATER HARDNESS: Soft and acidic to neutral

COMPATIBILITY WITH OTHER FISH: Moderate

Bleeding Heart Tetras, so called because of the red spot on their sides, are favourites among fish-keepers, and they take pride of place in many show-class planted aquariums. The male grows larger than the female and if it is kept in the right conditions will develop an extended dorsal fin.

They are a larger-than-average tetra and thus require a spacious tank with lots of space for swimming. Plant the tank, but leave space along the front. Soft, acidic

water conditions will help the fish develop its characteristic red marking. The young fish give no indication of the stunning appearance that they will have when they become adult.

Bleeding Heart Tetras are easy to feed and will accept a wide range of foods, relishing both frozen and live foods. They can be kept with a variety of community fish, including larger species such as gouramis. They are, however, too delicate to be mixed with the medium-sized cichlids. These fish rarely breed in aquariums.

Black Neon Tetra

iridescent • shoaling • peaceful • small

SCIENTIFIC NAME: *Hyphessobrycon herbertaxelrodi* • FAMILY: Characidae • ORIGIN: Brazil, Paraguay • NATURAL HABITAT: Streams and river tributaries • AVERAGE ADULT SIZE: 4 cm (1½ in) • COLOURS: Black body with a gold, neon, horizontal line stretching from the gill cover to the tail • SEXUAL DIFFERENCES: Females are larger and have fuller bodies • REPRODUCTION: Egg-scatterer • BREEDING POTENTIAL: Low • TANK LEVEL: Middle • FOOD: Small pieces of flake, frozen and live foods • PLANT FRIENDLY: Yes • SPECIAL NEEDS: A shoal of six or more EASE OF KEEPING: Moderate

Aquarium needs

MINIMUM TANK SIZE: 45 cm (18 in)
TEMPERATURE: 24–28°C (75–82°F)
PH: 6–7
WATER HARDNESS: Soft and acidic
COMPATIBILITY WITH OTHER FISH: Moderate

Black Neon Tetras are no less attractive than Neon Tetras (*Paracheirodon innesi*; page 75), and they can look very striking when kept in a large shoal. The neon stripe shows well in water that is stained by bogwood or shaded by overhanging vegetation.

They are well-behaved, small fish that are ideal for a mature, smaller aquarium in which they can be kept with tank mates that aren't too boisterous (such as some barbs and rainbowfish). Although a similar size to Neon Tetras, Black Neon Tetras grow more quickly and reach their full potential more regularly in the aquarium, and female fish develop noticeably fuller bodies. Add them only to tanks that are more than six weeks old.

Feed them regularly on slowly sinking foods and offer frozen *Daphnia* and bloodworms as occasional treats. Fish such as corydoras catfish make good tank mates, clearing up under the tetras, which won't take food from the bottom.

Planted tanks provide cover and security for this species, and they will look better if provided with soft, warm water.

Characins

Lemon Tetra

cute • peaceful • colourful • shoaling

SCIENTIFIC NAME: *Hyphessobrycon pulchripinnis* • FAMILY: Characidae • ORIGIN: Brazil (Tapajós and Tocantins river basins) • NATURAL HABITAT: Rivers, streams and their tributaries • AVERAGE ADULT SIZE: **4 cm (1½ in)**
COLOURS: Yellow body with a bright yellow anal fin bordered in black and a red streak through the eye
SEXUAL DIFFERENCES: Males have better defined colour on the anal fin • REPRODUCTION: Egg-scatterer • BREEDING POTENTIAL: Low • TANK LEVEL: Middle • FOOD: Small pieces of flake, frozen and live foods • PLANT FRIENDLY: Yes
SPECIAL NEEDS: A shoal of six or more • EASE OF KEEPING: Moderate

Characins

Aquarium needs

MINIMUM TANK SIZE: 60 cm (24 in)
TEMPERATURE: 24–28°C (75–82°F)
PH: 6–7
WATER HARDNESS: Soft and acidic to neutral
COMPATIBILITY WITH OTHER FISH: Moderate

Lemon Tetras can look rather insipid when they are first imported, but if they are kept in the right conditions both sexes turn a rich yellow colour, and males develop a thick, black edge on the anal fin.

For best results keep these fish in groups of six or more in a mature, planted aquarium with small, peaceful tank mates, such as other tetras and small catfish. Avoid large, boisterous tank mates.

The water should be soft and acidic. The species is undemanding – apart from the fact that the water quality must be consistently good. They are usually inexpensive to buy and make worthy additions to the community tank or a South American biotope tank.

Offer a variety of foods, including *Daphnia* and mosquito larvae. Like many tetras, Lemon Tetras will take food from the surface and middle water but will not pick up food from the bottom. Feed little and often (up to three times a day).

Spawning rarely occurs in the domestic tank, but the species is bred commercially in the Far East.

Red-eyed Tetra

striking • shoaling • hardy • dither fish

SCIENTIFIC NAME: *Moenkhausia sanctaefilomenae* • FAMILY: Characidae • ORIGIN: Widespread throughout South America, including Bolivia, Brazil, Paraguay, Peru • NATURAL HABITAT: Streams, rivers and lakes • AVERAGE ADULT SIZE: 8 cm (3 in) • COLOURS: Silver body with a white band and wider black band at the base of the tail; red eyes • SEXUAL DIFFERENCES: Females grow larger and have fuller bodies • REPRODUCTION: Egg-scatterer BREEDING POTENTIAL: Low • TANK LEVEL: Middle to top • FOOD: All foods, including flake, frozen and live foods PLANT FRIENDLY: Yes • SPECIAL NEEDS: A shoal of six or more • EASE OF KEEPING: Easy

Aquarium needs

MINIMUM TANK SIZE: 90 cm (36 in)
TEMPERATURE: 22–28°C (72–82°F)
PH: 6–7
WATER HARDNESS: Soft and acidic to medium hard and alkaline
COMPATIBILITY WITH OTHER FISH: Moderate

Red-eyed Tetras make some of the most impressive displays when they are kept in large shoals in larger aquariums. They shoal very tightly, and all the fish turn in the same direction at the same time. In large aquariums they will also swim near to the top of the tank, making them a good distraction for smaller cichlids, which might otherwise be rather boisterous with each other. (The term dither fish describes fish species that are tough enough and different enough to be used in numbers to distract mainly cichlid species from being too aggressive with each other, instead making them more protective of their fry and partners.)

Red-eyed Tetras grow large enough to be kept in groups with medium to large fish, but they should not be kept with long-finned fish because they may nip the fins. Their small teeth are clearly visible on close inspection. Their toughness makes them easy to keep, but they do prefer mature aquariums, and their slightly larger than average size and need to be kept in a shoal mean that they will be better in a tank that is 90 cm (36 in) or more long.

Characins

Cardinal Tetra

striking • shoaling • popular • small

SCIENTIFIC NAME: *Paracheirodon axelrodi* • FAMILY: Characidae • ORIGIN: Venezuela, Brazil, Colombia (River Negro) • NATURAL HABITAT: Blackwater streams and tributaries • AVERAGE ADULT SIZE: 5 cm (2 in) • COLOURS: Red lower half of the body is bordered by a blue-green, neon stripe above • SEXUAL DIFFERENCES: Females are larger and have fuller bodies • REPRODUCTION: Egg-scatterer • BREEDING POTENTIAL: Low • TANK LEVEL: Middle FOOD: Small foods, including flake, frozen and live foods • PLANT FRIENDLY: Yes • SPECIAL NEEDS: A shoal of six or more • EASE OF KEEPING: Moderate

Characins

Aquarium needs

MINIMUM TANK SIZE: 60 cm (24 in)
TEMPERATURE: 24–30°C (75–86°F)
PH: 6–7
WATER HARDNESS: Soft and acidic
COMPATIBILITY WITH OTHER FISH: Moderate

The Cardinal Tetra rivals the Neon Tetra for its colour and its ranking as one of the world's most popular tropical fish. Large shoals create a stunning display, and photographs of such groups are often used to promote tropical fish and fishkeep-

ing. The Cardinal Tetra is slightly more colourful than the Neon Tetra, with the red coloration stretching all along the lower half of the body, and it can grow a little bit larger too, although it rarely achieves its full size in captivity.

These fish require mature tanks with soft, warm water and no tank mates large enough to eat them. They do well in planted tanks, but their natural blackwater habitats in South America are devoid of plant life because of the highly acidic

water and low light levels. They are displayed at their best in South American biotope tanks containing bogwood, leaves and tannin-stained water.

Cardinal Tetras are bred in captivity only by professional breeders, and a proportion is still caught in the wild every year. The scattered eggs are light sensitive. Pairs can be sexed because the females become larger and fuller. Wild-caught fish are susceptible to the bacterial disease whitespot and should be quarantined before being added to the main tank.

Neon Tetra

tiny • peaceful • colourful • shoaling

SCIENTIFIC NAME: *Paracheirodon innesi* • FAMILY: Characidae • ORIGIN: Peru (upper Solimoes River system)
NATURAL HABITAT: Streams and rivers with clear or blackwater • AVERAGE ADULT SIZE: 4 cm (1½ in) • COLOURS:
Silver belly with a blue neon stripe across the top and a red tail • SEXUAL DIFFERENCES: Females have fuller
bodies and are slightly larger • REPRODUCTION: Egg-scatterer • BREEDING POTENTIAL: Low • TANK LEVEL: Middle
FOOD: Small pieces of flake, frozen and live foods • PLANT FRIENDLY: Yes • SPECIAL NEEDS: A shoal of six or more
EASE OF KEEPING: Moderate

Aquarium needs

MINIMUM TANK SIZE: 45 cm (18 in)
TEMPERATURE: 24–28°C (75–82°F)
PH: 6–7
WATER HARDNESS: Soft and acidic to
neutral
COMPATIBILITY WITH OTHER FISH: Moderate

The Neon Tetra is universally recognized even by non-fishkeepers, and
the species rivals goldfish and Guppies as one of the most popular
aquarium fish in the world. They
are small, peaceful characins, and
should not be kept with any large
fish, which might eat them.

Feed them little and often on foods
that sink slowly through the water
because they will not feed from the
bottom of the tank.

Keep them ideally at a high temperature – 27°C (81°F) – and soften
the water until the pH is less than 7.
The colour of fish kept in the wrong
water conditions may fade, and the
fish may succumb to whitespot
through stress. They are also not tolerant of nitrites, so test the water

before purchasing them and add
fish only to mature tanks.

Keep Neon Tetras with similarly
sized fish and plant the tank with
live plants to provide cover. They
rarely breed in home aquariums
because the eggs are light sensitive
and won't develop properly. The
fish often grow to just 2.5 cm (1 in)
long, and females can be identified
by their larger bellies.

Characins

Congo Tetra

striking • elegant • peaceful • subtle

SCIENTIFIC NAME: *Phenacogrammus interruptus* • FAMILY: Characidae • ORIGIN: Democratic Republic of Congo
NATURAL HABITAT: Rainforest streams and rivers • AVERAGE ADULT SIZE: 10 cm (4 in) • COLOURS: Rainbow-coloured
sheen on reflective scales; females are plainer • SEXUAL DIFFERENCES: Males grow larger and have extended
dorsal and caudal fins • REPRODUCTION: Egg-scatterer • BREEDING POTENTIAL: Moderate • TANK LEVEL: Middle
FOOD: Flake, frozen and live foods • PLANT FRIENDLY: Yes • SPECIAL NEEDS: Space to swim; groups • EASE OF
KEEPING: Moderate

Characins

Aquarium needs
MINIMUM TANK SIZE: 1.2 m (4 ft)
TEMPERATURE: 24–26°C (75–79°F)
PH: 6–7
WATER HARDNESS: Soft and acidic to neutral
COMPATIBILITY WITH OTHER FISH: Moderate

The Congo Tetra can be kept in similar conditions to its South American counterparts. It may eventually grow to a length of 10 cm (4 in), so a group will require a large tank.

The males grow larger than the females and develop all the colours of the rainbow on reflective scales on their flanks. Males also develop extended dorsal and caudal fins if they are given sufficient space to swim and non-boisterous tank mates. Male fish swim up and down the tank, showing off to each other, and can make an effective display. Females are plain and have deep bodies but are still charming in their own right.

Congo Tetras should be kept in a group, and the fish need plants to provide cover as they are a very skittish species. They have visible teeth, but do not present a threat to anything larger than mosquito larvae. These fish need soft, acidic to neutral water for their long-term care.

They do breed in aquariums, and the scattered eggs can be collected and raised by those fishkeepers who are prepared to look after them properly.

Other *Phenacogrammus* species are sometimes available but are not as popular or colourful.

Red Pacu

huge • peaceful • gregarious • nervous

SCIENTIFIC NAME: *Piaractus brachypomus* • FAMILY: Characidae • ORIGIN: Northern Brazil (Amazon and Orinoco Rivers) • NATURAL HABITAT: River systems and seasonally flooded forest • AVERAGE ADULT SIZE: 45 cm (18 in) • COLOURS: Juveniles mimic the Red-bellied Piranha; adult coloration is subdued black and olive SEXUAL DIFFERENCES: None • REPRODUCTION: Egg-scatterer • BREEDING POTENTIAL: Low TANK LEVEL: Middle • FOOD: Flake, pellets and sticks, fruit, nuts • PLANT FRIENDLY: No • SPECIAL NEEDS: A huge tank • EASE OF KEEPING: Moderate

Aquarium needs

MINIMUM TANK SIZE: 1.8 m (6 ft)
TEMPERATURE: 23–28°C (73–82°F)
PH: 6–7
WATER HARDNESS: Soft and acidic
COMPATIBILITY WITH OTHER FISH: Good

Red Pacu are sold in huge numbers for aquariums, and they are often mistaken (even by retailers) for Red-bellied Piranhas (*Pygocentrus nattereri*; page 78). They are sometimes even called vegetarian piranhas.

Their eventual size makes them unsuitable for aquariums. They are peaceful fish, which do best when kept in groups, but they are nervous and can hurt themselves against the glass if startled. They grow quickly and produce lots of waste, putting a strain on filtration systems.

Apart from their size, they are accommodating fish and can be kept with all sorts of other species, including other huge fish, such as arowanas and catfish, as well as with cichlids and even small fish.

They prefer soft, acidic water, similar to that of the River Amazon, but will tolerate well-filtered water with a high pH.

If you are tempted to buy one, the best advice must be: don't. Leave this fish in the shop and visit a public aquarium, where they are often on display in huge biotope aquariums.

The Black Pacu is similar, but it grows to 90 cm (36 in) long and can weigh up to 35 kg (77 lb).

Warning!
This species grows large.

Red-bellied Piranha

predatory • infamous • nervous • dangerous

SCIENTIFIC NAME: *Pygocentrus nattereri* • FAMILY: Characidae • OTHER NAME: Red Piranha • ORIGIN: Guyana
NATURAL HABITAT: Rivers that flood seasonally, trapping water in weedy pools and lakes • AVERAGE ADULT SIZE:
30 cm (12 in) • COLOURS: Juveniles are silver with black spots; adults are darker with the distinctive red belly
SEXUAL DIFFERENCES: None • REPRODUCTION: Egg-scatterer • BREEDING POTENTIAL: Low • TANK LEVEL: Middle
FOOD: Prawns, fish, meat-based foods and live food • PLANT FRIENDLY: Yes • SPECIAL NEEDS: A group; a mature
tank • EASE OF KEEPING: Moderate

Characins

Aquarium needs

MINIMUM TANK SIZE: 1.8 m (6 ft)
TEMPERATURE: 24–28°C (75–82°F)
PH: 6–7
WATER HARDNESS: Soft and acidic
COMPATIBILITY WITH OTHER FISH: Low

Red-bellied Piranhas are notorious all over the world for their skill at stripping flesh from animals in their native waters of South America. In the aquarium it is a different story, and piranhas are nervous, skittish fish that don't do a lot.

They must have a large tank with soft, acidic water and mature filtration. They are normally imported as spotted juveniles, and can be fed flake and mosquito larvae until they are about 5 cm (2 in) long, when they can be offered meatier foods, including shellfish. It is not

necessary to feed live fish to piranhas. They need to be kept in groups of six or more individuals of a similar size, as they will predate each other, and to prevent that must be well fed at all times.

They are not compatible with other fish because of their capable jaws. Treat with caution, and keep an eye on larger fish when carrying out tank maintenance. It is unwise to keep piranhas if young children are present, as the fish do bite.

Warning!
This species grows large.

Penguin Tetra

striking • shoaling • tolerant • easy to keep

SCIENTIFIC NAME: *Thayeria boehlkei* • FAMILY: Characidae • ORIGIN: Brazil, Peru (Amazon River basin)
NATURAL HABITAT: Streams and river tributaries • AVERAGE ADULT SIZE: 6 cm (2½ in) • COLOURS: Opaque body
coloration with a black line running horizontally across the body and into the lower half of the tail • SEXUAL
DIFFERENCES: Females are larger and have fuller bodies • REPRODUCTION: Egg-scatterer • BREEDING POTENTIAL:
Low • TANK LEVEL: Middle to top • FOOD: Flake, frozen and live foods • PLANT FRIENDLY: Yes • SPECIAL NEEDS:
A shoal of six or more • EASE OF KEEPING: Moderate

Aquarium needs

MINIMUM TANK SIZE: 75 cm (30 in)
TEMPERATURE: 22–28°C (72–82°F)
PH: 6–7
WATER HARDNESS: Soft and acidic to medium hard
COMPATIBILITY WITH OTHER FISH: Moderate

The Penguin Tetra is a striking fish, its common name deriving from the fact that it is largely black and white. Fish shoal in tight groups, and the black line running from behind the eye to the base of the tail stands out clearly when lots of fish are swimming together. They tend to swim in the same direction, and when there are many Penguin Tetras in the same tank they can make an eye-catching display. They swim at a slight angle, which accentuates the already curved black line on the body.

They grow larger than other tetras so can be mixed with slightly larger community fish, and they look best when kept in planted aquariums. These fish are easy to feed, accept-ing a variety of foods, and although they need a mature aquarium, they tolerate a wide temperature range.

They are not commonly bred in aquariums, but are bred commercially in the Far East.

Several species are known as Penguin Tetras, and the black and white coloration is also seen in *Hemiodopsis* characins, but *T. boehlkei* is the most widely available of these fish.

Spotted Headstander

plant eater • antisocial • attractive • unusual

SCIENTIFIC NAME: *Chilodus punctatus* • FAMILY: Chilodontidae • ORIGIN: Brazil, Guyana, Surinam, Venezuela
NATURAL HABITAT: Rivers and flooded forest areas with trees and leaf litter • AVERAGE ADULT SIZE: 10 cm (4 in)
COLOURS: Opaque body covered in rows of dark spots • SEXUAL DIFFERENCES: Hard to tell, but females may
develop slightly fuller bodies when they are mature • REPRODUCTION: Egg-scatterer • BREEDING POTENTIAL: Low
TANK LEVEL: Bottom • FOOD: Flake, frozen and vegetable matter • PLANT FRIENDLY: No • SPECIAL NEEDS: None
EASE OF KEEPING: Moderate

Characins

Aquarium needs

MINIMUM TANK SIZE: 90 cm (36 in)
TEMPERATURE: 24–28°C (75–82°F)
PH: 6–7
WATER HARDNESS: Soft and acidic to neutral
COMPATIBILITY WITH OTHER FISH: Moderate

Headstanders are a group of medium-sized characins from South America. They do as their name suggests, swimming in an inverted fashion with their heads close to the substrate. This adaptation has come about because the fish graze the river bottoms and flooded areas for food.

These fish are not as popular with fishkeepers as they could be for two main reasons. First, they like to eat plants, which means that they must be kept in a set-up without live plants or in a biotope containing bogwood and stones. Second, they can be antisocial with each other and with other occupants of the tank, and they may also nip fins.

The Spotted Headstander is one of the better behaved members of the group and is suitable for inclusion in a tank with larger fish, such as some peaceful cichlids and other larger characins. A large tank will help to minimize bad behaviour. A biotope tank can be particularly attractive, as the fish demonstrate their natural behaviour and hover, face down in groups, over the tank floor.

These fish prefer soft, acidic to neutral water with adequate, mature filtration. They are not commonly bred in captivity.

Six-barred Distichodus

large • unusual looking • attractive • plant eater

SCIENTIFIC NAME: *Distichodus sexfasciatus* • FAMILY: Citharinidae • ORIGIN: Democratic Republic of Congo
NATURAL HABITAT: Large rivers and also the margins of Lake Tanganyika • AVERAGE ADULT SIZE: 45 cm (18 in)
COLOURS: Six black vertical bars on an orange body and red fins • SEXUAL DIFFERENCES: Unknown
REPRODUCTION: Egg-scatterer • BREEDING POTENTIAL: Low • TANK LEVEL: Middle • FOOD: Flake, frozen and live
foods • PLANT FRIENDLY: No • SPECIAL NEEDS: A large tank; suitable tank mates • EASE OF KEEPING: Moderate

Aquarium needs

MINIMUM TANK SIZE: 1.8 m (6 ft)
TEMPERATURE: 24–26°C (75–79°F)
PH: 7
WATER HARDNESS: Soft and acidic to hard and alkaline
COMPATIBILITY WITH OTHER FISH: Moderate

The Six-barred Distichodus has sim-ilar markings to the Clown Loach (*Chromobotia macracanthus*; page 90). It is attractive, and small speci-mens are very appealing. They grow large, so need a suitable tank and filtration. In the wild they attain a length of 90 cm (36 in), but they rarely attain half that size in captiv-ity, which may be due to the limiting size of even large aquariums.

A group can be kept, but the fish must have grown up together. Tank mates should be chosen carefully because this species can be a trou-ble-maker. It may nip fins and whiskers and harass fish, including high-bodied fish of a similar shape. It is not too fussy about water hardness and is even kept in hard-water communities with rift lake cichlids. It will eat live aquarium plants and needs to be allowed a lot of swimming space.

The Long-nosed Distichodus (*Disti-chodus lususso*) is similar, but it does not grow as large and has a more slender profile.

Warning!
This species grows large.

Characins

Wolf Fish

antisocial • interesting • predatory • sedate

SCIENTIFIC NAME: *Hoplias malabaricus* • FAMILY: Erythrinidae • ORIGIN: River systems all over South America
NATURAL HABITAT: Shallows of fast-flowing rivers among leaf litter to the margins of lakes and slow-moving
rivers • AVERAGE ADULT SIZE: 45 cm (18 in) • COLOURS: Brown and beige markings with mottled fins • SEXUAL
DIFFERENCES: Females develop fuller bodies • REPRODUCTION: Egg-depositor • BREEDING POTENTIAL: Low • TANK
LEVEL: Bottom • FOOD: Meaty foods • PLANT FRIENDLY: Yes • SPECIAL NEEDS: Retreats • EASE OF KEEPING: Moderate
to hard

Characins

Aquarium needs

MINIMUM TANK SIZE: 1.5 m (6 ft)
TEMPERATURE: 22–28°C (72–82°F)
PH: 6–7
WATER HARDNESS: Soft and acidic to hard and alkaline
COMPATIBILITY WITH OTHER FISH: Low

Wolf Fish are specialized predators from the river systems of South America, where they lurk and then lunge at prey. They have prominent teeth and grow large, and they are respected even by piranhas in the wild.

Their coloration is dull but they have character and are impressive when they feed. They can be weaned on to dead foods, such as frozen fish and cockles; they should never be offered live fish, which is cruel and unnecessary. Tank mates should be chosen with care as they may end up on the menu if they are not large enough.

The tank set-up should consist of rocks and roots with some hardy plants to provide cover. The filtration system must be adequate for

these large fish, which prefer soft, acidic water.

Wolf Fish are shy when first introduced, but become bolder as they come to recognize feeding times. They are fast-growing fish but not that active, preferring to observe what is going on in the rest of the tank.

They have been bred in aquariums but the introduction of a pair usually ends in one fish being mauled. The fish is not one for beginners, but can be kept by experienced aquarists.

Warning!

This species grows large.

Marbled Hatchetfish

sensitive • interesting • surface swimmer • unusual looking

SCIENTIFIC NAME: *Carnegiella strigata strigata* • FAMILY: Gasteropelecidae • ORIGIN: Peru (Iquitos) • NATURAL HABITAT: Rivers and streams in forested areas • AVERAGE ADULT SIZE: 4 cm (1½ in) • COLOURS: Dark brown and silver-white patterning on the flank • SEXUAL DIFFERENCES: Females have fuller bodies • REPRODUCTION: Egg-scatterer • BREEDING POTENTIAL: Low • TANK LEVEL: Top • FOOD: Floating flake, frozen and live foods • PLANT FRIENDLY: Yes • SPECIAL NEEDS: A tight-fitting aquarium lid; surface cover • EASE OF KEEPING: Moderate

Aquarium needs

MINIMUM TANK SIZE: 60 cm (24 in)
TEMPERATURE: 24–28°C (75–82°F)
PH: 6–7
WATER HARDNESS: Soft and acidic
COMPATIBILITY WITH OTHER FISH: Moderate

Hatchetfish are bizarre-looking characins that have adapted to life just below the surface of the water. The fish's mouth is positioned at the top of its head so that it can pick off floating insects, and the dorsal fin is set far back on a flat dorsal profile. The strange 'hatchet' shape of the lower body is an adaptation and conceals large breast muscles attached to equally large pectoral fins, which enable the fish to leap out of the water when large predators approach from below.

The Marbled Hatchetfish is a desirable species that is suitable for mature aquariums. It prefers soft water with a low pH. To curb excessive jumping keep the fish only with other small fish and provide them with tall plants that stretch across the surface of the water to provide a feeling of security. Offer a diet consisting of lots of insect larvae and keep fish in groups of six or more.

The species is rarely bred in captivity (even by commercial breeders) and most are still caught in the wild. A spell in the quarantine tank, and medication, are therefore recommended before new fish are introduced to the main tank. Use a whitespot treatment as a precaution.

Characins

Splash Tetra

surface swimmer • peaceful • interesting • unusual

SCIENTIFIC NAME: *Copella arnoldi* • FAMILY: Lebiasinidae • ORIGIN: Guyana (lower Amazon River basin) and Colombia • NATURAL HABITAT: Streams with vegetation above • AVERAGE ADULT SIZE: 8 cm (3 in) • COLOURS: Golden-brown with some red edging to the tail • SEXUAL DIFFERENCES: Males are larger and have more flamboyant fins • REPRODUCTION: Egg-depositor • BREEDING POTENTIAL: Moderate • TANK LEVEL: Top • FOOD: Flake, frozen and live foods • PLANT FRIENDLY: Yes • SPECIAL NEEDS: Overhanging vegetation for spawning • EASE OF KEEPING: Moderate

Characins

Aquarium needs

MINIMUM TANK SIZE: 75 cm (30 in)
TEMPERATURE: 24–28°C (75–82°F)
PH: 6–7
WATER HARDNESS: Soft and acidic to medium hard
COMPATIBILITY WITH OTHER FISH: Moderate

Splash Tetras are well known for their breeding habits and have been filmed in their natural environment for nature documentaries. What makes them unique is an advanced form of parental care in which male and female fish leap from the surface of the water and place the fertilized eggs on the underside of an over-hanging leaf. They then splash the eggs frequently to keep them wet until the hatched fry drop into the water. This practice avoids the loss of eggs that would occur if they were simply scattered at the bottom.

Males are larger and have longer fins than females. Spawning can take place in captivity, and fish will utilize surfaces above the water, including cover glass. To condition the fish for spawning, keep females and males together in soft, acidic water and feed them on lots of frozen and live food. The best way to

observe their unique behaviour fully is to keep them in a tall tank, three-quarters filled with water, with over-hanging plants. A tall Amazon sword plant (*Echinodorus bleheri*), or even the leaves of a houseplant such as the Swiss cheese plant (*Monstera deliciosa*), would be natural looking and effective.

They can easily be mixed with other tetra species, and a tank filled with fish requiring similar water conditions is recommended. South American biotope aquariums with bogwood and tannin-stained water will suit their needs perfectly.

Hockeystick Pencilfish

peaceful • small • interesting • striking

SCIENTIFIC NAME: *Nannobrycon eques* • FAMILY: Lebiasinidae • ORIGIN: Brazil, Colombia (River Negro)
NATURAL HABITAT: Shallow areas of the main river and seasonally flooded ponds • AVERAGE ADULT SIZE: 5 cm
(2 in) • COLOURS: Dark brown lower body and lower half of the tail; light brown horizontal stripe and brown
back • SEXUAL DIFFERENCES: Males have better colour and are more slender • REPRODUCTION: Egg-scatterer
BREEDING POTENTIAL: Low • TANK LEVEL: Top • FOOD: Small pieces of flake, frozen and live foods • PLANT FRIENDLY:
Yes • SPECIAL NEEDS: A group; peaceful tank • EASE OF KEEPING: Moderate

Aquarium needs

MINIMUM TANK SIZE: 75 cm (30 in)
TEMPERATURE: 24–28°C (75–82°F)
PH: 6–7
WATER HARDNESS: Soft and acidic to medium hard
COMPATIBILITY WITH OTHER FISH: Moderate

Pencilfish are small characins, and they resemble elongated tetras. The Hockeystick Pencilfish comes from the blackwaters of Brazil, where it inhabits shallow waters along the shoreline of the River Negro. In the aquarium it will dwell at the surface in small groups and swim with its tail downwards. Its markings accentuate the swimming angle, and groups of fish swimming through a decorated tank can look quite striking.

They are peaceful fish that should be kept only with other small fish. If they are kept in mature aquariums with soft, acidic water and the right foods, the male fish will become distinct from the larger females and will spend a lot of time displaying in open water. They can be mixed with other pencilfish species or combined with other fish as part of a South American biotope tank. They make good community fish that provide movement in the upper water levels of the aquarium.

They are available as wild-caught fish, but they are also commercially bred in the Far East, although they rarely spawn in a domestic tank.

Characins

Flag-tail Prochilodus

large • peaceful • striking • algae eater

SCIENTIFIC NAME: *Semaprochilodus taeniurus* • FAMILY: Prochilodontidae • ORIGIN: Brazil, Colombia (Amazon River system) • NATURAL HABITAT: Main rivers of the Amazon basin where there is low visibility • AVERAGE ADULT SIZE: 30 cm (12 in) • COLOURS: Silver body with a black and white tail and red pelvic fins • SEXUAL DIFFERENCES: Females may develop fuller bodies when mature • REPRODUCTION: Egg-scatterer • BREEDING POTENTIAL: Low • TANK LEVEL: Middle • FOOD: Flake and frozen foods and vegetable matter • PLANT FRIENDLY: No SPECIAL NEEDS: A large tank • EASE OF KEEPING: Moderate

Characins

Aquarium needs

MINIMUM TANK SIZE: 1.8 m (6 ft)
TEMPERATURE: 24–26°C (75–79°F)
PH: 6–7
WATER HARDNESS: Soft and acidic to neutral
COMPATIBILITY WITH OTHER FISH: Good

Flag-tail Prochilodus have striking markings on their tails and spotted flanks, and they make stunning additions to large tanks. They are peaceful vegetarians. They will mix with any large fish, and because of their mainly vegetarian diet will not try to predate smaller fish.

They grow quickly, and the tank must be large if it is to hold a single specimen and huge to support a group. They prefer soft, acidic water and will require well-filtered, well-aerated water to stay healthy. Feed them on food sticks, flake, pellets and vegetable foods, such as algae wafers and *Spirulina*. They will eat live plants and are not so flighty that they need artificial plants for cover. They have been observed eating algae from the aquarium glass and are said to do a good job of cleaning surfaces, as their fleshy lips are adapted to rasp and graze.

Juvenile fish are slightly more colourful, but the adults are still splendid-looking fish.

They are not bred in captivity, either commercially or at home. As specimens are caught in the wild, quarantine is recommended.

Warning!
This species grows large.

Silver Dollar

deep bodied • peaceful • plant eater • dither fish

SCIENTIFIC NAME: *Metynnis argenteus* • FAMILY: Serrasalmidae • ORIGIN: Brazil, Guyana • NATURAL HABITAT: Rivers and areas of flooded forest • AVERAGE ADULT SIZE: 15 cm (6 in) • COLOURS: Metallic silver • SEXUAL DIFFERENCES: Males have a more developed anal fin • REPRODUCTION: Egg-scatterer • BREEDING POTENTIAL: Low TANK LEVEL: Middle • FOOD: Flake, frozen and live foods • PLANT FRIENDLY: No • SPECIAL NEEDS: A group; a large tank • EASE OF KEEPING: Easy

Aquarium needs

MINIMUM TANK SIZE: 1.5 m (5 ft)
TEMPERATURE: 24–28°C (75–82°F)
PH: 6–7
WATER HARDNESS: Soft and acidic to neutral
COMPATIBILITY WITH OTHER FISH: Good

Silver Dollars are popular fish. They are sometimes mistaken by newcomers to fishkeeping for piranhas, but they are safe with most small fish, although they are best kept in groups with larger fish. They can also be used as dither fish for cichlid pairs (see page 73).

They are hardy fish, which grow at an incredible rate. They are active and need plenty of space to swim. They are best kept in groups to make individual fish feel more secure. Although they prefer soft, acidic water, they will thrive in water with any pH as long as it is well filtered and mature.

Silver Dollars rarely breed in captivity, but adult fish will show signs of courtship behaviour if they are kept in the right conditions. Most are commercially bred in the Far East, but wild specimens are sometimes seen. Wild fish can have a parasite called blackspot, but this is carried by water birds and will usually disappear after several months spent in captivity.

These fish have many similar-looking relatives represented in small numbers in fishkeeping. Collectively known as disc characins, they can all be kept in the same way and will shoal loosely together.

Cyprinids

This huge group of fish families dominates the tropical and cold freshwaters of the world. With the exception of South America and Australia, these fish are widely distributed, and they are often important to local inhabitants for food, for the ornamental fish trade and for recreation in the form of fishing. Several of the major families contain popular ornamental species that are widely kept.

Fish families

The most important families for fishkeepers are Cobitidae, which contains species such as the Clown Loach (*Chromobotia macracanthus*; page 90) and the Coolie Loach (*Pangio kuhlii*; page 91); Cyprinidae, which contains nearly all other species, including barbs, rasboras and danios; and Gyrinocheilidae, which contains the Algae Eater (*Gyrinocheilus aymonieri*; page 109).

Of these families, Cyprinidae contains the most suitable inhabitants for the aquarium, and many of these

The Tiger Barb is a very popular choice for tropical aquariums.

species are among the most popular tropical freshwater fish, including the Tiger Barb (*Puntius tetrazona*; page 96), Zebra Danio (*Danio rerio*; page 99) and Red-tailed Black Shark (*Epalzeorhynchos bicolor*; page 102).

Most of these fish are bred commercially in the Far East, with only a small percentage being caught in the wild. Some new species do turn up every year, although most are of no great importance to fishkeepers because they lack vivid coloration. One recent rediscovery, however, was of the Rosy-line Shark (*Puntius denisonii*; page 105), whose coloration looks almost painted on; these fish can now be seen in nearly every aquatic store.

Aquarium care

Most cyprinids prefer water that is around 25°C (77°F) and neutral to slightly acidic. In the wild they live in habitats that range from small ponds and ditches, to lakes and rivers, to mountain streams. Most are active species, so will appreciate well-oxygenated water with some flow provided by the outlet from a power filter. Most can be safely kept with live plants, but larger species, such as the Tinfoil Barb (*Barbonymus schwanenfeldii*; page 95) and the Cigar Shark (*Leptobarbus hoeveni*; page 104), are

The Silver Shark is suitable only for the larger sizes of aquarium.

not plant friendly and should not be kept with small fish. The fish are mostly active and should be kept in as large an aquarium as you can accommodate. The majority are happiest when they are kept in groups containing male and female fish.

In the right conditions they can be undemanding and generally hardy fish that are suitable for beginners to tropical fishkeeping.

Recommended species

There are many recommended species for beginners, and the Zebra Danio is especially suitable. One of the hardiest tropical fish, it is tolerant of different water conditions, including cool, unheated aquariums. It is also small and easy to keep and breed. The Rosy Barb (*Puntius conchonius*; page 93) is another hardy, colourful species for cooler water, and easy to keep and breed.

Add with caution

Three large species are included in the descriptions in this section on cyprinids. These fish should not be added for the long term to tanks less than 1.5 m (5 ft). The Tinfoil Barb puts in a regular appearance at aquatic stores, re-homed when it reaches a length of 15 cm (6 in) and more. The Silver Shark (*Balantiocheilus melanopterus*; page 92) is also included in this category, yet it can and does grow to over 30 cm (12 in) long and is a nervous fish, to boot. Finally, the Cigar Shark can grow to 60 cm (24 in) in length and may predate smaller fish, so this is definitely one to avoid for the home aquarium.

Clown Loach

interesting • colourful • bottom dwelling • snail eater

SCIENTIFIC NAME: *Chromobotia macracanthus* • FAMILY: Cobitidae • ORIGIN: Borneo, Sumatra • NATURAL HABITAT: Stony streams and shallow rivers • AVERAGE ADULT SIZE: 15 cm (6 in) • COLOURS: Orange body with wide black vertical bars and a red tail • SEXUAL DIFFERENCES: None • REPRODUCTION: Egg-scatterer • BREEDING POTENTIAL: Low • TANK LEVEL: Bottom • FOOD: Live foods (snails, cockles) and tablet foods • PLANT FRIENDLY: Yes • SPECIAL NEEDS: Adequate food; a group • EASE OF KEEPING: Moderate

Cyprinids

Aquarium needs

MINIMUM TANK SIZE: 1 m (3 ft 3 in)
TEMPERATURE: 25–30°C (77–86°F)
PH: 6–7
WATER HARDNESS: Soft and acidic
COMPATIBILITY WITH OTHER FISH: Good

Clown Loaches are among the most popular tropical fish available, providing interest and movement in the lower layers of the water. The common name is a reference to their bizarre aquarium habits: they can be regularly seen lying on their sides, playing dead and winking at the tank owner. They also make audible clicking sounds as they communicate with each other, especially at feeding times.

Not many people believe that they can grow to 30 cm (12 in) in length, which would be an impressive sight, but it takes years for them to attain any size and many never grow to more than 15 cm (6 in) long.

With age comes sexual maturity, and the prospect of breeding them has been considered by thousands of

aquarists but achieved by none. There are reports of them turning into ferocious fish eaters before spawning, devouring tank mates for some much-needed protein, but these reports have not been confirmed.

Clown Loaches are good snail eaters and so can benefit the tank. They should be added only to mature tanks because they are intolerant of new tanks and are susceptible to catching whitespot.

When you are introducing these fish to your tank keep the temperature a few degrees warmer than usual and treat for whitespot as a precaution.

Coolie Loach

shy • unusual looking • burrower • popular

SCIENTIFIC NAME: *Pangio kuhlii* • FAMILY: Cobitidae • OTHER NAME: Kuhli Loach • ORIGIN: Vietnam • NATURAL HABITAT: Sand and rocks in streams and rivers • AVERAGE ADULT SIZE: 10 cm (4 in) • COLOURS: Yellow on lower body with wide, brown bands over the back • SEXUAL DIFFERENCES: Females have fuller bodies • REPRODUCTION: Egg-scatterer • BREEDING POTENTIAL: Low • TANK LEVEL: Bottom • FOOD: Mosquito larvae, tablet foods • PLANT FRIENDLY: Yes • SPECIAL NEEDS: Retreats • EASE OF KEEPING: Moderate

Aquarium needs

MINIMUM TANK SIZE: 60 cm (24 in)
TEMPERATURE: 24–28°C (75–82°F)
PH: 6–7
WATER HARDNESS: Soft to medium hard
COMPATIBILITY WITH OTHER FISH: Moderate

Coolie Loaches can be a surprising sight when they are first viewed in the aquarium store. They are usually part of a swirling mass of bodies in the rear corner of the tank. Some people find them endearing, others rather creepy, but they are popular fish none the less, and they do bring benefits to the aquarium. Their slender bodies are designed for digging, and they can squeeze themselves into small nooks and crannies to find food. This benefits the aquarium in that Coolie Loaches can get to places that other fish can't – under rocks and wood and among plant stems, for example – and can eat any leftover food that has accumulated there. The disadvantage of their body shape for the fishkeeper is that they may pen-

etrate filter bodies and can be almost impossible to catch without totally stripping the tank. They like to hide during the day and will be seldom seen.

The tank set-up should include plenty of hiding places, which may bring a sense of security for the fish. Cover the base of the tank with fine sand for burrowing and keep six or more individuals.

The very slim juveniles fatten up as they mature, and females are believed to have deeper bodies so that they can carry eggs, but these

fish have never been bred successfully. Many species are sold under the name Coolie Loach.

Cyprinids

Silver Shark

large • reflective • nervous • dither fish

SCIENTIFIC NAME: *Balantiocheilus melanopterus* • FAMILY: Cyprinidae • OTHER NAME: Bala Shark • ORIGIN: Borneo, Malaysia, Sumatra, Thailand • NATURAL HABITAT: Large rivers and lakes where the fish swims in midwater • AVERAGE ADULT SIZE: 35 cm (14 in) • COLOURS: Reflective silver scales and white fins bordered in black • SEXUAL DIFFERENCES: Females have fuller bodies • REPRODUCTION: Egg-scatterer • BREEDING POTENTIAL: Low • TANK LEVEL: Middle • FOOD: Flake, sticks and pellets, live and frozen foods • PLANT FRIENDLY: No SPECIAL NEEDS: A large tank • EASE OF KEEPING: Moderate

Cyprinids

Aquarium needs

MINIMUM TANK SIZE: 1.5 m (5 ft)

TEMPERATURE: 24–28°C (75–82°F)

PH: 6–8

WATER HARDNESS: Soft and acidic to hard and alkaline

COMPATIBILITY WITH OTHER FISH: Moderate

Silver Sharks are popular fish, but it is not widely known that they can grow large. A mature specimen 35 cm (14 in) long can be attained by anyone who can provide the fish with a large tank and the right foods and maintenance regime. Sadly, many don't reach that size and are stunted at around 15 cm (6 in) instead. At this size it is noted that they commonly eat small fish, such as Neon Tetras, and may browse on delicate live plants.

They are nervous fish that crash into the tank walls if they are frightened. A solution is to keep them in groups in well-decorated tanks where they will not be affected by

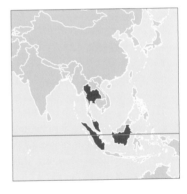

vibration, noise or sudden movements outside the tank.

Feeding Silver Sharks is easy, and they will grow quickly. They have never been bred and reared naturally in aquariums, but they are farmed in huge numbers in the Far East to meet the demand for them among fishkeepers.

They are compatible with other large fish and can be used as dither fish (see page 73) to distract over-attentive cichlids.

Warning!
This species grows large.

Rosy Barb

peaceful • hardy • colourful • active

SCIENTIFIC NAME: *Puntius conchonius* • FAMILY: Cyprinidae • ORIGIN: Afghanistan, northern India, Nepal, Pakistan • NATURAL HABITAT: Cool, fast-flowing streams • AVERAGE ADULT SIZE: 5 cm (2 in) • COLOURS: Females have gold-coloured bodies; males are red • SEXUAL DIFFERENCES: Colour as above • REPRODUCTION: Egg-scatterer BREEDING POTENTIAL: High • TANK LEVEL: Middle • FOOD: Flake, frozen and live foods • PLANT FRIENDLY: Yes SPECIAL NEEDS: None • EASE OF KEEPING: Easy

Aquarium needs

MINIMUM TANK SIZE: 90 cm (36 in)
TEMPERATURE: 18–26°C (64–79°F)
PH: 6–7.5
WATER HARDNESS: Soft to medium hard
COMPATIBILITY WITH OTHER FISH: Good

Rosy Barbs are excellent community fish and are recommended for beginners to fishkeeping and for new tanks. They can be mixed with all types of fish, from small tetras to medium-sized cichlids, and, as an added advantage, they are temperature tolerant and can be kept in unheated, temperate indoor aquariums.

They can grow to 10 cm (4 in) long but usually stay much smaller, averaging about 5 cm (2 in) in length. Because they are active fish they need a relatively spacious tank with areas of open water for swimming. The water quality should be good, but they are not too bothered about the pH of the water and only extremes should be avoided.

The sexes can be told apart by their coloration: males are red, females are pale yellow. The intensity of the males' colour will change with mood and maturity, and there are several colour variants available, including neon shades, but the happier they are, the more colourful they will be. Long-finned varieties are also available.

To breed Rosy Barbs, keep a group with more female than male fish and condition them by offering mosquito larvae. Add some bushy plants to the aquarium to act as

a spawning mop. Remove the eggs after spawning and raise them away from the parents.

Cyprinids

Black Ruby Barb

hardy • peaceful • easy to keep • active

SCIENTIFIC NAME: *Puntius nigrofasciatus* • FAMILY: Cyprinidae • ORIGIN: Sri Lanka • NATURAL HABITAT: Forest and hill streams; some ponds and lakes • AVERAGE ADULT SIZE: 6 cm (2½ in) • COLOURS: Females are brown with broad vertical bars; males are barred but with black fins and a red head when sexually active • SEXUAL DIFFERENCES: Females have fuller bodies; males are more colourful • REPRODUCTION: Egg-scatterer • BREEDING POTENTIAL: Moderate • TANK LEVEL: Middle • FOOD: Flake, frozen and live foods • PLANT FRIENDLY: Yes • SPECIAL NEEDS: A group • EASE OF KEEPING: Easy

Cyprinids

Aquarium needs

MINIMUM TANK SIZE: 75 cm (30 in)
TEMPERATURE: 24–26°C (75–79°F)
PH: 6–7.5
WATER HARDNESS: Soft and acidic
COMPATIBILITY WITH OTHER FISH: Good

Juvenile Black Ruby Barbs look quite plain and unassuming, but mature male fish can be stunning. The coloration changes from a brown base with broad black stripes to jet black with reflective-edged scales and a crimson head and breast with a red nose. In the right conditions the transformation can happen within days of purchase, and the fish will behave differently, with the males swimming with a sense of purpose and trying to attract females.

They are easy to keep and widely available, and they can be kept and bred by beginners. For best results, keep more females than males, decorate the tank with bog-

wood and hardy plants and offer a variety of foods. Black Ruby Barbs can be mixed with other barbs and other community fish, including gouramis, tetras and small catfish. They are well behaved and do not nip the fins of other fish.

The females develop deeper bodies as they mature and may well spawn in the aquarium. Place fine-leaved plants in the main tank to encourage the parents to spawn over them. Remove the eggs once they have been scattered by the parents, and raise them in a separate tank.

Tinfoil Barb

reflective • large • peaceful • shoaling

SCIENTIFIC NAME: *Barbonymus schwanenfeldii* • FAMILY: Cyprinidae • ORIGIN: Borneo, Singapore, Sumatra
NATURAL HABITAT: Rivers, streams and canals; flooded fields • AVERAGE ADULT SIZE: 30 cm (12 in) • COLOURS:
Silver body with red fins and a black edge on the tail fin • SEXUAL DIFFERENCES: Females have fuller bodies
REPRODUCTION: Egg-scatterer • BREEDING POTENTIAL: Low • TANK LEVEL: Middle • FOOD: Flakes, pellets, sticks and
frozen foods • PLANT FRIENDLY: No • SPECIAL NEEDS: A large tank; a group • EASE OF KEEPING: Easy

Aquarium needs

MINIMUM TANK SIZE: 1.8 m (6 ft)

TEMPERATURE: 24–26°C (75–79°F)

PH: 6–7.5

WATER HARDNESS: Soft to hard

COMPATIBILITY WITH OTHER FISH: Moderate

Tinfoil Barbs are popular tropical fish but they do have one flaw: their size. They reach lengths of 30 cm (12 in) or so, making them too big for most tanks. If they are provided with suitably large accommodation they are hardy, peaceful and easy to keep, and they can be mixed with nearly all other large tropical species, such as catfish and large cichlids.

Their bodies are a reflective silver, and mature fish have deep red fins. Albino forms are also available. As a group they look very striking, and their constant swimming motion up and down the tank is relaxing to watch.

They will readily consume all foods as they grow and may well eat the soft leaves of aquarium plants, so keep plastic plants as decoration or no plants at all.

Breeding is not common in the aquarium, perhaps because few fishkeepers have groups of large, sexually mature fish. The sexes are distinguished by the redder fins of males and the deeper bodies developed by females. If the fish are kept in good water and given a varied diet, spawning may take place.

They are not expensive fish, and aquarium stores will often have specimens of 15 cm (6 in).

Warning!
This species grows large.

Tiger Barb

striking • active • shoaling • popular

SCIENTIFIC NAME: *Puntius tetrazona* • FAMILY: Cyprinidae • ORIGIN: Borneo, Sumatra • NATURAL HABITAT: Rivers and streams with some flow • AVERAGE ADULT SIZE: 6 cm (2½ in) • COLOURS: Beige body with four black vertical bars, red fins and a red nose • SEXUAL DIFFERENCES: Females have fuller bodies; males are more colourful REPRODUCTION: Egg-scatterer • BREEDING POTENTIAL: Low • TANK LEVEL: Middle • FOOD: Flake, frozen and live foods • PLANT FRIENDLY: Yes • SPECIAL NEEDS: A group • EASE OF KEEPING: Moderate

Cyprinids

Aquarium needs

MINIMUM TANK SIZE: 90 cm (36 in)
TEMPERATURE: 24–26°C (75–79°F)
PH: 6–7.5
WATER HARDNESS: Soft to hard
COMPATIBILITY WITH OTHER FISH: Moderate

Tiger Barbs are popular fish, one of the species that are recognized in shops even by non-fishkeepers. They are, unfortunately, responsible for much misunderstanding about the whole barb group. Tiger Barbs may nip the fins of long-finned fish, such as Angelfish, Guppies and Siamese Fighting Fish.

To discourage fin-nipping, keep Tiger Barbs in groups of six or more in spacious tanks and feed them well on a range of foods. The larger the group, the less they will be inclined to bother other fish and the more they will congregate only with each other. Problems tend to occur only when fewer than six fish are kept together and temptation is put

their way. The antisocial behaviour by one member of the barb family has for decades led to the whole group being labelled, wrongly, as fin nippers.

Apart from that one slight flaw, Tiger Barbs are lovely fish to keep, and are available in green and albino variants in addition to the usual beige, black and red colour scheme. Female fish develop visibly fuller bodies as they mature, and males have more colourful fins. They often spawn in the main tank, but eggs should be removed for rearing to avoid predation.

Cherry Barb

peaceful • active • colourful • hardy

SCIENTIFIC NAME: *Puntius titteya* • FAMILY: Cyprinidae • ORIGIN: Sri Lanka • NATURAL HABITAT: Forest streams containing leaf litter • AVERAGE ADULT SIZE: 5 cm (2 in) • COLOURS: Females are lightly coloured with a brown stripe and brown flecks; males develop a red hue all over their bodies • SEXUAL DIFFERENCES: Colour as above REPRODUCTION: Egg-scatterer • BREEDING POTENTIAL: Moderate • TANK LEVEL: Middle • FOOD: Flake, frozen and live foods • PLANT FRIENDLY: Yes • SPECIAL NEEDS: A group • EASE OF KEEPING: Easy

Aquarium needs

MINIMUM TANK SIZE: 45 cm (18 in)
TEMPERATURE: 22–26°C (72–79°F)
PH: 6–7.5
WATER HARDNESS: Soft to medium hard
COMPATIBILITY WITH OTHER FISH: Good

Cherry Barbs are excellent community fish and are recommended for newly set up tanks and for newcomers to fishkeeping. They stay small and are often seen for sale at just 2.5 cm (1 in). The sexes may be easily differentiated (males turn bright red), and they may spawn in the community tank, although the adults should be separated from the eggs so they do not eat them.

These fish can be kept in small tanks. They benefit from live plants as decoration, and a decorated tank will show off the males' coloration. They are very active, but if they stop still for long enough you will be able to see the tiny barbels at the edge of their mouths.

Keep one male to every two females because they can be a little boisterous at times. Offer a variety of foods, including live or frozen foods, to bring the fish into condition. The drabber females remain brown in colour, but they still have charm and will develop fuller bodies at spawning time.

Their full size of 5 cm (2 in) may take some time to achieve, but it will be worth the wait as they are very rewarding fish.

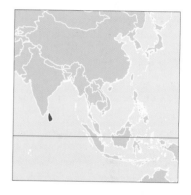

Cyprinids

Cyprinids

Pearl Danio

active • easy to keep • cute • shoaling

SCIENTIFIC NAME: *Danio albolineata* • FAMILY: Cyprinidae • ORIGIN: Burma (Myanmar), Laos, Sumatra, Thailand
NATURAL HABITAT: Shallow streams with fast-moving water • AVERAGE ADULT SIZE: 6 cm (2½ in) • COLOURS:
Opaque body with blue and pink near the tail • SEXUAL DIFFERENCES: Males are slimmer and more colourful
REPRODUCTION: Egg-scatterer • BREEDING POTENTIAL: High • TANK LEVEL: Top • FOOD: Flake, frozen and live foods
PLANT FRIENDLY: Yes • SPECIAL NEEDS: A group of six or more • EASE OF KEEPING: Easy

Aquarium needs

MINIMUM TANK SIZE: 45 cm (18 in)
TEMPERATURE: 20–24°C (68–75°F)
PH: 6–8
WATER HARDNESS: Soft to hard, acid to alkaline
COMPATIBILITY WITH OTHER FISH: Good

Pearl Danios are active fish, but they are easy to keep and suitable for beginners. They are tolerant of cooler temperatures, which means that they can be kept in unheated indoor aquariums.

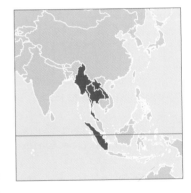

They swim constantly and rarely stop to reveal the tiny barbels at the sides of their mouths, which are characteristic of all danios.

They can be the first fish to be added to a new aquarium and they are tolerant of the mistakes that can be made by novice fishkeepers. Pearl Danios will accept all foods with vigour, and regular feeding will help to give them the energy they need for their constant movement. The tank should contain open water for swimming and some fine-leaved live plants, which may be used for spawning. The eggs are scattered among the plant leaves and can be reared away from the parents. These fish may well spawn frequently once they have reached maturity.

Male fish are smaller, more slender and more colourful than the larger, full-bodied females. They will mix with all other fish, apart from those that are large enough to eat them, and they are inexpensive and readily available. All retail stocks are commercially bred in the Far East.

Zebra Danio

active • hardy • shoaling • easy to keep

SCIENTIFIC NAME: *Danio rerio* • FAMILY: Cyprinidae • ORIGIN: India • NATURAL HABITAT: Rice paddies, streams and ditches • AVERAGE ADULT SIZE: 5 cm (2 in) • COLOURS: Blue-green horizontal stripes on a gold body with striped caudal and anal fins • SEXUAL DIFFERENCES: Females are larger and have fuller bodies; males are slimmer with more anal fin markings • REPRODUCTION: Egg-scatterer • BREEDING POTENTIAL: High • TANK LEVEL: Top • FOOD: Flake, frozen and live foods • PLANT FRIENDLY: Yes • SPECIAL NEEDS: Swimming space; keep in groups of six or more • EASE OF KEEPING: Easy

Aquarium needs

MINIMUM TANK SIZE: 45 cm (18 in)
TEMPERATURE: 18–24°C (64–75°F)
PH: 7–8
WATER HARDNESS: Soft to hard
COMPATIBILITY WITH OTHER FISH: Good

Zebra Danios are popular fish that are suitable for beginners because they are very hardy. They can tolerate fluctuations in temperature and can even be kept in an unheated indoor tank. They are permanently active and never stop swimming, so it is important to provide an area of free swimming space and some water movement from an internal power filter. They are surface swimmers that are always first to the food, so don't keep them with fish that will be out-competed by them at feeding time.

At first glance they don't look very colourful, but well-conditioned fish show deep blue horizontal bars and patterning appears in the fins.

They have been bred in their millions and have been line-bred to produce variants, including long-finned and golden varieties.

They have been the subject of experiment, and genetically modified fish have been produced to glow in the dark. The movement of such fish is controlled to prevent contamination of original wild stocks; these 'Glo' fish should not be purchased as it would only encourage the creation of more man-made mutants.

Siamese Algae Eater

algae eater • peaceful • sought after • subtle

SCIENTIFIC NAME: *Crossocheilus siamensis* • FAMILY: Cyprinidae • OTHER NAME: Siamese Flying Fox • ORIGIN: Malaysia, Thailand • NATURAL HABITAT: Streams and rivers that flood seasonally • AVERAGE ADULT SIZE: 15 cm (6 in) • COLOURS: White underside with a black horizontal stripe and brown back • SEXUAL DIFFERENCES: Unknown • REPRODUCTION: Egg-scatterer • BREEDING POTENTIAL: Low • TANK LEVEL: Bottom • FOOD: Algae, tablet and wafer foods • PLANT FRIENDLY: Yes • SPECIAL NEEDS: Algae-based foods • EASE OF KEEPING: Moderate

Cyprinids

Aquarium needs

MINIMUM TANK SIZE: 90 cm (36 in)
TEMPERATURE: 24–26°C (75–79°F)
PH: 6–7.5
WATER HARDNESS: Soft to hard
COMPATIBILITY WITH OTHER FISH: Good

The Siamese Algae Eater is much sought after by owners of planted aquariums because of its ability to remove algae from the leaves of plants. There may be some difficulty, however, in correctly identifying the species in aquatic stores. Other species are also known as the Siamese Flying Fox (this species' alternative common name), including *Epalzeorhnchos kalopterus* and *Garra* spp., but none of these fish is quite as well behaved as *C. siamensis*. The other species have more colour on the upper body, and *E. kalopterus* has more flamboyant fins, again with hints of colour.

The true Siamese Algae Eater looks quite slender and transparent in its juvenile form, and the black stripe does not run all the way through the tail. It can be combined with other fish of all sizes and will

help to keep the aquarium clean.

It will need to have its diet supplemented with algae-based tablet foods if there are not enough algae and grazing surfaces in the tank. To ensure that there is plenty of naturally occurring food, this species really needs a tank that is 90 cm (36 in) or more in length for its long-term care. The fish can be mixed with each other and kept in groups, and they will in time reach their full size of 15 cm (6 in) long.

They do not breed regularly in the domestic aquarium, but are bred in the Far East for sale in the West.

Giant Danio

impressive • attractive • active • dither fish

SCIENTIFIC NAME: *Devario aequipinnatus* • FAMILY: Cyprinidae • ORIGIN: India • NATURAL HABITAT: Fast-flowing streams and rivers with small boulders • AVERAGE ADULT SIZE: 10 cm (4 in) • COLOURS: Silver-gold body with blue striated patterning along the flanks • SEXUAL DIFFERENCES: Mature females have much fuller bodies and are less colourful • REPRODUCTION: Egg-scatterer • BREEDING POTENTIAL: Moderate • TANK LEVEL: Top • FOOD: Flake, frozen and live foods • PLANT FRIENDLY: Yes • SPECIAL NEEDS: Space to swim; a group of six or more • EASE OF KEEPING: Moderate

Aquarium needs

MINIMUM TANK SIZE: 1.2 m (4 ft)

TEMPERATURE: 24°C (75°F)

PH: 6–7

WATER HARDNESS: Soft to hard, acidic to alkaline

COMPATIBILITY WITH OTHER FISH: Good

Giant Danios are impressive medium-sized fish that are good additions to communities of other medium to large fish. Their silver-gold bodies and blue striated markings make them an attractive fish, and their eventual size means that they are big enough not to be eaten by larger fish, but not so big

that they predate smaller fish themselves. They can be used as dither fish, when their constant surface swimming and tight shoaling behaviour can act as a distraction to over-attentive male cichlids, thus saving their partners from harassment (see page 73).

They are bred in large numbers for fishkeepers around the world, but in recent years they have tended to show a lack of vitality and decreased resistance to disease. Moreover, fish bred in the Far East may well be

hybrids of related species rather than pure bred, so choose stock with care and quarantine new acquisitions for several weeks before adding them to your main tank.

They will spawn in the aquarium by scattering eggs over plants. Males can be distinguished by their slim bodies and better coloration.

The paramount requirement for Giant Danios is swimming space. Like their smaller cousins, they rarely, if ever, stop swimming.

Cyprinids

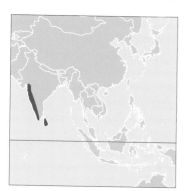

Red-tailed Black Shark

antisocial • striking • bottom dwelling • colourful

SCIENTIFIC NAME: *Epalzeorhynchos bicolor* • FAMILY: Cyprinidae • ORIGIN: Thailand (Mekong River basin)
NATURAL HABITAT: Rivers and streams; this species may be extinct in the wild • AVERAGE ADULT SIZE: 15 cm (6 in)
COLOURS: Matt black body and fins with a bright red tail; mature specimens develop a white tip to the dorsal fin
SEXUAL DIFFERENCES: Males have a pointed anal fin • REPRODUCTION: Egg-scatterer • BREEDING POTENTIAL: Low
TANK LEVEL: Bottom • FOOD: Algae, tablets and frozen foods • PLANT FRIENDLY: Yes • SPECIAL NEEDS: Retreats
EASE OF KEEPING: Moderate

Cyprinids

Aquarium needs

MINIMUM TANK SIZE: 1.2 m (4 ft)
TEMPERATURE: 24–26°C (75–79°F)
PH: 6–8
WATER HARDNESS: Around neutral, soft to medium hard
COMPATIBILITY WITH OTHER FISH: Moderate

The Red-tailed Black Shark is a well-known tropical fish that remains popular year after year.

It is, however, often misunderstood and can become a terror in a peaceful community tank. The key is to understand the needs of the fish. First and foremost, it is territorial. This is because it is naturally a grazing fish, and it must protect its food source from being grazed by other members of its own species and other species. In the aquarium it must not be mixed with its own species nor with other, similar-looking species, because it will attack them. In smaller tanks even red fish will occasionally be attacked because their colour annoys the resident Red-tailed Black Shark. To avoid problems, provide a spacious tank

and decorate it with plenty of rocks, wood, plants and caves, distributing them over the base of the tank to form boundaries. The fish will then be happy that it has areas in which to graze that will not be under threat from other fish.

Avoid mixing Red-tailed Black Sharks with other shark species and any other similar-looking fish.

Newly purchased fish will often look pale, but they will quickly develop depth in the body and the typical coloration of a jet black body with a crimson tail and a white tip to the dorsal fin.

Ruby Shark

antisocial • colourful • algae eater • bottom dwelling

SCIENTIFIC NAME: *Eplazeorhynchos frenatus* • FAMILY: Cyprinidae • OTHER NAME: Rainbow Shark • ORIGIN: Thailand (Bang Fai and Mae Khlong river basins) • NATURAL HABITAT: Rivers and streams that flood, spreading them over a wide area • AVERAGE ADULT SIZE: 15 cm (6 in) • COLOURS: Dark grey body with a blotch at the base of the tail and a line through the eye; the fins are all red • SEXUAL DIFFERENCES: Males have a black edge to the anal fin • REPRODUCTION: Egg-scatterer • BREEDING POTENTIAL: Low • TANK LEVEL: Bottom • FOOD: Algae-based tablets and sinking foods • PLANT FRIENDLY: Yes • SPECIAL NEEDS: Retreats • EASE OF KEEPING: Moderate

Cyprinids

Aquarium needs

MINIMUM TANK SIZE: 1.2 m (4 ft)
TEMPERATURE: 24–26°C (75–79°F)
PH: 6–8
WATER HARDNESS: Soft to medium hard
COMPATIBILITY WITH OTHER FISH: Moderate

Ruby Sharks resemble the Red-tailed Black Shark, but they have red on all their fins, whereas the Red-tailed Black Shark shows red only on its tail. The two species are similar in their behaviour and need to be kept as the only example of their species in the tank, with no similar-looking species included with them.

Decorate the tank with rocks and bogwood and use planting to break up areas of the tank and to create territories and areas for grazing.

The larger the tank, the more contented the shark will be, and a tall tank can be an advantage as other fish species can stay out of the way in the upper layers of water.

Ruby Sharks can be useful to fishkeepers because their grazing will remove some filamentous algae in the aquarium. They also provide colour and movement in the lower water layers.

The sexes are hard to tell apart, but mature males develop a darkened anal fin. They will come into good condition quickly given the right aquarium, water and temperature, and their colour will intensify from the washed-out red that they often display in the shops.

Breeding does not occur in aquariums, not least because of the fish's hatred of its own kind, but

they are bred in vast numbers in the Far East to supply fishkeepers in the West.

Cigar Shark

large • peaceful • shoaling • dither fish

SCIENTIFIC NAME: *Leptobarbus hoeveni* • FAMILY: Cyprinidae • OTHER NAME: Mad Fish • ORIGIN: Borneo, Sumatra, Malaysia, Thailand • NATURAL HABITAT: Large streams and rivers through forests that flood • AVERAGE ADULT SIZE: 45 cm (18 in) • COLOURS: Silver scales with red pelvic and anal fins and a red tail with a black edge • SEXUAL DIFFERENCES: Females have fuller bodies • REPRODUCTION: Egg-scatterer • BREEDING POTENTIAL: Low • TANK LEVEL: Middle • FOOD: Flake, pellets, sticks and fruit • PLANT FRIENDLY: No • SPECIAL NEEDS: A large tank • EASE OF KEEPING: Easy

Cyprinids

Aquarium needs

MINIMUM TANK SIZE: 1.8 m (6 ft)

TEMPERATURE: 24–26°C (75–79°F)

PH: 6–8

WATER HARDNESS: Soft to medium hard

COMPATIBILITY WITH OTHER FISH: Moderate

Cigar Sharks are often bought as innocent-looking juveniles at 5–8 cm (2–3 in) in length, but they grow quickly and are returned to the shop when they have grown to lengths of 15 cm (6 in) or so in just a few months. The reality is that they can grow very large indeed and must be kept in a big aquarium if they are to be properly cared for. A tank of 1.8 m (6 ft) is really the minimum size necessary to keep these fish, and ideally they need a tank that is 2.4 m (8 ft) or more long if you want to keep a group.

The alternative common name, Mad Fish, arose because in their native waters some of the fruit that falls into the water and is then ingested by the fish can affect their behaviour, causing them to swim very erratically, almost as if they were drunk.

In the aquarium their behaviour is calmer, but they are prone to jumping and a fish over 30 cm (12 in) long can easily injure itself and can accidentally break cover glasses.

Although large, they are peaceful. However, adults will eat small fish, so keep only with fish of similar sizes. They can be mixed with large fish such as Oscars (*Astronotus ocellatus*; page 139), and could be considered the ultimate dither fish for cichlid pairs in huge tanks (see page 73).

Warning!

This species grows large.

Rosy-line Shark

attractive • colourful • sensitive • expensive

SCIENTIFIC NAME: *Puntius denisonii* • FAMILY: Cyprinidae • OTHER NAME: Denison's Barb • ORIGIN: India • NATURAL HABITAT: Cool, fast-flowing mountain streams • AVERAGE ADULT SIZE: 15 cm (6 in) • COLOURS: White body with a black horizontal line and red flash from the nose to just below the base of the dorsal fin; the tail is marked with black and white • SEXUAL DIFFERENCES: Females have fuller bodies • REPRODUCTION: Egg-scatterer BREEDING POTENTIAL: Low • TANK LEVEL: Middle • FOOD: Flake, frozen and live foods • PLANT FRIENDLY: Yes SPECIAL NEEDS: A mature tank • EASE OF KEEPING: Moderate

Aquarium needs

MINIMUM TANK SIZE: 1.2 m (4 ft)
TEMPERATURE: 22–25°C (72–77°F)
PH: 7
WATER HARDNESS: Around neutral
COMPATIBILITY WITH OTHER FISH: Moderate

At present the Rosy-line Shark is enjoying an increase in popularity, largely because of the red coloration that runs along the upper body, which is so vivid that it could be mistaken for artificial colouring (a practice that should not be encouraged). In fact, the colour is perfectly natural and becomes more prominent and brighter with age.

Another characteristic that makes the species so popular is the accommodating nature of the fish, which can be combined with all peaceful species, including their own kind. They are also plant friendly and can be used in effective displays.

The disadvantages of the fish are their high cost, resulting from their popularity, and the fact that quantity rather than quality has been the criterion used in breeding, although they are now being commercially bred in the Far East. Just a few generations of tank-bred fish have already weakened the strain.

They need a tank that is large enough to keep a small group and provide open water for swimming. They also need plants as shelter. These fish will not tolerate high temperatures and very acidic water for long, so before you buy test the water and aerate it so that it holds its pH values. You must also ensure that the tank and filter are suitably mature;

many of these fish have succumbed to over-enthusiastic fishkeepers who know little about their proper care.

Cyprinids

Harlequin

small • active • shoaling • peaceful

SCIENTIFIC NAME: *Trigonostigma heteromorpha* • FAMILY: Cyprinidae • ORIGIN: Western Malaysia, Singapore, Sumatra, Thailand • NATURAL HABITAT: Forest streams with vegetation • AVERAGE ADULT SIZE: 4 cm (1½ in)

COLOURS: Brown body with an orange or pink hue and a large, black wedge shape on the rear half

SEXUAL DIFFERENCES: Females have larger, fuller bodies and less intense colour • REPRODUCTION: Egg-scatterer

BREEDING POTENTIAL: Low • TANK LEVEL: Middle • FOOD: Flake, frozen and live foods • PLANT FRIENDLY: Yes

SPECIAL NEEDS: A group of six or more • EASE OF KEEPING: Moderate

Cyprinids

Aquarium needs

MINIMUM TANK SIZE: 45 cm (18 in)
TEMPERATURE: 24–26°C (75–79°F)
PH: 6–7
WATER HARDNESS: Soft and acidic
COMPATIBILITY WITH OTHER FISH: Moderate

Harlequins are small rasboras, and they are excellent additions to a community tank with other small fish. They shoal tightly and swim in all areas of the tank, making attractive displays, and their uniform markings make large groups particularly effective.

Their size means that they are suitable for small tanks, but they do prefer planted aquariums, soft water and mature filtration. They can be mixed with all other fish, apart from those that are big enough to eat them, so avoid species that grow to 10 cm (4 in) in length.

Harlequins are rarely bred in aquariums – they spawn under the leaves of plants – but they are bred

commercially in the Far East. Mature fish must be chosen for sexual differences to be apparent: male fish have more intense colour and smaller, narrower bodies.

Easy to feed, they accept a wide range of small foods. The coloration can change depending on conditions; new fish may look washed out compared with those that have lived in a mature planted tank for years.

Similar species include *Rasbora espei* and *R. hengeli*, but they can be distinguished from these by the narrower, black, wedge-shaped mark on the flank.

Pygmy Rasbora

tiny • colourful • fragile • shoaling

SCIENTIFIC NAME: *Rasbora maculata* • FAMILY: Cyprinidae • ORIGIN: Malaysia, Singapore, Sumatra • NATURAL HABITAT: Sheltered forest streams • AVERAGE ADULT SIZE: 2.5 cm (1 in) • COLOURS: Red body with black spots near the anal and caudal fins and on the flanks • SEXUAL DIFFERENCES: Females are larger and have fuller bodies; males are more colourful • REPRODUCTION: Egg-scatterer • BREEDING POTENTIAL: Low • TANK LEVEL: Middle • FOOD: Small pieces of dry, frozen and live foods • PLANT FRIENDLY: Yes • SPECIAL NEEDS: A group; gentle filtration; small tank mates • EASE OF KEEPING: Moderate

Aquarium needs

MINIMUM TANK SIZE: 30 cm (12 in)
TEMPERATURE: 24–26°C (75–79°F)
PH: 6–7
WATER HARDNESS: Soft and acidic
COMPATIBILITY WITH OTHER FISH: Low

Tiny Pygmy Rasboras are among the smallest tropical fish available to fishkeepers. Their size can work against them in that they may be sucked into the inlets of power filters or eaten by larger fish. The advantage for the fishkeeper is that shoals can be kept in very small tanks.

These fish need air-powered foam filtration, fine-leaved plants and soft water. Tank mates should be equally tiny, and should include Midget Sucker Catfish (*Otocinclus affinis*; page 170) to clean up the bottom of the tank. They make impressive miniature displays, and are therefore suitable for keeping in any size of room.

Feed them little and often with flake, *Daphnia*, *Cyclops*, brine shrimp and mosquito larvae. They

do spawn in the aquarium but require very soft water with a low pH. Males are smaller and more colourful than the females, and eggs are scattered during spawning.

Keep groups of 12 of more fish, which will form shoals. They generally sell for half the price of even other small fish such as tetras, as so many can be packed into boxes for shipping to aquarists in the West.

Cyprinids

Scissortail

peaceful • shoaling • elegant • subtle

SCIENTIFIC NAME: *Rasbora trilineata* • FAMILY: Cyprinidae • ORIGIN: Borneo, Malaysia, Sumatra • NATURAL HABITAT: Slow-moving rivers, streams, lakes, ditches and canals, where the species dwells just below the surface eating insects • AVERAGE ADULT SIZE: 10 cm (4 in) • COLOURS: Opaque body (which may turn gold on maturity), tiny black edges to the scales and white and black markings on the tail • SEXUAL DIFFERENCES: Females are larger and develop fuller bodies • REPRODUCTION: Egg-scatterer • BREEDING POTENTIAL: Moderate • TANK LEVEL: Middle FOOD: Flake, frozen and live foods • PLANT FRIENDLY: Yes • SPECIAL NEEDS: A group • EASE OF KEEPING: Moderate

Aquarium needs

MINIMUM TANK SIZE: 90 cm (36 in)
TEMPERATURE: 24–26°C (75–79°F)
PH: 6–7
WATER HARDNESS: Soft and acidic to hard and alkaline
COMPATIBILITY WITH OTHER FISH: Good

Scissortails have been kept by aquarists for decades, but they have recently become less popular than other, more colourful fish. However, if they are kept in groups in planted aquariums the effect can be stunning, as they shoal quite tightly and all swim the same way, making an attractive display.

They are called Scissortail because of the black and white markings on the tail. When they are sitting motionless in midwater, their tails twitch occasionally, giving the effect of a pair of scissors.

Perfect community fish, they are peaceful, hardy and grow to a large enough size not to be eaten by fish such as adult Angelfish. They readily accept all foods, and if

kept in soft water can develop a golden sheen and reflective scales.

The sexes can be distinguished because female fish become larger and develop fuller bodies; males stay slender with more clearly defined markings. They have been bred in captivity, and mature fish may well spawn in the aquarium, scattering eggs among bushy plants. Unless the eggs are removed, however, they will be eaten by other fish.

The Greater Scissortail (*Rasbora caudimaculata*) looks similar but is a much rarer find in the shops.

Cyprinids

Algae Eater

algae eater • cleaner • peaceful • hardy

SCIENTIFIC NAME: *Gyrinocheilus aymonieri* • FAMILY: Gyrinocheilidae • ORIGIN: Thailand • NATURAL HABITAT: Fast-flowing rivers and streams • AVERAGE ADULT SIZE: 15 cm (6 in) • COLOURS: Brown back with a horizontal bar running from mouth to tail and a silver belly; a yellow form is available • SEXUAL DIFFERENCES: Males develop a thick spine around the eye • REPRODUCTION: Egg-scatterer • BREEDING POTENTIAL: Low • TANK LEVEL: Bottom • FOOD: Algae, tablet and sinking wafers • PLANT FRIENDLY: Yes • SPECIAL NEEDS: Grazing areas • EASE OF KEEPING: Easy

Aquarium needs

MINIMUM TANK SIZE: 90 cm (36 in)
TEMPERATURE: 20–28°C (68–82°F)
PH: 6–8
WATER HARDNESS: Soft to hard
COMPATIBILITY WITH OTHER FISH: Moderate

As their common name suggests, Algae Eaters are very effective at removing algae from all surfaces in the aquarium, including the tank glass. For this reason the species offers great benefits to the aquarium and to the fishkeeper.

Although some specimens are said to have grown to lengths of nearly

30 cm (12 in), most never grow to more than a few centimetres (inches) and so may be considered much easier to accommodate than large sucker-mouthed catfish. In an aquarium 90 cm (36 in) long, several individuals could be added to tackle algae and would clean the tank effectively with only the odd territorial squabble. Such is their grazing ability that if no algae is left extra food must be added in the form of sinking foods, so that the fish do not lose weight.

A golden form is widely available and is perhaps more popular than the original wild type, but both are inexpensive. They are hardy fish and will tolerate different temperatures and pH values in the aquarium. They are also tolerant of their companions and will mix with nearly all fish, from small tetras to large cichlids. The only disadvantage is that they have been known to 'graze' on the bodies of deep-bodied, slow-moving fish, but this could simply be a hungry fish looking for a new source of food.

Cyprinids

Rainbowfish

Rainbowfish inhabit the fresh and brackish waters of Australia, Madagascar, Papua New Guinea and Irian Jaya. They start life as small, silver fish, which could be easily overlooked in the aquatic store, but they go on to develop into beautifully coloured, active fish that would grace any aquarium. Some species, such as Boeseman's Rainbowfish (*Melanotaenia boesemani*; page 115), could stake a claim to being one of the most colourful freshwater fish species in the world.

Community fish

The Melanotaeniidae family make up the bulk of the rainbowfish species, which are all similar in temperament. They are deep-bodied, lively fish, which are generally well behaved, if a little boisterous at times, and are quite easy to keep and feed. They have huge appetites and will accept a wide range of dry and frozen and live foods. They are all plant friendly and appreciate some current in the tank in the form of an outlet from a power filter. They can be mixed with

> **TIP**
>
> **Many rainbowfish will not show colour in bare tanks, exploding into a rainbow of colours when presented with some decor to display in front of.**

each other or, ideally, with other medium-sized species, such as barbs. The males are more colourful and have deeper bodies than the females, and they display vigorously at breeding time, sometimes developing a flashing crest on the forehead.

The Threadfin Rainbowfish (*Iriatherina werneri*; page 114) is an altogether different-looking rainbowfish, with a slender body and delicate, elongated fins. It is very peaceful and would prefer to be with other similarly sized, delicate species, such as tetras or rasboras, rather than with its more robust cousins.

Breeding

All these fish are egg-scatterers, and they will predate their own eggs and fry if they are not removed from the tank.

In groups females should outnumber males, and mature males can sometimes harass females. The eggs

The Boeseman's Rainbowfish is very colourful when mature.

are typically scattered over fine-leaved plants, so fake 'spawning mops' can be made out of wool and placed in the tank to catch the eggs. To condition the fish for spawning offer a higher concentration of frozen foods and conduct several partial water changes.

The Threadfin Rainbowfish is a slender-bodied, delicate fish.

Other families

The Madagascan Rainbowfish (*Bedotia geayi*; page 112) can be kept with Melanotaeniidae rainbowfish in larger aquariums. A group of mature specimens, with their subtle coloration and sleek shapes, can make a stunning display. They may predate small fish but are fine kept with most similarly sized species. They do best in planted aquariums and will swim in a group in midwater.

Aquarium care

Most species of rainbowfish need a fairly large tank decorated with plants, rocks and bogwood. The pH and water hardness are not critical as long as extremes are avoided, but the water quality should be consistently good with low levels of nitrate.

Lighting can range from dim through to bright, and its level will depend chiefly on the requirements of the plants, though light tubes that bring out the rich colours of the fish are a good idea. They naturally inhabit clearwater lakes and creeks, and an aquascape mimicking that habitat will show them off best and make them feel at home.

Madagascan Rainbowfish

colourful • shoaling • peaceful • active

SCIENTIFIC NAME: *Bedotia geayi* • FAMILY: Bedotiidae • ORIGIN: Madagascar • NATURAL HABITAT: Lowland freshwater near to the coast • AVERAGE ADULT SIZE: 12 cm (5 in) • COLOURS: Opaque body with red fins and an iridescent sheen • SEXUAL DIFFERENCES: Males have more colourful fins • REPRODUCTION: Egg-scatterer BREEDING POTENTIAL: Low • TANK LEVEL: Middle • FOOD: Flake, frozen and live foods • PLANT FRIENDLY: Yes SPECIAL NEEDS: None • EASE OF KEEPING: Moderate

Rainbowfish

Aquarium needs

MINIMUM TANK SIZE: 90 cm (36 in)
TEMPERATURE: 22–25°C (72–77°F)
PH: 6–7
WATER HARDNESS: Soft and acidic
COMPATIBILITY WITH OTHER FISH: Moderate

Madagascan Rainbowfish are sought after because of their rich but subtle coloration, and they often take pride of place in planted display aquariums.

They are good community fish but may eat small fry when fully grown. Keep them in as large a tank as possible. Provide space for free swimming at the front of the tank, but decorate the rear and bottom with bogwood, rocks and hardy plants, which will show off the coloration to the greatest effect. In addition, the security that this shelter will afford the fish will encourage them to develop their colours.

They are well-behaved fish and should be kept in groups with other rainbowfish or medium-sized community fish such as barbs. They will take most foods but will achieve the best condition when they are

offered a range of foods, including lots of live or frozen foods.

Mature fish can look stunning, but it will take an investment of a few years on the part of the fish-keeper and perfect water quality to see them at their absolute best.

Sexual differences are apparent in mature fish, with males having darker coloration all around the dorsal, anal and caudal fins. Female fish have slightly fuller bodies with a paler belly region and less colourful fins. In the right conditions they may spawn in the aquarium but are rarely bred and raised by aquarists.

Red Rainbowfish

peaceful • attractive • shoaling • active

SCIENTIFIC NAME: *Glossolepis incisus* • FAMILY: Melanotaeniidae • ORIGIN: Irian Jaya (Lake Sentani) • NATURAL HABITAT: Hill lakes • AVERAGE ADULT SIZE: 15 cm (6 in) • COLOURS: Red body with some silver scales • SEXUAL DIFFERENCES: Females are more olive in colour; males have deeper bodies • REPRODUCTION: Egg-scatterer BREEDING POTENTIAL: Moderate • TANK LEVEL: Middle • FOOD: Flake, frozen and live foods • PLANT FRIENDLY: Yes SPECIAL NEEDS: Swimming space • EASE OF KEEPING: Moderate

Aquarium needs

MINIMUM TANK SIZE: 1 m (3 ft 3 in)
TEMPERATURE: 24–26°C (75–79°F)
PH: 7–8
WATER HARDNESS: Soft to medium hard
COMPATIBILITY WITH OTHER FISH: Moderate

Red Rainbowfish are beautiful, medium-sized community fish for the slightly larger tank. The males' coloration can change dramatically from the juveniles' reddish-silver through to bright red, crimson and dark burgundy as they mature. Some scales also become reflective silver, and the body shape becomes deeper, making the head look narrow. Females are not so colourful but should be added to keep the males displaying and showing their best colours.

The tank should contain live plants with bogwood and rocks on the bottom, but it should primarily be spacious and open so that the fish can freely swim the whole length of the aquarium. Offer a varied diet, including plenty of live and frozen foods, and change a proportion of the tank water frequently.

Combine with other rainbowfish for a stunning display, but do not include small tetras in the tank because they may find the rainbowfish too active and boisterous if they spawn.

Mature rainbowfish may well spawn in the aquarium, and eggs should be removed and raised away from the parents to avoid predation.

Rainbowfish

Threadfin Rainbowfish

elegant • sensitive • small • peaceful

SCIENTIFIC NAME: *Iriatherina werneri* • FAMILY: Melanotaeniidae • ORIGIN: Australia (Cape York, Queensland), Papua New Guinea • NATURAL HABITAT: Swamps and slow-moving creeks • AVERAGE ADULT SIZE: 5 cm (2 in) COLOURS: Grey body with black extended fins and a pink tail; the body can acquire a pinkish sheen • SEXUAL DIFFERENCES: Males develop extended fins and more colour • REPRODUCTION: Egg-scatterer • BREEDING POTENTIAL: Low • TANK LEVEL: Middle • FOOD: Flake, frozen and live foods • PLANT FRIENDLY: Yes • SPECIAL NEEDS: A group • EASE OF KEEPING: Moderate

Rainbowfish

Aquarium needs

MINIMUM TANK SIZE: 60 cm (24 in)
TEMPERATURE: 24–29°C (75–84°F)
PH: 6–7
WATER HARDNESS: Soft and acidic
COMPATIBILITY WITH OTHER FISH: Moderate

Although Threadfin Rainbowfish are in the same family as several other species of rainbowfish, they look altogether more fragile than their larger cousins and should be treated as such. Add them to quiet, mature aquariums with no boisterous fish.

They are well behaved and are excellent additions to a community of small fish. Their preference for soft, warm water would make them good companions for small tetras from South America. The tank should contain medium to heavy planting with live plants and have a gentle filtration system.

Offer them a variety of foods, including live foods that are small enough for their small mouths, such as *Daphnia*, brine shrimp and mosquito larvae.

Sexual differences are obvious in mature fish: males have flamboyant, extended fins; females have much shorter, less colourful fins. Males display to females by flickering their fins. To make their identification more difficult, many commercially bred batches of fish that arrive in aquarist shops contain just males. This could be to foil fishkeepers' attempts to breed them, which would increase supply and lessen demand. Threadfin Rainbowfish have been bred in captivity, but fry are rarely raised by amateur fishkeepers.

Boeseman's Rainbowfish

striking • active • colourful • peaceful

SCIENTIFIC NAME: *Melanotaenia boesemani* • FAMILY: Melanotaeniidae • ORIGIN: Irian Jaya (Vogelkop Peninsula)
NATURAL HABITAT: Large lakes • AVERAGE ADULT SIZE: 10 cm (4 in) • COLOURS: Blue body with a bright yellow rear
SEXUAL DIFFERENCES: Males develop deeper bodies and become more colourful • REPRODUCTION: Egg-scatterer
BREEDING POTENTIAL: Moderate • TANK LEVEL: Middle • FOOD: Flake, frozen and live foods • PLANT FRIENDLY: Yes
SPECIAL NEEDS: Space • EASE OF KEEPING: Moderate

Aquarium needs

MINIMUM TANK SIZE: 1 m (3 ft 3 in)
TEMPERATURE: 24–28°C (75–82°F)
PH: 7–8
WATER HARDNESS: Soft and acidic
COMPATIBILITY WITH OTHER FISH: Moderate

Boeseman's Rainbowfish, with their bright blue and yellow coloration, are among the most colourful of the tropical fish that are available to aquarists. The fish are often placed in display aquariums and are ambassadors for tropical fish, showing how colourful the fish can be.

Female fish are quite colourful, but the males become truly stunning and develop deep bodies and even more vivid shades. To maintain them at their best, decorate their tank with live plants, bogwood and rocks and provide areas for free swimming. Keep them in groups of males and females to encourage the males to display, and feed them a diet consisting of lots of live and frozen foods. Change a proportion of the tank water regularly. When they are in condition they may well spawn in the aquarium, mostly in the morning, but will quickly eat the eggs if they are not removed promptly.

These are well-behaved, medium-sized fish, which make perfect additions to a large community tank. Adults can be mixed with all other similarly sized rainbowfish or barbs, although they may be too boisterous for tanks containing small tetras.

Boeseman's Rainbowfish are long-lived fish, which improve with age,

so a long-term commitment by the fishkeeper will see them at their best.

Rainbowfish

Blue Rainbowfish

colourful • attractive • peaceful • active

SCIENTIFIC NAME: *Melanotaenia lacustris* • FAMILY: Melanotaeniidae • ORIGIN: Papua New Guinea (Lake Kutubu)
NATURAL HABITAT: Lake margins and tributaries • AVERAGE ADULT SIZE: 10 cm (4 in) • COLOURS: Blue body and
fins with a white belly • SEXUAL DIFFERENCES: Males develop deeper bodies and become more colourful, with
a gold crest on the head • REPRODUCTION: Egg-scatterer • BREEDING POTENTIAL: Moderate • TANK LEVEL: Middle
FOOD: Flake, frozen and live foods • PLANT FRIENDLY: Yes • SPECIAL NEEDS: None • EASE OF KEEPING: Moderate

Aquarium needs

MINIMUM TANK SIZE: 90 cm (36 in)
TEMPERATURE: 22–26°C (72–79°F)
PH: 7–8
WATER HARDNESS: Soft to medium hard
COMPATIBILITY WITH OTHER FISH: Good

Juvenile Blue Rainbowfish can be easily overlooked, because few people realize just how colourful they can become. In fact, like other rainbowfish, this species demonstrates perfectly that with time and the right conditions, unprepossessing juveniles can turn into stunning tropical fish that will grace any display with colour and movement.

The Blue Rainbowfish turns from a silvery juvenile to a deep-bodied adult with several shades of blue over its body and a gold crest running up from the snout to the dorsal fin. The crest, which can appear fluorescent, is sometimes flashed to passing females to get extra attention. Male fish may be distinguished

from females by their better colour and deeper body profile, and male fish that are several years old can be almost humpbacked. Females are plainer but are worth adding to encourage the males to display.

These fish need a spacious tank with live plants, rocks and bogwood as well as areas free of decoration in which they can swim. Mature fish may well spawn frequently in the main aquarium, but eggs and very small fry will be eaten by the parents in all but the most densely planted and largest aquariums.

Neon Dwarf Rainbowfish

peaceful • colourful • vivid • attractive

SCIENTIFIC NAME: *Melanotaenia praecox* • FAMILY: Melanotaeniidae • ORIGIN: Irian Jaya (Mamberambo River system) • NATURAL HABITAT: Rivers and streams with stony bottoms • AVERAGE ADULT SIZE: 6 cm (2½ in) • COLOURS: Pale blue scales with red fins • SEXUAL DIFFERENCES: Females are paler; males have more colour and deeper bodies • REPRODUCTION: Egg-scatterer • BREEDING POTENTIAL: Moderate • TANK LEVEL: Middle • FOOD: Flake, frozen and live foods • PLANT FRIENDLY: Yes • SPECIAL NEEDS: None • EASE OF KEEPING: Moderate

Aquarium needs

MINIMUM TANK SIZE: 75 cm (30 in)
TEMPERATURE: 24–28°C (75–82°F)
PH: 7–8
WATER HARDNESS: Soft to medium hard
COMPATIBILITY WITH OTHER FISH: Good

Neon Dwarf Rainbowish are both colourful and well behaved, and their eventual adult size of about 6 cm (2½ in) makes them ideal fish for a community tank. They are small enough to be mixed with tetras but large enough not to be bullied or eaten by medium to large fish.

Their ideal tank would include live plants together with bogwood and rocks on the tank bottom. Make sure there are open areas for swimming, and filter the water well, carrying out plenty of partial water changes. Offer a range of foods to obtain their best condition.

Keep these fish in groups of six or more, with a ratio of two females to every male. Males can be distinguished from females by the vivid red edging that develops on the fins. They also have deeper bodies and become light blue all over. Females are plainer and less deep in the body.

Mature fish will spawn readily in the aquarium, and fine-leaved plants can be placed strategically to catch the scattered eggs. To raise the fry it is best to remove them to avoid predation by the parents.

Labyrinths

The best-known and most recognizable fish in this group is the Siamese Fighting Fish (*Betta splendens*; page 121). Line-bred in captivity to produce stronger colours, longer fins and an enhanced instinct to fight, the fish kept in aquariums today no longer resemble the wild strain. Single specimens should be kept on their own, or they will tire themselves by displaying or be nipped at by other species.

Air breathers

What makes labyrinths fundamentally different from other groups is their ability to breathe air. They are known as labyrinths because they possess a labyrinth organ, which enables the fish to take in oxygen by gulping atmospheric air from the surface of the water, instead of the conventional way of extracting oxygen from the water by passing it over the gills. This adaptation has allowed these fish to penetrate bodies of water with low levels of dissolved oxygen and thus to take advantage of the insect and plant life within them. Labyrinths are mostly found across Southeast Asia, where they live in weed-choked canals, ditches, rivers and ponds.

Bubblenesters

With the exception of mouth-brooders, such as the Chocolate Gourami (*Sphaerichthys osphromenoides*; page 128), members of the Belontiidae family, such as the Dwarf Gourami (*Colisa lalia*; page 125), have a novel way of raising their young. The male blows a foam of tiny, sticky bubbles at the surface of the water, called a bubblenest. He may use plant stems to strengthen the nest and stop it from floating away. He then entices a female to swim up to him below the

nest, where they embrace and eggs and sperm are caught in the mass of bubbles. The male tends to the nest and replaces any fertilized eggs that fall out. When the fry are hatched they are tiny, and the time while their labyrinth organ develops can be difficult, but all species have been bred in captivity, and the breeding of gouramis in ponds was once the backbone of the ornamental fish industry in Singapore, a major fish-exporting country. Most species of gouramis make excellent aquarium fish.

Not for the home aquarium, the Giant Gourami reaches an enormous size.

Dwarf Gourami are good community fish that are available in a variety of colours.

Add with caution

Some labyrinths are not suitable for the average community aquarium. These include the Giant Gourami (*Osphronemus goramy*; page 135), a colossus of a fish that grows huge and has an appetite to match, and the Chocolate Gourami, which is just too delicate for most tanks, preferring very soft, acidic water and a diet of live foods. The Leopard-spotted Climbing Perch (*Ctenopoma acutirostre*; page 120) is a predatory anabantid and should not be kept with small fish, and the Paradise Fish (*Macropodus opercularis*; page 126) can be too spiteful and aggressive for most community tanks

TIP

In the aquarium, labyrinths such as Siamese Fighting Fish and gouramis must be able to breathe air through the surface of the water. If this is impossible – because the aquarium has been overfilled, for example – they can drown.

but is well suited to an unheated, heavily planted tank of its own. The Siamese Fighting Fish is also not one for the community tank, despite having been placed in them for decades. Most tanks are too deep, too powerfully filtered and too busy for all Siamese Fighting Fish, and they should be kept in tanks designed just for them.

Leopard-spotted Climbing Perch

predatory • camouflaged • unusual• quiet

SCIENTIFIC NAME: *Ctenopoma acutirostre* • FAMILY: Anabantidae • ORIGIN: Democratic Republic of Congo
NATURAL HABITAT: Tributaries of the River Congo • AVERAGE ADULT SIZE: 15 cm (6 in) • COLOURS: Yellow body
covered with large, brown blotches • SEXUAL DIFFERENCES: Males have spiny faces and gill covers, are more
colourful and have longer fins • REPRODUCTION: Floating eggs • BREEDING POTENTIAL: Low • TANK LEVEL: Middle
FOOD: Fish, meaty foods • PLANT FRIENDLY: Yes • SPECIAL NEEDS: Retreats • EASE OF KEEPING: Moderate

Labyrinths

Aquarium needs

MINIMUM TANK SIZE: 90 cm (36 in)
TEMPERATURE: 24–26°C (75–79°F)
PH: 6–7
WATER HARDNESS: Soft to medium hard
COMPATIBILITY WITH OTHER FISH: Moderate

Leopard-spotted Climbing Perch are members of a family that is known for its predatory tendencies and that can, reputedly, climb trees. Some of these fish are rather plain and are not popular with aquarists, but the Leopard-spotted Climbing Perch is one of the most attractive fish belonging to the group.

Climbing perch can leave the water in times of hardship to find new water holes, and one was once found in a tree, but this was more an exception than a regular occurrence. In the aquarium they should be provided with lots of cover from bogwood and live plants, and the lighting should be subdued. Filtration should be slow, but biologically effective, because predators produce ammonia-rich waste. Tank

mates should be peaceful, because these are not boisterous fish, but should be several centimetres (inches) long to avoid being on the climbing perch's menu.

When they are first introduced into the tank they will be reluctant feeders and the temptation will be to feed live fish, but they can and should be trained to take dead bait fish instead.

Several of these fish can be kept in a tank, but they are rarely bred in captivity and most are still wild caught. At close quarters the spiny gill covers can be seen on male fish.

Siamese Fighting Fish

colourful • slow swimmer • infamous • antisocial

SCIENTIFIC NAME: *Betta splendens* • FAMILY: Belontiidae • OTHER NAME: Betta • ORIGIN: Cambodia, Thailand
NATURAL HABITAT: Shallow waters of rivers and streams and rice paddies • AVERAGE ADULT SIZE: 6 cm (2½ in)
COLOURS: Red, blue and green variants available, bred from a drabber wild ancestor • SEXUAL DIFFERENCES:
Males are more colourful and have longer fins • REPRODUCTION: Bubblenester • BREEDING POTENTIAL: Moderate
TANK LEVEL: Top • FOOD: Flake, frozen and live foods • PLANT FRIENDLY: Yes • SPECIAL NEEDS: A quiet tank
EASE OF KEEPING: Moderate

Aquarium needs

MINIMUM TANK SIZE: 30 cm (12 in)
TEMPERATURE: 24–30°C (75–86°F)
PH: 6–7
WATER HARDNESS: Soft and acidic
COMPATIBILITY WITH OTHER FISH: Low

The Siamese Fighting Fish is well known among fishkeepers and non-fishkeepers the world over for its fearsome reputation for fighting. Males cannot be kept together because they attack each other within seconds of being introduced. This characteristic – along with longer fins and richer coloration – was enhanced by line-breeding the fish, but over the decades the aquarium strain has been weakened, and fish are not now quite as vicious as they used to be. They can even become victims themselves when other fish pull at their flowing fins, and an unhappy Siamese Fighting Fish will become listless and hang just below the surface of the water in a quiet corner.

What these fish really need is a tank set up just for them. It should be small and gently filtered by an air-powered sponge filter. The water should be warm and soft, and plants should be included. If you offer small amounts of *Daphnia* and mosquito larvae you should soon have a happier fish.

Females can be introduced to the tank, but this will whip up the male's aggression levels and he may pursue unripe females. In addition, females may squabble among themselves. The male blows a bubblenest in order to breed.

Labyrinths

Honey Gourami

small • quiet • subtle • peaceful

SCIENTIFIC NAME: *Colisa chuna* • FAMILY: Belontiidae • ORIGIN: Bangladesh, India • NATURAL HABITAT: Vegetation-edged ditches, ponds and lakes • AVERAGE ADULT SIZE: **5 cm (2 in)** • COLOURS: Orange body; males develop a black breast and yellow dorsal fin; females are paler with a horizontal brown bar • SEXUAL DIFFERENCES: As above • REPRODUCTION: Bubblenester • BREEDING POTENTIAL: Low • TANK LEVEL: Top • FOOD: Flake, frozen and live foods • PLANT FRIENDLY: Yes • SPECIAL NEEDS: Quiet tank • EASE OF KEEPING: Moderate

Labyrinths

Aquarium needs

MINIMUM TANK SIZE: **45 cm (18 in)**
TEMPERATURE: **24–28°C (75–82°F)**
PH: **6–7**
WATER HARDNESS: Soft and acidic
COMPATIBILITY WITH OTHER FISH: Moderate

Honey Gouramis look similar to Dwarf Gouramis (*Colisa lalia*; page 125), but are usually smaller. They are not line-bred to produce colour morphs, and mature males attain an orange coloration with a black breast and yellow dorsal fin. Females are plain, apart from a faint horizontal line midway up the body.

Honey Gouramis are peaceful fish, and they should not be kept with boisterous fish. They do not like excessively large or deep tanks, nor do they like power filtration. Instead, they should be kept in

smaller tanks with mature, air-powered filtration and soft, acidic water. Live plants will be appreciated, and floating plants are useful for providing cover and as somewhere to secure a bubblenest.

Combine them only with other small fish, such as rasboras or tetras. They do best when they are the only gourami species in the tank.

Offer small, frozen and live foods and crumbled flake. They have been bred in captivity but the fry are not easy to raise as they are tiny. They are bred commercially in the Far East for sale to fishkeepers in the West.

Banded Gourami

peaceful • subtle • shy • colourful

SCIENTIFIC NAME: *Colisa fasciata* • FAMILY: Belontiidae • ORIGIN: India, Bangladesh, Burma (Myanmar)
NATURAL HABITAT: Weedy rivers, lakes and ponds • AVERAGE ADULT SIZE: 10 cm (4 in) • COLOURS: Rusty coloured
body with turquoise stripes and cheeks • SEXUAL DIFFERENCES: Males are longer and much more colourful
REPRODUCTION: Bubblenester • BREEDING POTENTIAL: Low • TANK LEVEL: Middle, top • FOOD: Flake, frozen and
live foods • PLANT FRIENDLY: Yes • SPECIAL NEEDS: Plants, quiet tanks • EASE OF KEEPING: Moderate

Aquarium needs

MINIMUM TANK SIZE: 90 cm (36 in)
TEMPERATURE: 24–28°C (75–82°F)
PH: 6–7
WATER HARDNESS: Soft to medium hard
COMPATIBILITY WITH OTHER FISH: Moderate

Although it is sometimes known as the giant gourami, the Banded Gourami is not to be confused with the true Giant Gourami (*Osphronemus goramy*; page 135), which grows to around 70 cm (28 in) long. Instead, the Banded Gourami grows to only 10 cm (4 in) in length and is very similar in appearance to the Thick-lipped Gourami (*Colisa labiosa*; page 124).

These fish are relatively easy to care for provided that the tank has a mature filter, preferably soft acidic water, live plants and quiet tank mates. They are also best kept as the only gourami species in the tank as they are quite shy and will be more willing to show their rich colours if they feel secure.

The Banded Gourami may be distinguished from the Thick-lipped Gourami by its more rounded head. In addition, males and females have a thicker tail base. The sexes can be told apart because the males have better colour and more elongated bodies. Females have shorter fins.

In the right conditions they may breed in the aquarium, when the male will blow a bubblenest at the surface of the water. All gourami fry are very tiny and need suitably small foods, such as rotifers, if they are to survive.

Labyrinths

Thick-lipped Gourami

peaceful • subtle • graceful • quiet

SCIENTIFIC NAME: *Colisa labiosa* • FAMILY: Belontiidae • ORIGIN: India • NATURAL HABITAT: Rivers edged with vegetation • AVERAGE ADULT SIZE: 8 cm (3 in) • COLOURS: Rusty coloured or orange body with turquoise vertical stripes and a turquoise belly • SEXUAL DIFFERENCES: Males are larger, and more colourful and elongate REPRODUCTION: Bubblenester • BREEDING POTENTIAL: Low • TANK LEVEL: Middle, top • FOOD: Flake, frozen and live foods • PLANT FRIENDLY: Yes • SPECIAL NEEDS: Slow water flow • EASE OF KEEPING: Moderate

Labyrinths

Aquarium needs

MINIMUM TANK SIZE: 75 cm (30 in)
TEMPERATURE: 24–28°C (75–82°F)
PH: 6–7
WATER HARDNESS: Soft to medium hard
COMPATIBILITY WITH OTHER FISH: Good

The Thick-lipped Gourami is only occasionally seen in shops, although its cousin, the Dwarf Gourami (*C. lalia*; opposite), is much more popular and widely available. This is surprising because this species is

an ideal community fish, suitable for small and medium-sized tanks.

Fish in good condition are attractively marked with turquoise bands on a rusty coloured body, and the colours are intensified on males that wish to breed. In addition, an orange form is available. They look similar to the Banded Gourami (*Colisa fasciata*; page 123).

The ideal tank will be decorated with lots of live plants and bogwood, with trailing or floating plants

at the surface to aid bubblenest building. The water flow should be slow, and additional aeration is not necessary because, like all gouramis, Thick-lipped Gouramis can breathe atmospheric air.

They are well-behaved fish, which can be mixed with all smaller fish. Add them to the tank in sexed pairs: males are larger and more colourful, while females have shorter bodies. They occasionally breed in captivity but are not commonly bred in domestic aquariums, the great majority being bred commercially in the Far East.

Dwarf Gourami

peaceful • small • slow swimmer • colourful

SCIENTIFIC NAME: *Colisa lalia* • FAMILY: Belontiidae • ORIGIN: Borneo and India • NATURAL HABITAT: Ponds, drainage ditches and sluggish streams • AVERAGE ADULT SIZE: 5 cm (2 in) • COLOURS: Males are vertically striped in red and blue alternately and have blue cheeks; females are silver • SEXUAL DIFFERENCES: Males are larger and more colourful • REPRODUCTION: Bubblenester • BREEDING POTENTIAL: Low • TANK LEVEL: Top • FOOD: Flake, frozen and live foods • PLANT FRIENDLY: Yes • SPECIAL NEEDS: Quiet tank mates • EASE OF KEEPING: Moderate

Aquarium needs

MINIMUM TANK SIZE: 45 cm (18 in)
TEMPERATURE: 24–28°C (75–82°F)
PH: 6–7
WATER HARDNESS: Soft and acidic to neutral
COMPATIBILITY WITH OTHER FISH: Moderate

Dwarf Gouramis are peaceful fish that are suitable for quieter, smaller tropical tanks. They prefer slow water movement and planted aquariums with soft, warm water. Like many other members of the members of the Belontiidae family, they are bubblenesters and deposit their fertilized eggs into a sticky nest of bubbles blown by the male at the water surface.

Because gouramis have a labyrinth organ, enabling them to breathe atmospheric air, they must be able to reach the surface of the water in order to breathe.

Dwarf Gouramis are available in many different colours that have been developed for fishkeepers. Sadly, this line-breeding has weakened the strain somewhat, so take special care to provide mature aquariums with good water quality. If your fish are in their natural form, as found in the wild, you will be able to distinguish the colourful male fish from the plain females. With line-bred variants, females can be the same colour as males, but males are still larger and females have shorter bodies.

These fish may breed in the aquarium, but the tiny fry need special care.

Labyrinths

Paradise Fish

colourful • hardy • aggressive • snail eater

SCIENTIFIC NAME: *Macropodus opercularis* • FAMILY: Belontiidae • ORIGIN: China, Korea, Taiwan • NATURAL HABITAT: Rivers, streams and still waters with low oxygen content • AVERAGE ADULT SIZE: 10 cm (4 in) • COLOURS: Red and blue body colour is layered into vertical stripes • SEXUAL DIFFERENCES: Males are larger and more colourful and have longer fins • REPRODUCTION: Bubblenester • BREEDING POTENTIAL: Moderate • TANK LEVEL: Middle, top • FOOD: Flake, frozen and live foods • PLANT FRIENDLY: Yes • SPECIAL NEEDS: Dense planting for cover • EASE OF KEEPING: Easy

Labyrinths

Aquarium needs

MINIMUM TANK SIZE: 60 cm (24 in)
TEMPERATURE: 15–28°C (59–82°F)
PH: 6–7.5
WATER HARDNESS: Soft to medium hard
COMPATIBILITY WITH OTHER FISH: Low

Paradise Fish are famous for being perhaps the first tropical fish ever to be imported and kept in ornamental aquariums. The species is an air breather and tolerant of cool temperatures, factors that would have been crucial in its survival in captivity, while most other species would have perished on their journey to cooler countries.

They can be aggressive and are not safe to be kept with most peaceful, small community fish. Some individuals develop a taste for the eyes of other fish and can even remove them from catfish and other species. In addition, male fish should not be kept together as they fight.

On the plus side these are colourful, hardy fish. Their subtropical background means that they can be kept in simple, unheated aquariums, and they are great at eating nuisance snails. The tank should include dense planting to provide cover, and the fish also needs areas that are out of the line of sight of other Paradise Fish. Surface vegetation will be used for bubblenesting. Single-species tanks may be the best way to keep them.

Male fish are much more colourful than females and have longer fins. An albino form is also available.

Licorice Gourami

small • colourful • sensitive • unusual

SCIENTIFIC NAME: *Parosphronemus deissneri* • FAMILY: Belontiidae • ORIGIN: Malaysia, Singapore, Sumatra
NATURAL HABITAT: Shallow, blackwater streams with vegetation • AVERAGE ADULT SIZE: 3.5 cm (1½ in) • COLOURS:
Yellow body with thick, brown horizontal bars • SEXUAL DIFFERENCES: Males develop more colourful fins
REPRODUCTION: Cave-spawner • BREEDING POTENTIAL: Moderate • TANK LEVEL: Bottom • FOOD: Live and frozen
foods • PLANT FRIENDLY: Yes • SPECIAL NEEDS: Soft water • EASE OF KEEPING: Difficult

Aquarium needs

MINIMUM TANK SIZE: 45 cm (18 in)
TEMPERATURE: 24–28°C (75–82°F)
PH: 5–7
WATER HARDNESS: Soft and acidic
COMPATIBILITY WITH OTHER FISH: Moderate

Licorice Gouramis are sensitive, small gourami, which should be treated with extra care and not added to a normal community tank. They originate from blackwater areas of Southeast Asia – that is, their native waters are soft and acidic with a low mineral content and are stained brown from tannins leached from wood and leaves in surrounding forests. The pH can be as low as 5, and light penetration into this water is poor.

The tank for these fish should be small with air-powered filtration and a gentle flow of water. Set the temperature quite high and use reverse osmosis (RO) water to obtain soft, acidic water. Add bogwood to stain the water or filter it through peat. Use only one small, fluorescent light tube.

Live plants may not survive but floating plants would be beneficial and will help to cut down on light. These fish are cave-spawners, building a bubblenest on the underside of the cave. Feed the adults on frozen and live foods, because they will be reluctant to take dry foods.

If you are able to give these fish the special care they need, you may well be able to breed them.

Labyrinths

Chocolate Gourami

small • subtle • sensitive • quiet

SCIENTIFIC NAME: *Sphaerichthys osphromenoides* • FAMILY: Belontiidae • ORIGIN: Borneo, Malaysia, Sumatra
NATURAL HABITAT: Shallow, vegetation-edged forest streams • AVERAGE ADULT SIZE: 5 cm (2 in) • COLOURS: Brown
body with gold bars • SEXUAL DIFFERENCES: Males develop a yellow edge to the anal fin • REPRODUCTION:
Mouth-brooder • BREEDING POTENTIAL: Moderate • TANK LEVEL: Middle • FOOD: Flake, frozen and live foods
PLANT FRIENDLY: Yes • SPECIAL NEEDS: Soft, acidic water • EASE OF KEEPING: Difficult

Labyrinths

Aquarium needs

MINIMUM TANK SIZE: 45 cm (18 in)
TEMPERATURE: 25–30°C (77–86°F)
PH: 5–7
WATER HARDNESS: Soft and acidic
COMPATIBILITY WITH OTHER FISH: Moderate

Chocolate Gouramis would be more readily available were it not for the difficulty of keeping them alive in aquariums. They are bred commercially for aquarists but do not do well in captivity because they need very acidic water. Even if this is provided, they sometimes die prematurely from bacterial infections.

If you come across healthy specimens, set up a tank especially for them with very soft, acidic, warm water and feed them on lots of frozen and live foods. The tank does not have to be large or have powerful filtration; a mature air-powered sponge filter will suffice. If they make it past their first few weeks in captivity they seem to become hardier and more tolerant of less acidic water.

These fish can be bred in captivity, the female carrying the eggs in her mouth.

If you are mixing Chocolate Gouramis with other species, choose quiet species that like the same water conditions – Cardinal Tetras, for example – but quarantine the gouramis for several weeks.

Because of their sensitivity they are not recommended for beginners and should be kept only by experienced aquarists.

Pearl Gourami

colourful • peaceful • subtle • graceful

SCIENTIFIC NAME: *Trichogaster leeri* • FAMILY: Belontiidae • ORIGIN: Borneo, Malaysia, Sumatra • NATURAL HABITAT: Still waters with floating plants • AVERAGE ADULT SIZE: 12 cm (5 in) • COLOURS: Lace pattern over a gold background • SEXUAL DIFFERENCES: Males develop a red breast and a longer dorsal fin • REPRODUCTION: Bubblenester • BREEDING POTENTIAL: Low • TANK LEVEL: Middle, top • FOOD: Dry, frozen and live foods • PLANT FRIENDLY: Yes • SPECIAL NEEDS: More females than males • EASE OF KEEPING: Moderate

Aquarium needs

MINIMUM TANK SIZE: 90 cm (36 in)
TEMPERATURE: 24–28°C (75–82°F)
PH: 6–7
WATER HARDNESS: Soft to medium hard
COMPATIBILITY WITH OTHER FISH: Good

Pearl Gouramis are wonderfully coloured community fish, and they make good additions to a slightly larger community tank. They swim in a graceful manner and bring peace and relaxation to the aquarium. They prefer mature aquariums with still water, and their colours will be shown off best in a planted tank with soft, warm water. Decorate the tank quite heavily to provide cover.

These fish can be kept in groups, and the more colourful males should be outnumbered by females to prevent them becoming boisterous on occasions. Males can be identified by their long dorsal fin. Females have a short, rounded dorsal fin.

They can be fed on a range of foods, including all dry foods, but they relish feeds of red mosquito larvae. They can be bred in the aquarium, and a bubblenest is built on the surface of the water and anchored to live plants. They do not generally spawn, however, and it would take a special effort by the owner (and a separate tank) to get them to spawn successfully and then raise the fry. They are bred in ponds in the Far East in their thousands for sale in the West.

Labyrinths

Moonlight Gourami

large • reflective • graceful • peaceful

SCIENTIFIC NAME: *Trichogaster microlepsis* • FAMILY: Belontiidae • ORIGIN: Cambodia, Thailand • NATURAL HABITAT: Shallow vegetated ponds and lakes • AVERAGE ADULT SIZE: 15 cm (6 in) • COLOURS: Reflective silver SEXUAL DIFFERENCES: Males have darker ventral fins • REPRODUCTION: Bubblenester • BREEDING POTENTIAL: Low TANK LEVEL: Middle • FOOD: Flake, frozen and live foods • PLANT FRIENDLY: Yes • SPECIAL NEEDS: A large tank EASE OF KEEPING: Moderate

Labyrinths

Aquarium needs

MINIMUM TANK SIZE: 1.2 m (4 ft)
TEMPERATURE: 25–28°C (77–82°F)
PH: 6–7
WATER HARDNESS: Soft and acidic
COMPATIBILITY WITH OTHER FISH: Good

Moonlight Gouramis have been kept by aquarists for decades, and are well suited to larger aquariums with medium-sized to large companions. They are not as popular as they once were; this could be because of poor initial acclimatization, which affects the supply chain to the fishkeeper. They are hardy once properly acclimatized, but when first imported they are susceptible to bacterial infection, so quarantine is recommended, and any changes to the pH and hardness of the water should be made gradually. Larger fish are stronger and a better choice at the aquarium store.

These fish need as large a tank as possible because they can reach their full length of 15 cm (6 in) in captivity. Decorate the tank with bogwood and live plants but leave plenty of room for free swimming. A group of Moonlight Gouramis can look particularly effective in a tank decorated with lots of fine-leaved plants and a light substrate, because their highly reflective scales can reflect the colours in the tank. They will accept a range of foods, and should be active swimmers once they have settled.

They can be bred and will build a large bubblenest, but they are mostly bred commercially in the Far East.

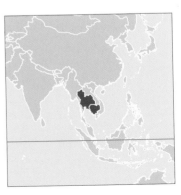

Three-spot Gourami

hardy • graceful • colourful• boisterous

SCIENTIFIC NAME: *Trichogaster trichopterus* • FAMILY: Belontiidae • ORIGIN: Burma (Myanmar), Malaysia, Sumatra, Thailand, Vietnam • NATURAL HABITAT: Margins of sluggish rivers with low visibility and dense vegetation
AVERAGE ADULT SIZE: 12 cm (5 in) • COLOURS: Light blue body with blue spots or striations, depending on the variety; a gold form is available • SEXUAL DIFFERENCES: Males have extended dorsal fins; females are shorter
REPRODUCTION: Bubblenester • BREEDING POTENTIAL: Low • TANK LEVEL: Middle, top • FOOD: Flake, frozen and live foods • PLANT FRIENDLY: Yes • SPECIAL NEEDS: More females than males • EASE OF KEEPING: Moderate

Aquarium needs

MINIMUM TANK SIZE: 90 cm (36 in)
TEMPERATURE: 24–28°C (75–82°F)
PH: 6–7
WATER HARDNESS: Soft to medium hard
COMPATIBILITY WITH OTHER FISH: Good

Three-spot Gouramis are medium-sized fish that are suitable for medium to large community tanks. They are hardy fish that have been kept by aquarists for decades, and they would have been one of the few blue species available in the early years. They are now available in a golden form, and there is also a striated form called the Opaline Gourami.

They are best kept in groups with several females to one male as the males can be boisterous and harass single females and other males. Apart from that, they are safe to be mixed with fish as small as Neon Tetras (*Paracheirodon innesi*; page 75) and as large as Tinfoil Barbs (*Barbonymus schwanenfeldii*; page 95) and adult Silver Sharks (*Balantiocheilus melanopterus*; page 92).

They do need a well-decorated tank that provides cover in the form of live plants, which will also be utilized for bubblenests. They do not like a strong flow of water in the tank, so if you are using power filtration, provide an area wihout a strong current. Feed them on a range of foods, including mosquito larvae. Soft water will condition the fish for breeding. Males have an extended dorsal fin; females have a short, rounded dorsal fin and also develop fuller bodies.

Labyrinths

Sparkling Gourami

tiny • fragile • sensitive • cute

SCIENTIFIC NAME: *Trichopsis pumila* • FAMILY: Belontiidae • ORIGIN: Cambodia, Sumatra, Thailand, Vietnam
NATURAL HABITAT: Stagnant ponds and ditches with floating plants • AVERAGE ADULT SIZE: 3.5 cm (1½ in)
COLOURS: Tiny blue dots on a white body and blue and red speckled fins • SEXUAL DIFFERENCES: Males have a
pointed dorsal fin • REPRODUCTION: Bubblenester • BREEDING POTENTIAL: Low • TANK LEVEL: Middle • FOOD: Small
foods, flake, frozen and live • PLANT FRIENDLY: Yes • SPECIAL NEEDS: A small tank • EASE OF KEEPING: Moderate

Labyrinths

Aquarium needs

MINIMUM TANK SIZE: 30 cm (12 in)
TEMPERATURE: 24–28°C (75–82°F)
PH: 6–7
WATER HARDNESS: Soft and acidic
COMPATIBILITY WITH OTHER FISH: Moderate

Sparkling Gouramis are tiny tropical fish, which are usually offered
for sale when they are around 1 cm
(½ in) long, when they are often
overlooked and mistaken for tetras
or rasboras.

Because of their diminutive size,
the tank should be set up especially
for them, and they will do better in a
smaller aquarium. The tank should
be filtered gently by an air-powered
sponge filter. Heating should be
slightly warmer than normal, and
the water should be soft and acidic
with a low pH. Decorate the tank
with small, fine-leaved plants so that
some of the surface is covered, too.

The fish can be added in a group
of six or more, which should contain

a mixture of males and females,
from which a pair should form. The
male builds a bubblenest before the
pair spawns.

Offer Sparkling Gouramis small
foods, such as *Daphnia* and
mosquito larvae, and as the adults
grow their coloration should become
more apparent. They can be mixed
with other fish but would be better
combined with other tiny species or
none at all. Suitable companions
would include the Pygmy Rasbora
(*Rasbora maculata*: page 107) and
Pygmy Corydoras (*Corydoras pygmaeus*; page 163).

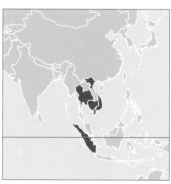

Croaking Gourami

small • subtle • unusual• sensitive

SCIENTIFIC NAME: *Trichopsis vittata* • FAMILY: Belontiidae • ORIGIN: Eastern India, Malaysia, Thailand, Vietnam
NATURAL HABITAT: Ditches, ponds, flooded fields and densely vegetated shallow water • AVERAGE ADULT SIZE:
6 cm (2½ in) • COLOURS: Beige body with brown horizontal stripes covered in a colourful sheen • SEXUAL
DIFFERENCES: Males have redder anal fins • REPRODUCTION: Bubblenester • BREEDING POTENTIAL: Low • TANK
LEVEL: Middle • FOOD: Flake, frozen and live foods • PLANT FRIENDLY: Yes • SPECIAL NEEDS: Quiet tanks • EASE OF
KEEPING: Moderate

Aquarium needs

MINIMUM TANK SIZE: 60 cm (24 in)
TEMPERATURE: 24–28°C (75–82°F)
PH: 7
WATER HARDNESS: Soft to medium hard
COMPATIBILITY WITH OTHER FISH: Good

Croaking Gouramis are so called because the male fish makes a croaking sound when it is enticing the female at spawning time. They don't enjoy huge popularity, and from a distance don't look that colourful, but close up they have subtle coloration and make good additions to smaller community aquariums.

Their bodies are a different shape from that of most deep-bodied gouramis. They have a shallower body, rather like that of their smaller cousin, the Sparkling Gourami. They are adult at just over 5 cm (2 in) long, but when imported they are much smaller and it will take a trained eye to spot them in the busy tanks at the aquatic store.

They prefer heavily planted aquariums with soft, warm water and a slow form of filtration, like that from an air-powered sponge filter. The water quality should be good and a proportion should be changed regularly, as they can be susceptible to bacterial infection if they are kept in less than perfect conditions.

They can be mixed with other similarly sized fish, but are best kept as the only gourami species in the aquarium.

They can be bred in the aquarium, but all other fish should be removed if you want the fry to survive.

Labyrinths

Kissing Gourami

unusual • large • peaceful • algae eater

SCIENTIFIC NAME: *Helostoma temminckii* • FAMILY: Helostomatidae • ORIGIN: Thailand, Java • NATURAL HABITAT: Sluggish waters with dense vegetation • AVERAGE ADULT SIZE: 20 cm (8 in) • COLOURS: Pink; the natural form is green • SEXUAL DIFFERENCES: Females develop fuller bodies • REPRODUCTION: Floating eggs • BREEDING POTENTIAL: Low • TANK LEVEL: Middle • FOOD: Algae, flake and frozen foods • PLANT FRIENDLY: No • SPECIAL NEEDS: A large tank • EASE OF KEEPING: Moderate

Labyrinths

Aquarium needs

MINIMUM TANK SIZE: 1.2 m (4 ft)
TEMPERATURE: 24–28°C (75–82°F)
PH: 7
WATER HARDNESS: Soft to hard
COMPATIBILITY WITH OTHER FISH: Good

The family Helostomatidae is monotypic and contains only this species.

Kissing Gouramis are so named because two fish may appear to 'kiss' each other with their enlarged lips. The kissing is not from passion, however, but is more a test of strength. The lips are used naturally to graze algae and vegetable matter and may also be used to eat soft-leaved plants in the aquarium. Algae-covered surfaces will be cleaned to an extent, but the fish should not be relied on to clean all surfaces thoroughly.

They grow large and become more elongated as they grow, so must be kept in a big tank. Unlike the bubblenesting gouramis, they produce floating eggs.

The pink coloration is not natural, but was line-bred from the green colour that wild fish possess.

There is also a 'balloon' form, which has a much shortened body and an appealing appearance, but

this has been developed from a mutation and should not be endorsed, as many other tropical fish species could suffer the same fate.

Giant Gourami

huge • pet fish • hardy • occasionally territorial

SCIENTIFIC NAME: *Osphronemus goramy* • FAMILY: Osphronemidae • ORIGIN: China, India, Indonesia, Thailand
NATURAL HABITAT: Slow-moving rivers, canals and lakes with low oxygen levels and dense vegetation; they have
been introduced into many waters as a food fish • AVERAGE ADULT SIZE: 70 cm (28 in) • COLOURS: Grey with white
head; some fish show a pink coloration in the tail • SEXUAL DIFFERENCES: Males develop longer fins and bigger teeth
REPRODUCTION: Bubblenester • BREEDING POTENTIAL: Low • TANK LEVEL: Middle • FOOD: Sticks, pellets, fruit, vegetables,
live food, worms • PLANT FRIENDLY: No • SPECIAL NEEDS: A huge tank; responsible owners • EASE OF KEEPING: Easy

Aquarium needs

MINIMUM TANK SIZE: 2.4 m (8 ft)
TEMPERATURE: 24–30°C (75–86°F)
PH: 6–7.5
WATER HARDNESS: Soft to hard
COMPATIBILITY WITH OTHER FISH: Moderate

Giant Gouramis are large, intelligent fish that can be kept in aquariums and will make good pets, but – and it's a big but – they can grow to over 60 cm (24 in) long in captivity, making a huge tank necessary if you wish to keep one. You must take a responsible attitude before purchasing a Giant Gourami. There are many adult specimens in the world that have been given up by fish-keepers who could not commit to the necessary tank size or to the length of time that these fish live for, which can be 20 years.

If you are a dedicated keeper and prepared to give them a long-term home, they can be very rewarding animals and will hand feed. They eat many human foods, including bananas, tomatoes, apples and lettuce. They also eat cockles, mussels, whitebait and earthworms.

These fish produce copious amounts of waste and need an adequately filtered aquarium. They are very hardy and can breathe air (an adaptation that helps such big fish survive in natural and aquarium waters that are poor in oxygen). They can be mixed with other fish, but the odd individual (possibly a male) can become very territorial and will attack the glass when viewed.

Warning!
This species grows large.

Cichlids

The fish in this group are mostly colourful and active, and are popular with many fishkeepers because of their flamboyant finnage, boldness and the unique behaviour that some cichlids exhibit in rearing their young. They are more intelligent than most other fish and tend to think before they swim, moving around the aquarium with a real sense of purpose. Not all cichlids can be kept together nor can they be kept with some other kinds of fish – and some can be downright antisocial. Because the type of water in which they live is paramount, they are often divided into two main groups: soft-water cichlids and hard-water cichlids.

Soft-water cichlids

Soft-water cichlids inhabit the river systems of South America and West and Central Africa. The rivers feed through tropical rainforest and are softened and acidified by the tannic and humic acids produced by the wood and leaves that fall into them. The water can often

The Discus, from South America, is the most famous soft-water cichlid.

be stained brown by these acids, when it is known as blackwater, or it may contain so much sediment that visibility is poor.

They are at the mercy of predators from the air and the water, so some of these fish are camouflaged, but also uniquely marked so that they can recognize each other in the gloom. Males, of course, also need to look good enough to attract a mate in the breeding season.

They can be small fish like the Cockatoo Cichlid (*Apistogramma cacatuoides*; page 138), or large like the Oscar (*Astronotus ocellatus*; page 139), or shy and demanding to keep like the Discus (*Symphysodon* spp.; page 155).

They all relish foods such as mosquito larvae and form pairs in order to lay eggs and raise their young. These cichlids can be aggressive when they are rearing young, but outside the breeding season they can be mixed with other similarly sized non-cichlid species.

Hard-water cichlids

This group of cichlids can be further divided into Central American species, such as the Firemouth Cichlid (*Thorichthys meeki*; page 156), and East African rift-lake cichlids, such as the Frontosa (*Cyphotilapia frontosa*; page 142).

Central American cichlids mostly inhabit shallow, fast-flowing rivers or large lakes. They are all pair-

The Fairy Cichlid needs hard water and a rocky environment.

Cichlids

forming substrate spawners and will ferociously defend their young. They are easy to feed and undemanding but can be too aggressive for delicate tank mates. Their tanks should be decorated with rocks and wood to create territories and potential spawning sites. The Firemouth Cichlid can be particularly recommended for novice fishkeepers.

The East African rift lakes include Lakes Malawi and Tanganyika, and although the water chemistry of the two lakes is similar, the fish species found in each lake are quite different. Nearly all Malawi cichlids are maternal mouth-brooders – that is, the female fish incubates large eggs in her mouth and does not form a pair bond with the male. Many Tanganyika cichlids are also maternal mouth-brooders, but some are pair-forming, substrate

TIP

A good cichlid for novice fishkeepers to begin with is the Kribensis (*Pelvicachromis pulcher*; page 152). It is a small, colourful, pair-forming cichlid from West Africa, which can be kept with smaller fish and will take up residence in a suitable cave. It is plant friendly and easy to breed.

spawners – that is, they lay eggs on a surface and protect the eggs and fry from predators. Substrate spawners include the rock-dwelling Julie (*Julidochromis* spp.; page 145) and the Fairy Cichlid (*Neolamprologus brichardi*; page 148), a prolific spawner that is straightforward to keep and can be recommended for beginners.

Cockatoo Cichlid

small • quiet • subtle • sensitive

SCIENTIFIC NAME: *Apistogramma cacatuoides* • FAMILY: Cichlidae • ORIGIN: South America (Amazon River basin) • NATURAL HABITAT: Small, quiet tributaries • AVERAGE ADULT SIZE: 7 cm (2¾ in) • COLOURS: Beige body with a dark, horizontal stripe, red fins, a spotted tail fin and green facial markings • SEXUAL DIFFERENCES: Males are larger and have more flamboyant fins • REPRODUCTION: Egg-depositor • BREEDING POTENTIAL: Moderate • TANK LEVEL: Bottom • FOOD: Live and frozen foods • PLANT FRIENDLY: Yes • SPECIAL NEEDS: Soft water; a quiet tank • EASE OF KEEPING: Difficult

Cichlids

Aquarium needs
MINIMUM TANK SIZE: 60 cm (24 in)
TEMPERATURE: 24–26°C (75–79°F)
PH: 6–7
WATER HARDNESS: Soft and acidic
COMPATIBILITY WITH OTHER FISH: Moderate

Cockatoo Cichlids belong to the *Apistogramma* genus of dwarf cichlids. They prefer to be kept in quiet tanks with no boisterous companions and in soft, acidic water with gentle filtration.

The Cockatoo Cichlid is a particularly attractive representative of the group. The males have elaborate red fins, and they grow larger than the females, which are plainer. The males also develop a wide mouth. They should be kept in pairs in tanks decorated with plants and bogwood, and flowerpots or empty coconut shells should be added to provide caves for spawning. Adults should be conditioned on live and frozen foods.

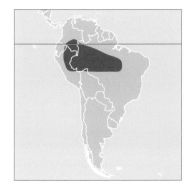

To obtain suitable soft water for the species use reverse osmosis (RO) water. Use a simple air-powered sponge filter to provide the filtration.

If the tank is carefully prepared to take account of the fish's needs before purchase, there should be no problems. But these are sensitive fish, and if their exacting requirements aren't met they may last for only a few weeks in a more generalized aquarium.

They are commercially bred in Europe and are available in a double-red form, which is even more red than the normal form.

Oscar

large • antisocial • popular • pet fish

SCIENTIFIC NAME: *Astronotus ocellatus* • FAMILY: Cichlidae • ORIGIN: Brazil, Colombia, Peru • NATURAL HABITAT: Sluggish backwaters of the main rivers with tree roots • AVERAGE ADULT SIZE: 35 cm (14 in) • COLOURS: Black and grey with orange markings and a spot on the tail • SEXUAL DIFFERENCES: None • REPRODUCTION: Egg-depositor • BREEDING POTENTIAL: Low • TANK LEVEL: Middle • FOOD: Fish, sticks, pellets and worms • PLANT FRIENDLY: No • SPECIAL NEEDS: A large, well-filtered tank • EASE OF KEEPING: Easy

Aquarium needs

MINIMUM TANK SIZE: 1.5 m (5 ft)
TEMPERATURE: 24–28°C (75–82°F)
PH: 6–7
WATER HARDNESS: Soft and acidic
COMPATIBILITY WITH OTHER FISH: Low

Oscars are big fish with big personalities and they make great pets, but they must have large living quarters and power filtration to cope with their waste. They quickly learn to respond to the person who feeds them and can develop a bond with the owner, just as a cat or dog would, but this is because they are driven by their stomachs, not by affection.

In the wild these are ambush predators, who eat anything that falls in the water. The 'eye spot' on the tail is a defence against piranha attack, the fish sticking its tail towards danger.

In the aquarium young Oscars are very competitive, and bully and try to eat other fish. They should be kept on their own in a large tank decorated with bogwood, rocks and artificial plants; alternatively, if they grow up in a group and form a pair, the pair can be kept together. They can be mixed with tough catfish, such as *Glyptoperichthys* sp. (page 167), or kept with big non-cichlids, such as Tinfoil Barbs (*Barbonymus schwanenfeldii*; page 95).

In addition to the usual colouring, albino forms are available, and red and red tiger-patterned varieties.

Warning!
This species grows large.

Cichlids

Baensch's Aulonocara

colourful • peaceful • sedate • pretty

SCIENTIFIC NAME: *Aulonocara baenschi* • FAMILY: Cichlidae • ORIGIN: Africa (Lake Malawi) • NATURAL HABITAT: Rocky areas and over sand in open water • AVERAGE ADULT SIZE: 15 cm (6 in) • COLOURS: Orange flanks and a blue face • SEXUAL DIFFERENCES: Males are colourful with yellow spots on the anal fin; females are plain REPRODUCTION: Maternal mouth-brooder • BREEDING POTENTIAL: Moderate • TANK LEVEL: Middle • FOOD: Flake, frozen and live foods • PLANT FRIENDLY: Yes • SPECIAL NEEDS: A peaceful cichlid tank • EASE OF KEEPING: Moderate

Cichlids

Aquarium needs

MINIMUM TANK SIZE: 90 cm (36 in)
TEMPERATURE: 24–26°C (75–79°F)
PH: 7.5–8.2
WATER HARDNESS: Hard and alkaline
COMPATIBILITY WITH OTHER FISH: Moderate

Aulonocara spp. are also known as peacock cichlids, and *A. baenschi* has an orange adult coloration, whereas most are a variation on blue. Although they are from Lake Malawi, these cichlids are much more peaceful than the competitive rock-dwelling cichlids (mbuna) that are found in that lake, and they have evolved to eat plankton rather than the algae on rocks.

The tank should be fairly open, with a few rocks, and tough plants such as Java Moss (*Vesicularia dubyana*) can be included. Water quality must be good, and the bottom should have a layer of fine sand.

The sexes can be easily told apart as adults because only the males become brightly coloured; females remain drab with shorter fins.

The male Baensch's Aulonocara should be the main attraction in the tank. Ideally, it should be the only *Aulonocara* species in the tank (to avoid hybridization) and should be surrounded by a harem of females. Other non-cichlids can be added, but a biotope tank containing other peaceful Malawi cichlids and perhaps some Malawi *Synodontis* catfish is the best option.

Because their diet is not strictly herbivorous, a variety of frozen foods can be offered, including bloodworms, brine shrimp and *Mysis* shrimp.

Convict Cichlid

aggressive • territorial • prolific • hardy

SCIENTIFIC NAME: *Cryptoheros nigrofasciatus* • FAMILY: Cichlidae • ORIGIN: Throughout Central America
NATURAL HABITAT: Rivers and lakes; introduced into many waters outside their natural range • AVERAGE ADULT
SIZE: 15 cm (6 in) • COLOURS: Grey with black vertical bars • SEXUAL DIFFERENCES: Males are larger and may
develop a nuchal hump; females attain colourful bellies • REPRODUCTION: Egg-depositor • BREEDING POTENTIAL:
High • TANK LEVEL: Middle • FOOD: Dry, frozen and live foods • PLANT FRIENDLY: No • SPECIAL NEEDS: Spawning sites
EASE OF KEEPING: Easy

Aquarium needs

MINIMUM TANK SIZE: 90 cm (36 in)
TEMPERATURE: 24–26°C (75–79°F)
PH: 7–8
WATER HARDNESS: Neutral to hard and alkaline
COMPATIBILITY WITH OTHER FISH: Moderate

Anyone who wants to begin keeping cichlids should acquire some Convict Cichlids, which will be everything that everyone thinks a cichlid should be. They are well-built, stocky little fish when first purchased, and they swim around the decoration in the tank with a real sense of purpose. They will eat almost anything and will tolerate most temperatures and pH, although they are best kept in water with a high pH and a temperature that isn't too hot.

Male fish become larger than females and have slightly longer fins and black vertical stripes. Females have shorter bodies, and when they are sexually mature they develop a lovely green and yellow belly.

If you have a male and a female in the same tank they will breed. They form a pair and take up residence in a cave or under decoration, where the female will lay eggs and the male will fertilize them. If your Convict Cichlids suddenly become more aggressive and the female more secretive, they probably have spawned. When the fry are born they will be hidden for a few days until they are free swimming, and then the pair will take them out into the tank to find food. The problems can now begin, however, because any other fish in the tank will be seen as a threat and a potential fry eater, even if they are not. Breeding pairs should be separated from other fish in the aquarium.

Frontosa

large • striking • sedate • expensive

SCIENTIFIC NAME: *Cyphotilapia frontosa* • FAMILY: Cichlidae • ORIGIN: Africa (Lake Tanganyika) • NATURAL HABITAT: Very deep water over sand and rock • AVERAGE ADULT SIZE: 35 cm (14 in) • COLOURS: Black and white vertical body stripes • SEXUAL DIFFERENCES: Males develop a large nuchal hump and longer fins • REPRODUCTION: Maternal mouth-brooder • BREEDING POTENTIAL: Low • TANK LEVEL: Middle • FOOD: Shellfish, fish, food sticks PLANT FRIENDLY: Yes • SPECIAL NEEDS: A large tank • EASE OF KEEPING: Moderate

Cichlids

Aquarium needs

MINIMUM TANK SIZE: 1.8 m (6 ft)
TEMPERATURE: 24–26°C (75–79°F)
PH: 7.5–8.2
WATER HARDNESS: Hard and alkaline
COMPATIBILITY WITH OTHER FISH: Moderate

Frontosas are large, predatory cichlids. In the wild they live in the depths and suck up small fish while they sleep. They are striking, with broad black and white stripes and large nuchal humps. Their tank should be large enough to hold five or six adults, and the water should be well filtered and maintained. The lighting should be subdued, and the tank mostly open water.

They are not predatory fish in captivity and should be kept on their own or with other large fish that won't steal their food, as they are often

slow to eat. The ideal group consists of one male and several females, and the females should have shelter away from the male if they are carrying eggs and fry. They don't usually breed in aquariums, so a female holding fry can be seen as a success. Young Frontosas are sought after.

Offer them cockles, mussels, prawns, whitebait and some food sticks, but too much dry food may cause Frontosas to float, a condition that should be avoided.

Warning!
This species grows large.

Jewel Cichlid

colourful • attractive • predatory • sometimes aggressive

SCIENTIFIC NAME: *Hemichromis* spp. • FAMILY: Cichlidae • ORIGIN: Cameroon, Ivory Coast, Togo, Nigeria
NATURAL HABITAT: Shallow rivers in forested areas • AVERAGE ADULT SIZE: 10 cm (4 in) • COLOURS: Red with tiny
blue dots all over the body • SEXUAL DIFFERENCES: Males are more elongated with more pointed dorsal and
anal fins • REPRODUCTION: Egg-depositor • BREEDING POTENTIAL: Moderate • TANK LEVEL: Middle • FOOD: Dry,
frozen and live foods • PLANT FRIENDLY: Yes • SPECIAL NEEDS: None • EASE OF KEEPING: Moderate

Aquarium needs

MINIMUM TANK SIZE: 90 cm (36 in)
TEMPERATURE: 24–28°C (75–82°F)
PH: 6–7
WATER HARDNESS: Soft and acidic to medium hard
COMPATIBILITY WITH OTHER FISH: Moderate

Jewel Cichlids are popular, medium-sized cichlids from West Africa. There are several species regularly available that look quite similar, including *Hemichromis guttatus*, *H. bimaculatus* (illustrated) and *H. lifalili*.

They are red fish, and the iridescent spots on the gill covers and down the flanks make them look very attractive. In nature they will eat anything from insects to small fish, so they should not be kept with small fish such as Neon Tetras in the aquarium.

Their tank should contain rocks and bogwood, so that they can create territories, as well as tough live plants, such as Java Moss (*Vesicularia dubyana*) and Java Fern (*Microsorium pteropus*). Filtration should be provided by an internal or external power filter, which will also provide some flow in the water. These fish need neutral or lower pH, and the water should be soft and acidic.

Male fish are larger than the females, which have shorter bodies and are squarer in the belly region when mature. If a pair forms and the water conditions are suitable they may well spawn. A breeding pair will become aggressive towards their tank mates in defence of their brood, so they should be segregated or removed to another empty tank.

Outside the breeding season Jewel Cichlids can be mixed with other tough, medium-sized fish, such as barbs, rainbowfish and characins.

Severum

large • peaceful • tolerant • plant eater

SCIENTIFIC NAME: *Heros efasciatus* • FAMILY: Cichlidae • ORIGIN: Brazil, Peru, Columbia • NATURAL HABITAT: Rivers and lakes with vegetation in the margins • AVERAGE ADULT SIZE: 25 cm (10 in) • COLOURS: Gold, green with a black vertical bar near to the tail • SEXUAL DIFFERENCES: Males have markings on their faces and longer fins REPRODUCTION: Egg-depositor • BREEDING POTENTIAL: Low • TANK LEVEL: Middle • FOOD: Sticks, pellets and frozen foods • PLANT FRIENDLY: No • SPECIAL NEEDS: A large tank • EASE OF KEEPING: Moderate

Cichlids

Aquarium needs

MINIMUM TANK SIZE: 1.2 m (4 ft)
TEMPERATURE: 24–30°C (75–86°F)
PH: 6–7
WATER HARDNESS: Soft and acidic
COMPATIBILITY WITH OTHER FISH: Moderate

There are four species in the *Heros* genus, including *Heros notatus*, *H. severus* and *H. appendiculatus* as well as *H. efasciatus* (illustrated). *H. efasciatus* is the most commonly available; the other three species are usually much rarer and more expensive.

Severums are long-term favourites and are available in a golden and a natural green form. They grow large but remain relatively peaceful and will mix with all fish except those that are very small, such as Neon Tetras. They are tolerant of hard water but will do best with a low pH, when they may breed.

Male fish may be distinguished from females by their longer pelvic

and anal fins and striated gill covers (even on the gold form).

They do have a taste for plants, so should be kept with artificial plants or none at all. They can be kept in groups in large tanks, and tall tanks are a better choice as they are high-bodied fish. Decorate the aquarium with bogwood and sand for an authentic Amazon tank.

Their herbivorous nature means that they will benefit from being fed something with some vegetable content, so feed algae-based foods and *Spirulina* food sticks and tablets as well as other cichlid foods.

Julie

small • secretive • patterned • rock dwelling

SCIENTIFIC NAME: *Julidochromis* spp. • FAMILY: Cichlidae • ORIGIN: Africa (Lake Tanganyika) • NATURAL HABITAT: Vertical rocky escarpments • AVERAGE ADULT SIZE: 10 cm (4 in) • COLOURS: Yellow underside with thick black markings all over the back and into the dorsal fin • SEXUAL DIFFERENCES: Females become larger REPRODUCTION: Egg-depositor • BREEDING POTENTIAL: Moderate • TANK LEVEL: Middle • FOOD: Flake, frozen and live foods • PLANT FRIENDLY: Yes • SPECIAL NEEDS: Rocks • EASE OF KEEPING: Moderate

Aquarium needs

MINIMUM TANK SIZE: 75 cm (30 in)
TEMPERATURE: 24–26°C (75–79°F)
PH: 7.5–8.2
WATER HARDNESS: Hard and alkaline
COMPATIBILITY WITH OTHER FISH: Moderate

Julies are small, rock-dwelling cichlids from Lake Tanganyika, and they are represented by five species in fishkeeping: *Julidochromis transcriptus, J. dickfeldi, J. ornatus, J. regani* and *J. marleri* (illustrated). They are similar-looking species, which live and behave in the same way, and *J. regani* and *J. marleri* may turn out to be the same species. In the aquarium they need hard, alkaline water that is well filtered and maintained. The decor should consist simply of lots of rocks piled on top of each other.

Juvenile Julies are hard to sex, so a group should be added to the tank. Sadly, when a pair forms they will kill the other Julies left in the tank. They are secretive spawners that have quite small broods, and any interference with the tank may cause the parent fish to 'divorce' and try to kill each other.

They can be mixed with other Tanganyikan cichlids, but under-populate the tank for long-term stability. They will eat some flake, but are better fed on small frozen foods. They eat quite selectively, so add a small catfish to help to clear up any uneaten food.

Julies rarely leave the rocks and are able to swim upside down when travelling around them.

Cichlids

Zebra Cichlid

active • colourful • aggressive • rock dwelling

SCIENTIFIC NAME: *Metriaclima zebra* • FAMILY: Cichlidae • ORIGIN: Africa (Lake Malawi) • NATURAL HABITAT: Areas containing large boulders • AVERAGE ADULT SIZE: 15 cm (6 in) • COLOURS: Blue and white vertical stripes; there are a number of geographical colour variations • SEXUAL DIFFERENCES: Males have yellow spots on the anal fins and longer dorsal and anal fins • REPRODUCTION: Maternal mouth-brooder • BREEDING POTENTIAL: Moderate • TANK LEVEL: Middle • FOOD: Herbivore flake, some frozen foods • PLANT FRIENDLY: No • SPECIAL NEEDS: Rocks; other mbuna • EASE OF KEEPING: Moderate

Cichlids

Aquarium needs

MINIMUM TANK SIZE: 1.2 m (4 ft)
TEMPERATURE: 24–26°C (75–79°F)
PH: 7.5–8.2
WATER HARDNESS: Hard and alkaline
COMPATIBILITY WITH OTHER FISH: Moderate

Zebra Cichlids represent a group of colourful, rock-dwelling cichlids, called mbuna, from Lake Malawi. The lake is similar to an inland, fresh-water sea and is edged by rocky cliffs and sandy beaches. The mbuna

cichlids live in and around the rocks, where they graze algae.

The water is clear, and the males' bright colours are used to attract a mate. Other males, other species and females that don't wish to mate are chased away because they may be competition for the resident male's algae patch. This aggressive nature has to be controlled in the aquarium, and experienced aquarists found out the hard way that the only way to keep mbuna success-

fully was to overcrowd them so that one male couldn't hold territory for very long.

In an aquarium of 1.2 m (4 ft), 20 mbuna and above of the same size and different species can be kept to suppress aggression. Add lots of rock and stock two females to every male.

Male fish have prominent yellow spots on the anal fin. These spots, known as egg spots, are used during spawning as egg dummies. The females hold the eggs and subsequent fry for about 25 days and do not eat during that time. No pair bond is formed between the parents.

Ram

small • pretty • colourful • sensitive

SCIENTIFIC NAME: *Mikrogeophagus ramirezi* • FAMILY: Cichlidae • OTHER NAME • Dwarf Butterfly Cichlid • ORIGIN: Colombia and Venezuela (Orinoco River) • NATURAL HABITAT: Sheltered tributaries • AVERAGE ADULT SIZE: 7 cm (2¾ in) • COLOURS: Yellow body with a black blotch and blue spangling, red-edged fins and black dorsal spike
SEXUAL DIFFERENCES: Males are larger and have an extended dorsal fin ray; females develop a rounded pink belly
REPRODUCTION: Egg-depositor • BREEDING POTENTIAL: Moderate • TANK LEVEL: Bottom • FOOD: Flake, frozen and live foods • PLANT FRIENDLY: Yes • SPECIAL NEEDS: Soft water; a mature tank • EASE OF KEEPING: Difficult

Aquarium needs

MINIMUM TANK SIZE: 60 cm (24 in)
TEMPERATURE: 24–28°C (75–82°F)
PH: 6–7
WATER HARDNESS: Soft and acidic
COMPATIBILITY WITH OTHER FISH: Moderate

Rams are beautiful dwarf cichlids from South America. Their good looks and small size make them a popular choice with fishkeepers, but they do need extra care.

The tank should be mature and should contain soft, acidic water and plenty of decoration, such as plants and bogwood, to provide cover. Tank mates, which should also prefer soft water and which should be small and not boisterous, could include tetras and small South American catfish.

Offer Rams small quantities of frozen and live foods, such as mosquito larvae, and occasional feeds of flake.

The sexes can be distinguished by the extended dorsal fin on the males; females have a pink belly.

There is a gold form, which is very pretty; the females have a pink belly like the species.

Keep Rams in pairs, but only one pair per 60 sq cm (2 sq ft) of tank bottom. They may spawn in the aquarium in a shallow pit in the substrate, but the fry are not often raised to adulthood. They are bred in large numbers all over the world for aquarists, but those bred in Europe are often the best.

Cichlids

Fairy Cichlid

prolific • territorial• sensitive • rock dwelling

SCIENTIFIC NAME: *Neolamprologus brichardi* • FAMILY: Cichlidae • OTHER NAME: Brichard's Lamprologus

ORIGIN: Africa (Lake Tanganyika) • NATURAL HABITAT: Rocky areas with caves • AVERAGE ADULT SIZE: 10 cm (4 in)

COLOURS: Grey body with white-edged fins • SEXUAL DIFFERENCES: Slight but males are a little larger

REPRODUCTION: Egg-depositor • BREEDING POTENTIAL: High • TANK LEVEL: Middle • FOOD: Flake, frozen and live

foods • PLANT FRIENDLY: Yes • SPECIAL NEEDS: Rocks and retreats • EASE OF KEEPING: Moderate

Cichlids

Aquarium needs

MINIMUM TANK SIZE: 90 cm (36 in)

TEMPERATURE: 24–26°C (75–79°F)

PH: 7.5–8.2

WATER HARDNESS: Hard and alkaline

COMPATIBILITY WITH OTHER FISH: Moderate

Fairy Cichlids are small, rock-dwelling cichlids from Lake Tanganyika in Africa. It is a huge lake, almost like a freshwater sea, that has been inhabited mostly by cichlids. Fairy Cichlids belong to a group of cichlids known as Lamprologines, which are mostly quite small and are suitable for aquariums.

The water in Lake Tanganyika, although fresh, is very hard and alkaline, and all Tanganyikan cichlids need that hard water if they are to thrive. They will not tolerate any ammonia and nitrite or high levels of nitrate in the water, so the tank should be well filtered and regularly maintained. The tank decor should consist solely of rocks piled on top of each other, and the fish will stay close to these.

Males and females are hard to tell apart, so purchase a group, feed them little and often and

leave them to pair off. Once paired, Fairy Cichlids will spawn under some rocks and fiercely protect the fry once hatched. Moreover, as the fry grow the parents may spawn again and again, with the first lot of fry helping to defend the subsequent broods as they grow. The result is a colony of related fish that help each other along but that may need thinning out every so often so that they do not take over the whole tank.

Fairy Cichlids can be mixed with other Tanganyikan cichlids in a biotope tank.

Ocellatus

small • interesting • bold • shell dwelling

SCIENTIFIC NAME: *Neolamprologus ocellatus* • FAMILY: Cichlidae • ORIGIN: Africa (Lake Tanganyika) • NATURAL HABITAT: Beds of empty snail shells on sand • AVERAGE ADULT SIZE: 5 cm (2 in) • COLOURS: Brown with a blue or orange sheen • SEXUAL DIFFERENCES: Males are larger with a bigger head • REPRODUCTION: Egg-depositor BREEDING POTENTIAL: Moderate • TANK LEVEL: Bottom • FOOD: Flake, frozen and live foods • PLANT FRIENDLY: Yes SPECIAL NEEDS: Shells • EASE OF KEEPING: Moderate

Aquarium needs

MINIMUM TANK SIZE: 60 cm (24 in)
TEMPERATURE: 23–26°C (73–79°F)
PH: 7.5–8.2
WATER HARDNESS: Hard and alkaline
COMPATIBILITY WITH OTHER FISH: Moderate

These small, shell-dwelling cichlids from Lake Tanganyika make up in character what they lack in size. In nature they inhabit vast beds of empty shells that come from a type of snail that lives in the lake. The shell beds build up because the hard alkaline water preserves them. The Lamprologine group are rock- and cave-dwellers anyway, so Ocellatus and some other species have adapted to use these shells as their homes.

The aquarium should have a sandy bottom with empty snail shells – use apple snail or edible snail shells – and some rocks to break up territories along the bottom. Make sure that the water is hard and alkaline. It should be well filtered but with a gentle flow.

When you add groups of these fish to the tank the larger males will take up residence over the shells and invite females to live and spawn in them. Males can be aggressive with each other and even with you, and it is startling when such a tiny fish attacks your hand as you clean the tank. They can be kept with other Tanganyikan cichlids, but the tank will work best if it is underpopulated.

In addition to the brown species (illustrated), there are a blue form and a gold form, which are appealing fish with big eyes and iridescent flanks.

Cichlids

Venustus

predatory • patterned • large • striking

SCIENTIFIC NAME: *Nimbochromis venustus* • FAMILY: Cichlidae • ORIGIN: Africa (Lake Malawi) • NATURAL HABITAT: Rocky and open water areas • AVERAGE ADULT SIZE: 25 cm (10 in) • COLOURS: Large gold rings on a green background • SEXUAL DIFFERENCES: Males develop a gold crest and blue face • REPRODUCTION: Maternal mouth-brooder • BREEDING POTENTIAL: Moderate • TANK LEVEL: Middle • FOOD: Fish, shellfish, foodsticks • PLANT FRIENDLY: No • SPECIAL NEEDS: A large tank • EASE OF KEEPING: Moderate

Cichlids

Aquarium needs

MINIMUM TANK SIZE: 1.5 m (5 ft)
TEMPERATURE: 24–26°C (75–79°F)
PH: 7.5–8.2
WATER HARDNESS: Hard and alkaline
COMPATIBILITY WITH OTHER FISH: Moderate

This cichlid often stands out because of the pattern on its body rather than its coloration, but a mature male in breeding condition will also have a blue sheen and a gold crest.

These tough all-rounders can be kept with cichlids (mbuna) from Malawi but to the detriment of the mbuna, because Venustus are predatory and may eat small fish and fry. In addition, they grow larger than most available species from Malawi, with males growing to 25 cm (10 in) long.

The aquarium must be large to accommodate them and contain some rocks, although an open bed of sand will be fine. The filtration system

must be adequate to break down the waste that these fish produce. The water should be hard and alkaline.

Keep Venustus in a group with several females to one male. *Synodontis* catfish (see pages 171–3) can be included to scavenge the bottom, and other large 'haps' can be suitable tank mates. 'Hap' is short for *Haplochromis* – the former name for about half the cichlids in Lake Malawi. The name is now used for cichlids from Lake Victoria, but still applies to many Malawi cichlids, including Venustus. All these cichlids are maternal mouth-brooders.

Polleni

colourful • predatory • interesting • threatened in the wild

SCIENTIFIC NAME: *Paratilapia* spp. • FAMILY: Cichlidae • ORIGIN: Madagascar • NATURAL HABITAT: Rivers and large lakes with clear water • AVERAGE ADULT SIZE: 25 cm (10 in) • COLOURS: Jet black with gold spots • SEXUAL DIFFERENCES: Males are larger with longer fins • REPRODUCTION: Egg-depositor • BREEDING POTENTIAL: Low TANK LEVEL: Middle • FOOD: Fish, shellfish, foodsticks • PLANT FRIENDLY: No • SPECIAL NEEDS: A large tank; excellent water quality • EASE OF KEEPING: Moderate

Aquarium needs

MINIMUM TANK SIZE: 1.5 m (5 ft)
TEMPERATURE: 24–28°C (75–82°F)
PH: 6–7
WATER HARDNESS: Soft and acidic to medium hard
COMPATIBILITY WITH OTHER FISH: Moderate

Paratilapia species have been available to aquarists only in the last few years, but they have attracted a lot of attention from cichlid keepers, not only because of their jet black bodies and iridescent markings but also because of their conservation status. They occur naturally in Madagascar,

a country whose wildlife is threatened because of both deforestation and the introduction of alien species.

In the wild all *Paratilapia* species are endangered, and the cichlids of Madagascar are of further interest to science because they are from ancient cichlid lineages that are most like their marine ancestors. The future of Polleni in captivity is safe because many are kept by aquarists around the world, but attempts to

reintroduce the fish into the wild have not been successful because they are slow to grow and breed.

To keep them in the home you must provide a large tank with one male and several females; males are larger and better coloured. The fish form pairs loosely and are egg-depositors, laying the eggs in a slimy mass which they do not protect vigorously. Spawning will occur only in soft, acidic water.

Cichlids

Kribensis

colourful • dwarf cichlid • bottom dwelling • pair forming

SCIENTIFIC NAME: *Pelvicachromis pulcher* • FAMILY: Cichlidae • ORIGIN: Western Cameroon, Nigeria • NATURAL HABITAT: Rivers with a sandy substrate • AVERAGE ADULT SIZE: 10 cm (4 in) • COLOURS: Pale body with a brown horizontal line and back; the gill cover is yellow; both males and females may have spots in the top of the tail SEXUAL DIFFERENCES: Males are larger and have an extended dorsal fin; females develop pink bellies REPRODUCTION: Egg-depositor • BREEDING POTENTIAL: Moderate • TANK LEVEL: Bottom • FOOD: Flake, frozen and live foods • PLANT FRIENDLY: Yes • SPECIAL NEEDS: Caves and retreats • EASE OF KEEPING: Moderate

Cichlids

Aquarium needs

MINIMUM TANK SIZE: 75 cm (30 in)
TEMPERATURE: 24–26°C (75–79°F)
PH: 6–7
WATER HARDNESS: Soft and acidic
COMPATIBILITY WITH OTHER FISH: Good

Kribensis are a good species to start with if you are interested in keeping (and breeding) cichlids. They are a dwarf cichlid – that is, they do not grow longer than 10 cm (4 in) – and

they can be kept with small fish such as tetras without risk of their eating their smaller companions.

The tank's decor should include caves and hiding places surrounded by live plants and bogwood. The water should ideally be soft and acidic, although they are not too fussy, but the filters should be mature. They are mostly bottom-dwelling fish, so the bogwood and rocks should be arranged to create territories.

Condition the fish by feeding them on frozen and live foods, and a pair will soon form. Females develop a pink belly and are smaller than the males. Males develop longer fins. The pair become secretive when they are choosing a spawning site and spawning. They will be visibly more aggressive to tank mates once the fry are swimming freely because other fish may try to eat the young. At this stage, the pair and fry are best segregated by a divider from the other fish in the tank or even moved to another tank.

Edward's Mbuna

colourful • aggressive • territorial • rock dwelling

SCIENTIFIC NAME: *Pseudotropheus socolofi* • FAMILY: Cichlidae • ORIGIN: Africa (Lake Malawi) • NATURAL HABITAT: Rocky outcrops and large boulders • AVERAGE ADULT SIZE: 15 cm (6 in) • COLOURS: Blue all over with black-edged fins • SEXUAL DIFFERENCES: Males have yellow spots on the anal fin and slightly longer fins
REPRODUCTION: Maternal mouth-brooder • BREEDING POTENTIAL: Moderate • TANK LEVEL: Middle • FOOD: Flake and some frozen foods • PLANT FRIENDLY: No • SPECIAL NEEDS: Rocks; an overcrowded mbuna tank • EASE OF KEEPING: Moderate

Aquarium needs

MINIMUM TANK SIZE: 1.2 m (4 ft)
TEMPERATURE: 24–26°C (75–79°F)
PH: 7.5–8.2
WATER HARDNESS: Hard and alkaline
COMPATIBILITY WITH OTHER FISH: Moderate

The bright blue coloration makes this a popular species for Malawi cichlid tanks. These fish can be aggressive, however, and so should be added only once the tank is almost fully populated. It is also a good idea to stock these fish as juveniles because adults are more aggressive and will fight.

Keep two females or more with each male and put them in a large tank with plenty of rockwork to provide hiding places.

Water requirements are the same for all Malawi cichlids: the water should be hard and alkaline, and well filtered and maintained. Any live plants will be eaten by these fish, but live plants are not, in any case, a natural part of the rocky biotope so are not necessary.

The sexes can be distinguished because the males have prominent yellow 'egg spots' on the anal fin. The female mouth-broods the eggs before spitting out the large fry among the rockwork.

As with all mbuna, these fish should not have a diet that is too rich. Offer low-protein dry foods together with *Spirulina* algae and occasional feeds of frozen *Mysis* shrimp. A period of fasting once a week will encourage them to pick algae off the rocks.

Cichlids

Angelfish

elegant • popular • slow moving • sometimes aggressive

SCIENTIFIC NAME: *Pterophyllum scalare* • FAMILY: Cichlidae • ORIGIN: Brazil, Colombia, Ecuador, Peru • NATURAL HABITAT: Deep, slow-moving stretches of rivers and permanent lakes • AVERAGE ADULT SIZE: 15 cm (6 in) • COLOURS: Silver body with black, vertical bars • SEXUAL DIFFERENCES: Females have a squarer belly profile between the pelvic and anal fins • REPRODUCTION: Egg-depositor • BREEDING POTENTIAL: Moderate • TANK LEVEL: Middle FOOD: Flake, frozen and live foods • PLANT FRIENDLY: Yes • SPECIAL NEEDS: Tall tank • EASE OF KEEPING: Moderate

Cichlids

Aquarium needs

MINIMUM TANK SIZE: 90 cm (36 in)
TEMPERATURE: 24–28°C (75–82°F)
PH: 6–7
WATER HARDNESS: Soft and acidic to neutral
COMPATIBILITY WITH OTHER FISH: Moderate

Angelfish are a mainstay of tropical fishkeeping, and their long fins and compressed bodies make them instantly recognizable. They are available in many colour forms, including golden, marble, silver, ghost and koi, and there is also a variety with even longer fins called the Veiltail Angelfish.

Decades of commercial line-breeding have produced all the varieties but weakened the strain somewhat and affected the adults' breeding behaviour. It is now common for breeding pairs of Angelfish repeatedly to eat their eggs after laying them. This is because the link between parent and offspring has been broken by commercial breeders removing the eggs from the parents' care and raising them artificially.

To reinvigorate your captive stocks, mix some wild fish into a group. This will not only strengthen genetically weak lines but will also make it more likely that parents will care for the fry without any help.

To encourage egg laying, keep Angelfish in a tall tank and provide them with vertical surfaces, such as large plant leaves and rocks, on which the eggs may be laid.

The sexes are difficult to distinguish, so let a pair form naturally from a group of youngsters. Separate them when they become adult and more aggressive.

As they mature, Angelfish turn more cichlid-like and may become territorial and eat small fish. However, it is also important to take care not to mix them with fish that may nip their fins.

Discus

majestic • elegant • peaceful • sensitive

SCIENTIFIC NAME: *Symphysodon* spp. • FAMILY: Cichlidae • ORIGIN: Brazil, Colombia, Peru • NATURAL HABITAT: Deep rivers with fallen trees for shelter • AVERAGE ADULT SIZE: 15 cm (6 in) • COLOURS: Brown body with turquoise striations around the dorsal and anal fins • SEXUAL DIFFERENCES: None • REPRODUCTION: Egg-depositor • BREEDING POTENTIAL: Low • TANK LEVEL: Middle • FOOD: Frozen and live foods, granulated dry foods PLANT FRIENDLY: Yes • SPECIAL NEEDS: Soft, acidic, warm water • EASE OF KEEPING: Difficult

Aquarium needs

MINIMUM TANK SIZE: 1.2m (4ft)
TEMPERATURE: 27–30°C (81–86°F)
PH: 6–7
WATER HARDNESS: Soft and acidic
COMPATIBILITY WITH OTHER FISH: Moderate

Discus are high-bodied cichlids from South America, and their natural habitat is the very warm, soft and acidic water in the Amazon River system. There are several species and colour variants, and wild fish have been crossed and line-bred to create the many aquarium versions we see in the shops.

Many fishkeepers aspire to keep and breed Discus successfully, but they are demanding fish. They need warm, acidic water that is free of ammonia and nitrite and to be fed several times a day to maintain their health and vigour.

Juveniles should be kept in groups of five or more, and pairs may form within the group. Eggs are laid if conditions are good, but tank-bred fish often eat the eggs after laying them.

Adults need tall tanks to accommodate them, and they should be mixed only with peaceful fish that enjoy the same water conditions, such as characins and small catfish.

Cichlids

Firemouth Cichlid

colourful • territorial • substrate sifter • sensitive

SCIENTIFIC NAME: *Thorichthys meeki* • FAMILY: Cichlidae • ORIGIN: Guatemala, Mexico • NATURAL HABITAT: Slow-moving rivers with a sand substrate • AVERAGE ADULT SIZE: 15 cm (6 in) • COLOURS: Blue body with a red throat
SEXUAL DIFFERENCES: Males have redder throats and longer dorsal and anal fins • REPRODUCTION: Egg-depositor
BREEDING POTENTIAL: Moderate • TANK LEVEL: Middle • FOOD: Dry, frozen and live foods • PLANT FRIENDLY: Yes
SPECIAL NEEDS: Retreats and spawning sites • EASE OF KEEPING: Moderate

Aquarium needs

MINIMUM TANK SIZE: 90 cm (36 in)
TEMPERATURE: 22–26°C (72–79°F)
PH: 7–8
WATER HARDNESS: Medium hard
COMPATIBILITY WITH OTHER FISH: Moderate

These colourful cichlids can be added to larger community aquariums containing medium-sized and large fish. They will take up a territory and may be aggressive if a pair forms and spawns in the tank, but outside the breeding season they are more peaceful than other Central American cichlids.

The tank should include some large items of decor, such as rocks, bogwood and pieces of slate, and it should be filtered with power filtration. If you add live plants, make sure they are hardy species and protect their roots from the digging activities of the fish.

Stock a group of juveniles and let a pair form naturally, removing any

non-adults when that occurs. Offer the fish a variety of foods, including food sticks, pellets, mosquito larvae and chopped-up earthworms. A poor diet can lead to a condition called hole in the head.

Male fish have a redder throat and longer fins; females have a fuller belly and shorter body, but juveniles are hard to sex.

Firemouth Cichlids have been kept by aquarists for a long time, but they are not as hardy as they once were and should be kept in good water that is free of pollutants if they are to thrive.

Dubois' Tropheus

unusual looking • attractive • sensitive • aggressive

SCIENTIFIC NAME: *Tropheus duboisi* • FAMILY: Cichlidae • ORIGIN: Africa (Lake Tanganyika) • NATURAL HABITAT: Areas of open water lined by boulders at the shore • AVERAGE ADULT SIZE: 13 cm (5 in) • COLOURS: Black body with a white vertical stripe and a blue head; juveniles are jet black with attractive white spots • SEXUAL DIFFERENCES: Males develop a concave head profile; females' heads are convex • REPRODUCTION: Maternal mouth-brooder • BREEDING POTENTIAL: Low • TANK LEVEL: Middle • FOOD: *Spirulina* algae, spinach, some frozen foods • PLANT FRIENDLY: No SPECIAL NEEDS: Excellent water; strictly controlled diet; the right tank mates • EASE OF KEEPING: Difficult

Aquarium needs

MINIMUM TANK SIZE: 1.2 m (4 ft)
TEMPERATURE: 24–26°C (75–79°F)
PH: 8–8.2
WATER HARDNESS: Hard and alkaline
COMPATIBILITY WITH OTHER FISH: Low

Dubois' Tropheus are maternal mouth-brooding cichlids from Lake Tanganyika, and they have evolved to eat algae from the large submerged rocks in the lake.

These cichlids do not always take well to captivity because they need excellent water quality, they are aggressive towards each other, and they can suffer from all sorts of digestive problems if they are fed the wrong foods. The algae they eat in the wild is very poor in nutrients, and these fish have specialized stomachs to process a continuous supply of poor-quality foods. In captivity, most tropical fish are fed once or twice a day on high-protein flake, which is far too rich for these cichlids to digest properly. Offer your fish flake made from *Spirulina*

algae, which is lower in protein and better for them than normal aquarium flake. You can also give them spinach, which is another low-protein, high-roughage food.

Their aggression can be dealt with by setting up a large tank specially for them and stocking them in groups of ten or more. Females should outnumber males by two or three to one, and each male should have a pile of rocks to call his own. If they are kept in small numbers they will chase and kill each other.

Despite these problems, they are popular fish and regarded as a

challenge by experts. Juveniles, with their striking jet black coloration and white spots, are especially attractive in appearance.

Catfish

Catfish are a varied group, with representatives in all tropical areas. There is huge variation in size, with species such as the Pygmy Corydoras (*Corydoras pygmaeus*; page 163) and the Midget Sucker Catfish (*Otocinclus affinis*; page 170) at just a few centimetres (inches) long, right up to Pangasius (*Pangasius hypopthalmus*; page 174) and the Red-tailed Catfish (*Phractocephalus hemioliopterus*; page 175) at more than 1 m (3 ft) in length and tipping the scales at nearly 23 kg (50 lb) in weight. Although some catfish don't look very pretty, they have admirers all over the world and among all those interested in any aspect of keeping freshwater fish.

Scavengers

Many catfish species are known for their skills at cleaning up the aquarium. The specialized mouths of sucker-mouthed catfish, members of the Loricariidae family, can be put to use in the aquarium as algae eaters. To claim that they eat fish waste is another matter, however, because large sucker-mouthed catfish, known as plecs, contribute to the waste in the tank by producing copious amounts of droppings as they graze, making power filtration and large water changes necessary.

Some catfish, like corydoras, can help to eat any food that falls to the bottom of the tank. They are also community fish and are recommended for a mature aquarium that contains smaller fish. Their larger, African equivalent are the *Synodontis* species from the Mochokidae family, whose large, tough representatives, such as the Decorated Synodontis (*Synodontis decorus*; page 171) can be added to tanks containing large and boisterous fish to help scavenge the bottom for food particles.

Predators

The group is not without its predators, and any catfish with a wide mouth and long whiskers is adapted to catch and eat fish. This includes the Pictus Catfish (*Pimelodus pictus*; page 176) and the Red-tailed Catfish, so tank mates should be chosen with care and should be about twice the size of the mouth of these fish if they are to be safe from predation.

Non-specialist fish eaters may also be opportunistic enough to take small fish at night while they sleep – for this reason *Synodontis* spp. are not to be trusted with fish that are a lot smaller than themselves. At the other end of the scale there are the loricariids that could not catch a fish if they tried because their mouths are

Corydoras catfish make great scavengers for the community tank.

Catfish

Synodontis Catfish are useful scavengers in larger aquariums.

totally unsuitable for the purpose, and they are incapable of premeditated pursuit and capture of prey, even though they are often blamed for it when they are found grazing on a corpse in the morning.

Requirements

This is such a diverse group that it is difficult to summarize their requirements, but these fish do have certain characteristics in common. The first major requirement that all catfish have is to be able to hide. Many are creatures of the night in their natural habitat and will not appreciate sparsely decorated tanks and bright lighting. Catfish such as the Twig Catfish (*Farlowella acus*; page 166) and the Banjo Catfish (*Dysichthys coracoideus*; page 160) give us clues as to their natural habitat as they have evolved to resemble it, and many catfish find a pile of bogwood pieces or a cave made out of rocks a source of comfort, as they know that they can escape there to get out of sight.

With the exception of the Cuckoo Catfish (*Synodontis multipunctatus*; page 172), all species described on the following pages would be happier in slightly acidic, soft water with a layer of fine sand on the bottom of the tank. Originally from Lake Tanganyika, the Cuckoo Catfish prefers hard, alkaline water with a pH of 7.5–8.2. It can be kept with Malawi and Tanganyika cichlids in a rocky aquarium.

Banjo Catfish

bizarre looking • camouflaged • secretive • nocturnal

SCIENTIFIC NAME: *Dysichthys coracoideus* • FAMILY: Aspredinidae • ORIGIN: South America (throughout the Amazon River basin) • NATURAL HABITAT: Shallow waters with wood and leaf litter on fine sand and mud
AVERAGE ADULT SIZE: 15 cm (6 in) • COLOURS: Beige and brown • SEXUAL DIFFERENCES: None • REPRODUCTION: Egg-scatterer • BREEDING POTENTIAL: Low • TANK LEVEL: Bottom • FOOD: Live and frozen foods • PLANT FRIENDLY: Yes • SPECIAL NEEDS: Shelter; the right foods • EASE OF KEEPING: Moderate

Catfish

Aquarium needs

MINIMUM TANK SIZE: 75 cm (30 in)
TEMPERATURE: 22–28°C (72–82°F)
PH: 6–7
WATER HARDNESS: Soft and acidic
COMPATIBILITY WITH OTHER FISH: Moderate

Banjo Catfish demonstrate well the diversity of the catfish group. The species shows extreme specialization and adaptation to its environment. Their camouflage has developed to mimic the leaf litter and driftwood in the River Amazon, and they spend long periods dormant and hidden.

To care for them properly in the aquarium an Amazon biotope set-up, with sand, bogwood and leaf litter, would be ideal and would show them off to the best advantage. Leaves from beech and oak trees are suitable; boil them to sterilize them and make them sink.

Banjo Catfish prefer subdued lighting, and this may encourage more activity in the day. Smallish, peaceful tank mates are recommended, but these fish are natural carnivores and an adult Banjo Catfish could eat a fish the size of a

Neon Tetra, so the tank mates should not be too small.

The water should be soft and acidic and mature, and because Banjo Catfish are wild caught these conditions will help them to acclimatize more quickly. You should make sure that they undergo a period of quarantine.

Offer these fish foods such as mosquito larvae, placed right in front of them to encourage them to feed. Once they get used to being fed that way they are perfectly straightforward to keep and can then be hand fed.

Common Brochis

peaceful • scavenger • shoaling • bottom dwelling

SCIENTIFIC NAME: *Brochis splendens* • FAMILY: Callichthyidae • ORIGIN: Brazil, Ecuador and Peru (Amazon River basin) • NATURAL HABITAT: Vegetated areas over a muddy bottom • AVERAGE ADULT SIZE: 8 cm (3 in) • COLOURS: Metallic green • SEXUAL DIFFERENCES: Females are larger and have fuller bodies • REPRODUCTION: Egg-depositor BREEDING POTENTIAL: Moderate • TANK LEVEL: Bottom • FOOD: Tablet foods, sinking foods • PLANT FRIENDLY: Yes SPECIAL NEEDS: Clean substrate • EASE OF KEEPING: Moderate

Aquarium needs

MINIMUM TANK SIZE: 90 cm (36 in)
TEMPERATURE: 22–28°C (72–82°F)
PH: 6–7
WATER HARDNESS: Soft and acidic to neutral
COMPATIBILITY WITH OTHER FISH: Good

Common Brochis look very similar to their cousins the corydoras, but have slightly larger, deeper bodies. They make excellent community fish and can be kept with small and medium-sized community species.

They shoal and scavenge food particles from the bottom of the tank, and tanks containing Brochis or corydoras do tend to have less detritus on the bottom. This is no excuse for lack of maintenance, however, as dirty gravel can cause their delicate barbels to be eroded and damaged, as can sharp gravel. The ideal substrate is soft silver sand, accompanied by some smooth stones and bogwood to mimic their natural environment.

The water should ideally be soft and acidic with some current provided by power filtration. Live plants can be added, but they will prefer to reside in an open area of sand, so don't plant the aquarium too heavily.

The fish will browse on all sinking foods and are also partial to frozen foods, such as mosquito larvae. Common Brochis are long lived and may spawn in the aquarium, sticking their eggs on to the aquarium glass.

Similar species include the Giant Brochis (*Brochis britzkii*) and Long-nosed Brochis (*Brochis multiradiatus*).

Catfish

Panda Corydoras

bottom swimmer • substrate scavenger • peaceful • shoaling

SCIENTIFIC NAME: *Corydoras panda* • FAMILY: Callichthyidae • ORIGIN: Peru (upper Amazon River) • NATURAL HABITAT: Cool, shallow tributaries • AVERAGE ADULT SIZE: 5 cm (2 in) • COLOURS: Beige with a black eye stripe, dorsal fin and patch by the base of the tail • SEXUAL DIFFERENCES: Females are larger and have fuller bodies REPRODUCTION: Egg-depositor • BREEDING POTENTIAL: Moderate • TANK LEVEL: Bottom • FOOD: Tablet and frozen foods • PLANT FRIENDLY: Yes • SPECIAL NEEDS: A group • EASE OF KEEPING: Moderate

Catfish

Aquarium needs

MINIMUM TANK SIZE: 60 cm (24 in)
TEMPERATURE: 20–26°C (68–79°F)
PH: 6–7
WATER HARDNESS: Soft and acidic to neutral
COMPATIBILITY WITH OTHER FISH: Good

Panda Corydoras are striking fish, beneficial to the tank and safe with small fish, and they do not grow large. The common name comes from their dark eye spots, said to resemble those of the Giant Panda.

They need a tank that includes an open area of fine sand on the bottom, with smooth stones and bogwood around the edges to provide cover. Live plants can be included, and ferns tied to wood look particularly attractive. The water should be soft and acidic but not too warm, and a power filter will provide enough filtration.

Keep a group of five or more Panda Corydoras so that they feel secure. Other corydoras species can be included with them in large

tanks, and they will all loosely shoal together. Any small to medium tank mates are fine, but fish that suit the water conditions and don't eat food off the tank bottom (such as tetras) are best.

Juvenile Panda Corydoras look stunning and are very appealing. When they get older the white coloration on the body begins to take on a beige tinge, but they are still attractive. Mature females are slightly larger with fuller bodies than males, and they may well spawn in the aquarium, leaving adhesive eggs stuck to the glass.

Pygmy Corydoras

tiny • shoaling • peaceful • midwater swimmer

SCIENTIFIC NAME: *Corydoras pygmaeus* • FAMILY: Callichthyidae • ORIGIN: Brazil (Madeira River basin)
NATURAL HABITAT: Tributaries joining the main river • AVERAGE ADULT SIZE: 2.5 cm (1 in) • COLOURS: Opaque
underbelly with a grey back and black horizontal line across the midsection • SEXUAL DIFFERENCES: Females are
larger and have fuller bodies • REPRODUCTION: Egg-depositor • BREEDING POTENTIAL: Low • TANK LEVEL: Middle
FOOD: Flake and frozen foods • PLANT FRIENDLY: Yes • SPECIAL NEEDS: A group; good water quality • EASE OF
KEEPING: Moderate

Aquarium needs

MINIMUM TANK SIZE: 45 cm (18 in)
TEMPERATURE: 22–26°C (72–79°F)
PH: 6–7
WATER HARDNESS: Soft and acidic
COMPATIBILITY WITH OTHER FISH: Moderate

Pygmy Corydoras are not only one of the smallest corydoras, but they are also one of the smallest tropical fish available. In fact, they are frequently sold when they are smaller than their maximum size, often being exported at a length of less than 1 cm (½ in). Unless there are hundreds of them in a tank, they can easily be overlooked in the aquatic store.

To make an effective display a group of 12 or more is needed. They are inexpensive to buy, and some stores will have special offers if you purchase a number of them. They do better in groups and should be kept in tanks with other small fish, such as tetras.

The tank set-up should consist of a smooth, sandy bottom with some decoration, such as bogwood and live plants. To the amazement of many new owners, the Pygmy Corydoras will leave the sand and shoal in midwater for extended periods, and they sometimes even shoal with tetras and other small characins. This behaviour adds to their endearing qualities, and the individual fish look appealing, too.

They need water that is soft and acidic and not too warm. Don't keep them in tanks with boisterous fish or overly powerful filtration because they will quickly tire from swimming.

The vast majority are caught in the wild, so keep your new acquisitions in quarantine for several weeks before adding them to the main aquarium.

Bristlenose Catfish

striking • peaceful • algae eater • sometimes prolific

SCIENTIFIC NAME: *Ancistrus temminckii* • FAMILY: Loricariidae • ORIGIN: Suriname • NATURAL HABITAT: Rivers with mud banks • AVERAGE ADULT SIZE: 15 cm (6 in) • COLOURS: Brown patches through to black, depending on mood • SEXUAL DIFFERENCES: Mature males have bristles on their noses • REPRODUCTION: Egg-depositor BREEDING POTENTIAL: Moderate • TANK LEVEL: Bottom • FOOD: Peas, cucumber, tablet foods, algae • PLANT FRIENDLY: No • SPECIAL NEEDS: Algae • EASE OF KEEPING: Moderate

Aquarium needs

MINIMUM TANK SIZE: 90 cm (36 in)
TEMPERATURE: 24–28°C (75–82°F)
PH: 6–7
WATER HARDNESS: Soft and acidic to hard and alkaline
COMPATIBILITY WITH OTHER FISH: Good

Bristlenose Catfish are a good community species and more suitable for the aquarium, in terms of size, than Sailfin Plecs (*Glyptoperichthys gibbiceps*; page 167) and Common Plecs (*Liposarcus multiradiatus*; page 169).

They are bred commercially in eastern Europe and are usually available in stores when they are quite small. In the right conditions, they may also breed in the aquarium; to encourage this provide lots of caves and pipes in which the adults can deposit eggs.

The pH and hardness of the water are not usually critical; these fish can even be effective algae eaters in a tank full of rift-lake African cichlids, who prefer hard, alkaline water. If you want your fish to breed, however, the pH should be low as in their natural environment. A pair that has spawned in the aquarium can turn out to be prolific, and aquatic shops

may well take youngsters in part exchange for food or other items.

They can be kept with some tough plants, such as Java Fern (*Microsorium pteropus*), but they will eat soft-stemmed plants such as Green Cabomba (*Cabomba caroliniana*).

It is not possible to distinguish the sex of youngsters, but when they reach about 8 cm (3 in) long males develop bristles around the face. All male *Ancistrus* catfish develop the bristlenose, and several similar species may be sold under the same name. They all need the same sort of conditions.

Golden Nugget Plec

colourful • striking • algae eater • shy

SCIENTIFIC NAME: *Baryancistrus* sp. L018 • FAMILY: Loricariidae • ORIGIN: Brazil (Rio Xingu) • NATURAL HABITAT: Rocky areas in the main river • AVERAGE ADULT SIZE: 10 cm (4 in) • COLOURS: Black with yellow spots and yellow-edged dorsal and caudal fins • SEXUAL DIFFERENCES: Unknown • REPRODUCTION: Egg-depositor
BREEDING POTENTIAL: Low • TANK LEVEL: Bottom • FOOD: Algae, tablet and sinking wafers • PLANT FRIENDLY: No
SPECIAL NEEDS: Retreats • EASE OF KEEPING: Moderate

Aquarium needs

MINIMUM TANK SIZE: 90 cm (36 in)
TEMPERATURE: 22–26°C (72–79°F)
PH: 6–7
WATER HARDNESS: Soft and acidic to neutral
COMPATIBILITY WITH OTHER FISH: Good

Golden Nugget Plecs are one of the more recent discoveries that are categorized by L-numbers. The L stands for Loricariidae, and the numbering system was created in the late 20th century to catalogue the myriad of sucker-mouthed catfish newly discovered in the Amazon basin. Along

with lots of brown and grey catfish came some outstanding and vividly coloured species, which became instantly popular.

Golden Nugget Plecs can be kept in mature aquariums, with power filtration to provide flow and oxygen in the tank. The decor can simply consist of bogwood, rocks and sand, because their natural environment does not contain live plants and they would chew on soft plant stems.

They are very shy and can be safely mixed with all other fish as they do not predate small fish and their armoured bodies protect them from larger fish.

Catfish

Twig Catfish

unusual looking • camouflaged • peaceful • interesting

SCIENTIFIC NAME: *Farlowella acus* • FAMILY: Loricariidae • ORIGIN: Brazil (Amazon River basin) • NATURAL HABITAT: Fast-flowing streams with rocks and driftwood • AVERAGE ADULT SIZE: 15 cm (6 in) • COLOURS: Brown and beige SEXUAL DIFFERENCES: Males develop bristles around the nose • REPRODUCTION: Egg-depositor • BREEDING POTENTIAL: Low • TANK LEVEL: Bottom • FOOD: Algae, tablet foods • PLANT FRIENDLY: Yes • SPECIAL NEEDS: Bogwood; soft water EASE OF KEEPING: Moderate

Catfish

Aquarium needs

MINIMUM TANK SIZE: 90 cm (36 in)
TEMPERATURE: 24–26°C (75–79°F)
PH: 6–7
WATER HARDNESS: Soft and acidic to neutral
COMPATIBILITY WITH OTHER FISH: Good

Twig Catfish are great examples of fish diversity – they look far removed from the stereotypical fish shape. They come from the Amazon River system and have evolved to resemble the driftwood and sunken logs that are found in abundance in the rivers and streams there.

Despite their fragile appearance, they come from fast-flowing water, which can be easily replicated in the aquarium using power filtration. Unlike some loricariid catfish, they seldom hide and can be seen in the daytime on bogwood or attached to the vertical stems of live plants.

They are good community fish because they present no threat to small fish, yet their appearance and length make them suitable for

including with larger fish without fear of them being attacked.

Their ideal aquarium would be decorated with smooth rocks and bogwood with a fine sand substrate. Live plants can be added, and the long leaves of *Vallisneria* spp. will provide extra refuge. Water should be soft and acidic, and they should be offered tablet food and algae.

Twig Catfish have been bred in captivity, and the male fish can be identified by the bristles on the sides of their nose. Wild-caught specimens are often available at adult size.

Sailfin Plec

large • impressive • patterned • algae eater

SCIENTIFIC NAME: *Glyptoperichthys gibbiceps* • FAMILY: Loricariidae • ORIGIN: Peru (upper Amazon River basin)
NATURAL HABITAT: Rivers containing wood and a mud substrate • AVERAGE ADULT SIZE: 50 cm (20 in) • COLOURS:
Orange body with large brown spots covering the body and fins • SEXUAL DIFFERENCES: Females develop fuller
bodies when they are carrying eggs • REPRODUCTION: Egg-depositor • BREEDING POTENTIAL: Low • TANK LEVEL:
Bottom • FOOD: Algae, vegetable matter, tablet and wafer foods • PLANT FRIENDLY: No • SPECIAL NEEDS: A large
tank • EASE OF KEEPING: Easy

Aquarium needs

MINIMUM TANK SIZE: 1.5 m (5 ft)
TEMPERATURE: 23–28°C (73–82°F)
PH: 6–7.5
WATER HARDNESS: Soft and acidic to
hard and alkaline
COMPATIBILITY WITH OTHER FISH: Good

The Sailfin Plec is an impressive fish
that displays its patterned dorsal fin.
It is a similar species to the Common
Plec (*Liposarcus multiradiatus*; page
169) and can be kept in the same
way. It does, however, grow even
bigger and broader than the Common Plec, and a tank 1.5 m (5 ft)

long by 60 cm (24 in) wide must be
considered a minimum size for the
long-term care of the species.

Decor should be sturdy, and live
plants should not be included
because they will be eaten. To obtain
the best condition offer a varied diet,
including tablet and wafer foods and
also cucumber and squashed peas.

Sailfin Plecs can be kept with tiny
species, such as Neon Tetras, and
with large, aggressive species.
They will not predate small fish,
although they are often blamed for

it when they are found grazing on a
fish corpse. They should, however,
be the only plec included in the tank
because mature specimens will scuf-
fle with other plecs for territory and
hiding places.

They do not breed in aquariums,
but they are bred commercially in
the Far East. Juveniles are cheap
and readily available, which makes
them popular.

Warning!

This species grows large.

Zebra Plec

colourful • striking • secretive • expensive

SCIENTIFIC NAME: *Hypancistrus zebra* L046 • FAMILY: Loricariidae • ORIGIN: Brazil (River Xingu) • NATURAL HABITAT: Rocks and driftwood at depth • AVERAGE ADULT SIZE: 6 cm (2¼ in) • COLOURS: Black and white • SEXUAL DIFFERENCES: Males have longer cheek bristles • REPRODUCTION: Egg-depositor • BREEDING POTENTIAL: Low TANK LEVEL: Bottom • FOOD: Algae, mosquito larvae, tablet foods • PLANT FRIENDLY: No • SPECIAL NEEDS: Soft water; retreats; the right food • EASE OF KEEPING: Moderate

Catfish

Aquarium needs

MINIMUM TANK SIZE: 90 cm (36 in)
TEMPERATURE: 23–26°C (73–79°F)
PH: 6–7
WATER HARDNESS: Soft and acidic to neutral
COMPATIBILITY WITH OTHER FISH: Good

Zebra Plecs are popular among fishkeepers because of their vivid markings, but their popularity has led to the species being overfished in the wild and availability has become poor. They are bred in captivity, but not in sufficient numbers to supply demand, and they remain very expensive.

If you manage to obtain one you may be disappointed to find that it likes nothing better than to hide under bogwood for most of the day. One way to encourage it to come out is to place food near where it is lurking and feed it at the same time every day. Eventually, it may be persuaded to venture out more often.

The aquarium should be decorated with rocks and bogwood to provide shelter. It is acceptable not to include any plants at all because they would not be present in the Zebra Plec's natural environment, although your fish may nibble at plants at night. The water should be soft and acidic, and power filtration should always be used to ensure the water quality.

These fish can be mixed with a wide range of other fish, but should not be kept with too many other plecs as they will squabble for territory and food.

Common Plec

large • hardy • algae eater • easy to keep

SCIENTIFIC NAME: *Liposarcus multiradiatus* • FAMILY: Loricariidae • ORIGIN: Bolivia, Paraguay, Peru • NATURAL HABITAT: Slow-moving waters containing algae and detritus • AVERAGE ADULT SIZE: 45 cm (18 in) • COLOURS: Brown with brown or black dots covering the whole body • SEXUAL DIFFERENCES: Females become fuller with eggs REPRODUCTION: Egg-depositor • BREEDING POTENTIAL: Low • TANK LEVEL: Bottom • FOOD: Algae, tablet foods PLANT FRIENDLY: No • SPECIAL NEEDS: A large tank; efficient filtration • EASE OF KEEPING: Easy

Aquarium needs

MINIMUM TANK SIZE: 1.5 m (5 ft)
TEMPERATURE: 20–28°C (68–82°F)
PH: 6–8
WATER HARDNESS: Soft and acidic to hard and alkaline
COMPATIBILITY WITH OTHER FISH: Good

The Common Plec is not a *Plecostomus* at all but is, in fact, a member of the *Liposarcus* genus. However, it is known around the world as a plec. The fish is as old as tropical fishkeeping, and has stood the test of time because of its overall hardiness and adaptability. It is tolerant of pH and temperature and will grow in all but the worst conditions. Its eventual size does work against it, however, and stores are inundated with specimens 30 cm (12 in) long, which have outgrown their accommodation.

They are excellent algae eaters (they may also eat soft plant stems) and will graze all surfaces; they can often be viewed from underneath, stuck to the front glass.

Common Plec are messy fish which produce copious faeces as they graze. This, combined with their armoured bodies, can ruin an aquascape unless precautions are taken, and decor should be sufficiently large and well anchored that it is not knocked over. They must have tanks that are wide enough to allow them turn around their inflexible bodies.

In the absence of algae, offer tablet foods and sinking food wafers, because plecs will lose weight in tanks that are too clean. Fish that try to take food from the surface may also be hungry.

Warning!

This species grows large.

Catfish

Midget Sucker Catfish

small • shoaling • algae eater • active

SCIENTIFIC NAME: *Otocinclus affinis* • FAMILY: Loricariidae • ORIGIN: Southern Brazil, Peru, Bolivia • NATURAL HABITAT: Streams containing driftwood and leaves • AVERAGE ADULT SIZE: 4 cm (1½ in) • COLOURS: Beige and brown • SEXUAL DIFFERENCES: Females are larger and broader • REPRODUCTION: Egg-depositor • BREEDING POTENTIAL: Low • TANK LEVEL: All levels • FOOD: Algae, tablet foods • PLANT FRIENDLY: No • SPECIAL NEEDS: The right food • EASE OF KEEPING: Moderate

Aquarium needs

MINIMUM TANK SIZE: 60 cm (24 in)
TEMPERATURE: 24–28°C (75–82°F)
PH: 6–7
WATER HARDNESS: Soft and acidic to neutral
COMPATIBILITY WITH OTHER FISH: Moderate

Otocinclus is a genus of dwarf catfish, all of which are suitable for keeping in the home aquarium. The Midget Sucker Catfish is one of the smallest and most readily available species, and it is kept by many fish-keepers because of its liking for algae. This fish will graze all surfaces for algae, including gravel, rocks, bogwood and aquarium glass. It will also graze algae from plant leaves, and while grazing may damage the large leaves of the Amazon Sword (*Echinodorus* sp.), which this herbivorous fish finds tasty, too.

Otocinclus species can be mixed with other small fish, and a shoal of five or six individuals is the best choice of algae eater for small tanks.

They need soft, acidic water and a mature tank with no boisterous fish. Their coloration can gain a golden hue once they have settled, and they will be active in the daytime and not seek refuge like L-number plecs do (see page 165). In the absence of any algae in the tank feed them on algae-based tablet foods.

These fish are still caught in the wild and exported from South America, so quarantine newly acquired fish unless they have been in the store for a month or more.

Decorated Synodontis

large • striking • robust • patterned

SCIENTIFIC NAME: *Synodontis decorus* • FAMILY: Mochokidae • ORIGIN: Cameroon • NATURAL HABITAT: Large rivers with rocks and wood in flowing water • AVERAGE ADULT SIZE: 30 cm (12 in) • COLOURS: Black and white with a stripy tail • SEXUAL DIFFERENCES: Males may have an extended dorsal fin • REPRODUCTION: Egg-depositor
BREEDING POTENTIAL: Low • TANK LEVEL: Bottom • FOOD: Sinking tablet and frozen foods • PLANT FRIENDLY: Yes
SPECIAL NEEDS: A large tank • EASE OF KEEPING: Moderate

Aquarium needs

MINIMUM TANK SIZE: 1.5 m (5 ft)
TEMPERATURE: 24–28°C (75–82°F)
PH: 6–7
WATER HARDNESS: Soft and acidic to neutral
COMPATIBILITY WITH OTHER FISH: Moderate

The Decorated Synodontis is becoming increasingly popular and widely available, as it is now commercially bred in eastern Europe.

Its markings are very striking, and some fish – possibly males – develop extended dorsal fins. They do grow large, however, and in the long term

are not suitable for tanks of less than 1.5 m (5 ft). Like many *Synodontis* species, these fish will grow quickly when added to the main tank. They are also long-lived – 20 years or more – and large specimens may not be easy to re-home at aquatic stores.

They will predate small fish, so large, similarly sized fish are the best tank mates. They can be kept with boisterous fish, and will eat any scraps of food that fall their way. They will tend to squabble with other

Synodontis species, including their own kind, so one in a tank is best.

The tank can be loosely decorated with rocks and bogwood arranged to provide cover. Live plants are not necessary, but if they are included tough ferns and potted plants are the best choices. Although they are bred commercially, aquarium spawnings are rare.

Warning!

This species grows large.

Catfish

Cuckoo Catfish

shade loving • interesting • attractive • expensive

SCIENTIFIC NAME: *Synodontis multipunctatus* • FAMILY: Mochokidae • ORIGIN: Africa (Lake Tanganyika) • NATURAL HABITAT: Vegetated margins and rocky areas • AVERAGE ADULT SIZE: 13 cm (5 in) • COLOURS: Silver with black spots • SEXUAL DIFFERENCES: Male has visible genitalia • REPRODUCTION: Mouth-brooding cichlid surrogate BREEDING POTENTIAL: Moderate • TANK LEVEL: Bottom • FOOD: Flake, frozen foods • PLANT FRIENDLY: Yes • SPECIAL NEEDS: Alkaline water; shelter • EASE OF KEEPING: Moderate

Catfish

Aquarium needs

MINIMUM TANK SIZE: 90 cm (36 in)
TEMPERATURE: 22–26°C (72–79°F)
PH: 7.5–8.2
WATER HARDNESS: Hard and alkaline
COMPATIBILITY WITH OTHER FISH: Moderate

The Cuckoo Catfish is so named because of its strange breeding method. Pairs congregate around mouth-brooding cichlids that are spawning and drop in their own fertilized eggs just as the female cichlid picks up her own eggs. Once in the cichlid's mouth, the predatory fry eat the cichlid fry until they are spat out by the cichlid and released into the water. The result is a small number of well-developed catfish that have been incubated by another species. In nature, a cichlid called *Ctenochromis horei* is usually the host fish, but they are not common in aquariums, and it has been found that the Cuckoo Catfish will spawn and use many cichlids from Lake Malawi as hosts instead.

The tank set-up should consist of lots of caves constructed from rock piles. The water should be hard and alkaline, and a group of cichlids should be added as surrogates if you want the Cuckoo Catfish to breed. These could include Zebra Cichlids (*Metriaclima zebra*; page 146), which are known to have been surrogate hosts in the past, or, from Lake Tanganyika, *Ctenochromis horei*, but they are not only rare but aggressive and hard to keep.

Upside-down Catfish

unusual looking • camouflaged • shade loving • interesting

SCIENTIFIC NAME: *Synodontis nigriventris* • FAMILY: Mochokidae • ORIGIN: Rwanda, Democratic Republic of Congo (Congo River basin) • NATURAL HABITAT: Sheltered stretches with overhanging vegetation • AVERAGE ADULT SIZE: 8 cm (3 in) • COLOURS: Brown with white dots and mottled fins • SEXUAL DIFFERENCES: Females have fuller bodies • REPRODUCTION: Egg-depositor • BREEDING POTENTIAL: Low • TANK LEVEL: Bottom • FOOD: Flake and frozen foods • PLANT FRIENDLY: Yes • SPECIAL NEEDS: Retreats and shady areas • EASE OF KEEPING: Moderate

Aquarium needs

MINIMUM TANK SIZE: 60 cm (24 in)
TEMPERATURE: 22–28°C (72–82°F)
PH: 6–7.5
WATER HARDNESS: Soft and acidic to neutral
COMPATIBILITY WITH OTHER FISH: Good

This fish is so called because it swims upside down for much of the time, which enables it to reach food that would otherwise be inaccessible. The underside of the fish, which in many similar fish is white, is camouflaged like its back, so it is not so visible to predators when viewed from above. This swimming action is used by many *Synodontis* species, but no species does it to quite the same extent.

When you are buying fish be aware, also, that many similar-looking *Synodontis* species may be wrongly offered for sale as Upside-down Catfish, but they will grow larger than that species and will not be as sociable. The differences are hard to discern, but the armour

around the head of the true Upside-down Catfish is quite prominent and any spotting on the body is blotchy rather than well defined. This species rarely attains its maximum size of 10 cm (4 in), but other species grow regularly to a length of over 15 cm (6 in).

The tank should be well decorated with large pieces of bogwood to provide cover, but it does not have to be planted. Any small to medium-sized tank mates will be safe, although very small fry will be eaten.

The species is largely nocturnal, but low lighting levels combined

with lots of cover and feeding at the same time every day may encourage them to become active in the daytime.

Pangasius

large • nervous • shark like • metallic

SCIENTIFIC NAME: *Pangasius hypopthalmus* • FAMILY: Pangasiidae • ORIGIN: Thailand (Mekong River basin)
NATURAL HABITAT: Large rivers along migratory patterns • AVERAGE ADULT SIZE: 60 cm (24 in) • COLOURS: Grey with a metallic sheen • SEXUAL DIFFERENCES: Unknown • REPRODUCTION: Egg-scatterer • BREEDING POTENTIAL: Low
TANK LEVEL: Middle • FOOD: All dry and frozen foods, fish • PLANT FRIENDLY: Yes • SPECIAL NEEDS: A large tank; a group • EASE OF KEEPING: Moderate

Catfish

Aquarium needs

MINIMUM TANK SIZE: 1.8 m (6 ft)
TEMPERATURE: 23–26°C (73–79°F)
PH: 7–7.5
WATER HARDNESS: Soft and acidic to hard and alkaline
COMPATIBILITY WITH OTHER FISH: Moderate

Pangasius come with a warning to potential owners not only because of their eventual size but also because they are not well suited to domestic aquariums. They can grow to 90 cm (36 in) long, and they are also very nervous fish,

prone to darting across the tank and hitting the glass with full force.

The proper care of those fish that are already in aquariums must be a priority. First, they must be kept in a large tank. The water should be well filtered and maintained, with some flow from the filter, because these fish need exercise. Second, they should be kept in groups, because they are a shoaling fish and a number of individuals may add to the feeling of security. Third, an effort should be made to make the tank boundaries visible in order to avoid

collisions. This can be achieved by sticking three-dimensional sheets to the back and sides of the tank. Planting at the sides will also help.

Although it may be hard to believe, *Pangasius hypopthalmus* is one of the smaller members of the genus. *P. gigas* is one of the largest fresh-water fish in the world – growing to over 2 m (6 ft 6 in) long – and it is critically endangered in its natural habitat by pressures from over-fishing and industry.

Warning!

This species grows large.

Red-tailed Catfish

huge • impressive • predatory • demanding

SCIENTIFIC NAME: *Phractocephalus hemioliopterus* • FAMILY: Pimelodidae • ORIGIN: Brazil, Guyana and Venezuela (Amazon River basin) • NATURAL HABITAT: Flood waters; widespread throughout the main river system in turbid waters • AVERAGE ADULT SIZE: 1.2 m (4 ft) • COLOURS: Dark grey with a white horizontal band and red tail • SEXUAL DIFFERENCES: Unknown • REPRODUCTION: Egg-scatterer • BREEDING POTENTIAL: Low • TANK LEVEL: Bottom • FOOD: Fish, shellfish • PLANT FRIENDLY: Yes • SPECIAL NEEDS: A huge tank; powerful filtration; serious, long-term commitment • EASE OF KEEPING: Moderate

Aquarium needs

MINIMUM TANK SIZE: 3.6 m (12 ft)
TEMPERATURE: 24–28°C (75–82°F)
PH: 6–7
WATER HARDNESS: Soft and acidic
COMPATIBILITY WITH OTHER FISH: Low

The Red-tailed Catfish is a huge and iconic tropical fish that still attracts people who want to try to keep one in an aquarium, some without proper regard for its long-term needs.

It is a South American species and a predator. They are appealing enough when they are juveniles – but so are lions and tigers! With its huge size comes a huge appetite and a phenomenal growth rate, from a juvenile about 5 cm (2 in) long to an adult 1.2 m (4 ft) long. Bear its potential length in mind if you are tempted to buy one: a catfish 1.2 m (4 ft) long will need an aquarium that is several times longer and at least as wide as itself when it is stretched out fully from front to back. An aquarium measuring 3.6 x 1.2 x 1.2 m (12 x 4 x 4 ft) will hold over 5,000 litres

(about 1,100 gallons) of water and weigh in excess of 5 tonnes. This is not within the budget or capabilities of most fishkeepers.

Huge tanks require powerful filtration systems and large-scale water changes – and involve enormous costs. If you still want one, start saving and do your fellow fishkeepers a favour by rescuing a 60-cm (2-ft) long sub-adult that has outgrown someone's tank. There are thousands of unwanted Red-tailed Catfish around the world.

Warning!
This species grows large.

Pictus Catfish

metallic • shark like • shoaling • active

SCIENTIFIC NAME: *Pimelodus pictus* • FAMILY: Pimelodidae • ORIGIN: Colombia (upper River Amazon basin)
NATURAL HABITAT: Areas of large rivers with strong undercurrents • AVERAGE ADULT SIZE: 13 cm (5 in) • COLOURS:
Silver with black spots • SEXUAL DIFFERENCES: None • REPRODUCTION: Egg-scatterer • BREEDING POTENTIAL: Low
TANK LEVEL: Bottom • FOOD: Flake, frozen foods, fish • PLANT FRIENDLY: Yes • SPECIAL NEEDS: A group; a large tank
EASE OF KEEPING: Moderate

Catfish

Aquarium needs

MINIMUM TANK SIZE: 1.2 m (4 ft)
TEMPERATURE: 22–26°C (72–79°F)
PH: 6–7
WATER HARDNESS: Soft and acidic
COMPATIBILITY WITH OTHER FISH: Moderate

Pictus Catfish are popular with fish-keepers who like the metallic, shark-shaped form of some tropical fish. The good news is that these fish remain medium sized, and groups can be accommodated in larger tanks. The bad news is that they do predate smaller fish, so medium-sized tank mates of 5 cm (2 in) and over are advised. Remember: any catfish with long whiskers is a fish eater; catfish with short, underslung barbels, like those on corydoras, are safe with small fish.

The tank should have fine sand on the base together with some smooth stones and bogwood. Plants can be included, but there should be plenty of room for swimming.

These fish prefer soft, acidic water, and there should be some filter flow for exercise, because they are very active fish that will swim the length of the tank. They will accept all foods with vigour, and frozen fish can be chopped up and offered as a treat. Big groups of these catfish in large tanks can make a stunning display.

If you are catching the fish, beware of the pectoral fins, which are sharp enough to pierce the skin and nearly always get caught in the net fabric, making for a bumbled catching and potential stress for the fish.

Glass Catfish

sleek • unusual looking • peaceful • fragile

SCIENTIFIC NAME: *Kryptopterus minor* • FAMILY: Siluridae • ORIGIN: Malaysia, Thailand • NATURAL HABITAT: Clear streams with aquatic vegetation • AVERAGE ADULT SIZE: 8 cm (3 in) • COLOURS: Translucent • SEXUAL DIFFERENCES: None • REPRODUCTION: Egg-scatterer • BREEDING POTENTIAL: Low • TANK LEVEL: Middle • FOOD: Small frozen and live foods • PLANT FRIENDLY: Yes • SPECIAL NEEDS: Good water quality; peaceful tank mates • EASE OF KEEPING: Moderate

Aquarium needs

MINIMUM TANK SIZE: 75 cm (30 in)
TEMPERATURE: 22–26°C (72–79°F)
PH: 7–7.5
WATER HARDNESS: Soft and acidic to medium hard
COMPATIBILITY WITH OTHER FISH: Moderate

Glass Catfish look strange at first. Their see-through bodies enable you to see their internal organs and bones. When viewed close up they cannot be described as pretty, but as a group in a well-decorated tank the effect can be dramatic.

They don't look or act like catfish because they are not thickset and armoured, nor are they adapted for life on the bottom. They are constant swimmers, waggling their tails but mostly hovering in the same spot.

If you are to keep them properly the aquarium should be mature with no boisterous tank mates or large fish. The lighting should be subdued, and there should be a gentle current in the tank for them to swim against. The water should be well maintained and temperature and pH extremes should be avoided. They should be kept in groups and fed little and often on small frozen and live foods such as mosquito larvae, because they are not partial to flake.

These fish look and are delicate, and they are best kept only by experienced fishkeepers. They should definitely not be bought as a gimmick for a new tank.

Killifish

Killifish are small, colourful fish that live in most of the tropical freshwater habitats of the world. They are well known for the annual species such as Rachow's Nothobranch (*Nothobranchius rachovii*; page 183), which inhabit semi-permanent pools that dry up at the height of the dry season, killing all the fish that live there. The killifish survival strategy is to lay eggs in the mud at the bottom of the pool. The eggs are protected and lie dormant under the surface of the mud until the rainy season. When the pool refills with water and becomes habitable again, the eggs hatch and the process begins once more.

Annual fish

Annual fish can be kept and bred in captivity, as long as the eggs are given a resting period. You should set up a small tank with a heater and air-operated filter, and sprinkle peat across the bottom of the tank. When the eggs have been laid they can be removed along with the peat and stored in moist conditions in plastic bags in the dark. The resting time will vary from species to species, but the unique aspect of this phenomenon is that the eggs can be sent to other enthusiasts by post, for them to then start a new colony. This self-sufficient pastime can be incredibly satisfying, with a network of breeders distributing fish in this way.

Rachow's Nothobranch is one of the most beautiful of all tropical fish.

Adult annual fish

There are some drawbacks to keeping annual fish, which you need to consider before you decide that these are the fish for you. First, only the male fish are colourful, and they are very aggressive towards other males of their species. Second, they are not that easy to keep because they demand mostly live foods and will be reluctant to take flake. Third, what seems like an ideal way to keep and breed fish will require a special effort on the part of the owner, and beginners are unlikely to succeed the first time they try.

TIP

Join a killifish society if these fish interest you. The other members will be able to steer you in the right direction and advise you about keeping and breeding them.

Non-annual fish

Annual fish represent only a fraction of killifish species, and those that inhabit permanent bodies of water have not had to take such extreme measures to survive. One of the largest species lives in the huge Lake Tanganyika. The Tanganyika Lamp Eye (*Lamprichthys tanganicanus*; page 185) can grow to 15 cm (6 in) in length and will live for several years. They are a demanding species and need a large tank and perfect conditions if they are to thrive.

Two much hardier species are the colourful Golden Wonder (*Aplocheilus lineatus*; page 182) and the Florida Flag Fish (*Jordanella floridae*; page 184). The first brings colour and movement to the upper water in tanks with medium-sized community fish, and the second can be kept in cool-water aquariums and even outdoor ponds in the summer months. All non-annual killifish lay eggs in a more normal fashion and can be raised artificially with a little fishkeeping skill.

Above: The Golden Wonder is a hardy non-annual fish that is suitable for beginners.

Below: The Tanganyika Lamp Eye requires a large tank to thrive.

Cape Lopez Lyretail

small • colourful • delicate • sensitive

SCIENTIFIC NAME: *Aphyosemion australe* • FAMILY: Aplocheilidae • ORIGIN: Togo, Nigeria, Cameroon, Rwanda, Democratic Republic of Congo • NATURAL HABITAT: Marshland • AVERAGE ADULT SIZE: 6 cm (2¼ in) • COLOURS: Yellow body with red spots and a yellow- and white-edged tail fin • SEXUAL DIFFERENCES: Males are much more colourful and larger • REPRODUCTION: Egg-scatterer • BREEDING POTENTIAL: Moderate • TANK LEVEL: Middle FOOD: Frozen and live foods • PLANT FRIENDLY: Yes • SPECIAL NEEDS: Peat substrate for breeding • EASE OF KEEPING: Moderate

Killifish

Aquarium needs

MINIMUM TANK SIZE: 45 cm (18 in)
TEMPERATURE: 21–24°C (70–75°F)
PH: 6–7
WATER HARDNESS: Soft and acidic
COMPATIBILITY WITH OTHER FISH: Moderate

Mature males of this species have yellow bodies and display a yellow- and white-tipped, lyre-shaped tail. This is an annual species, which in the wild is found in temporary pools in forests in western Africa. When the pools start to dry up, the parent fish spawn, leaving eggs in the mud. When the rains come, a new pool is formed and the fish grow.

They need an aquarium with mature, air-powered filtration and a temperature that is on the cool side of the range indicated. The water quality should be good, and the water

itself should be soft and acidic. Cover the bottom of the tank with a layer of peat into which the fish may lay their eggs. The tank can be heavily planted; include floating plants to provide areas of shade.

Add one male only to the tank together with several females, because males will fight and are too boisterous if there is only one female. Other fish can be added, but they must be peaceful, and they may prevent the killifish from breeding.

These fish are often reluctant to accept flake and should be fed frozen or live foods little and often.

Steel Blue Killifish

small • colourful • attractive • beginner's killifish

SCIENTIFIC NAME: *Aphyosemion gardneri* • FAMILY: Aplocheilidae • ORIGIN: Nigeria • NATURAL HABITAT: Swamp terrain in forested areas • AVERAGE ADULT SIZE: 8 cm (3 in) • COLOURS: Blue-green body with red flecks and a yellow-edged tail • SEXUAL DIFFERENCES: Males are more colourful and larger • REPRODUCTION: Egg-scatterer
BREEDING POTENTIAL: Moderate • TANK LEVEL: Middle • FOOD: Flake, frozen and live foods • PLANT FRIENDLY: Yes
SPECIAL NEEDS: Several females to each male • EASE OF KEEPING: Moderate

Aquarium needs

MINIMUM TANK SIZE: 60 cm (24 in)
TEMPERATURE: 24–28°C (75–82°F)
PH: 6–7
WATER HARDNESS: Soft and acidic to neutral
COMPATIBILITY WITH OTHER FISH: Moderate

The Steel Blue Killifish is one of the easier killifish to keep, but it will do better with a little specialist care. It is an annual fish that will accept some flake as well as frozen and live foods. Males do not tolerate each other, and only one male should be added to a tank with several

females. The males can be distinguished because they are larger and more colourful than the females.

It's important to avoid extremes with these fish. The tank should have a mature, air-powered filter. Set the heater thermostat to about 25°C (77°F), and make sure that the water pH and hardness are around neutral.

The decor should consist of a layer of peat on the tank bottom with live plants to provide cover and

some shade. Bogwood can also be used as decoration. The tank can be heavily planted and made to look like a small pond.

In the wild the pools that they inhabit dry up; the eggs stay moist under the mud until the rains come and the fry hatch. When they breed in captivity eggs are laid in peat, which can be removed and stored. Other species can be added to the tank, but will interrupt breeding.

Killifish

Golden Wonder

colourful • popular • surface dwelling • predatory

SCIENTIFIC NAME: *Aplocheilus lineatus* • FAMILY: Aplocheilidae • ORIGIN: Western India • NATURAL HABITAT: Flood plains, rice paddies, streams and ditches • AVERAGE ADULT SIZE: 10 cm (4 in) • COLOURS: Males are yellow; females are plain • SEXUAL DIFFERENCES: Males are larger and more colourful • REPRODUCTION: Egg-scatterer BREEDING POTENTIAL: Moderate • TANK LEVEL: Top • FOOD: Flake, frozen and live foods • PLANT FRIENDLY: Yes SPECIAL NEEDS: None • EASE OF KEEPING: Moderate

Aquarium needs

MINIMUM TANK SIZE: 75 cm (30 in)

TEMPERATURE: 22–26°C (72–79°F)

PH: 6–7.5

WATER HARDNESS: Soft and acidic to medium hard

COMPATIBILITY WITH OTHER FISH: Moderate

Male Golden Wonders are colourful, popular fish, but what many people do not realize is that this species grows to 10 cm (4 in) long and can eat fish the size of Neon Tetras.

The fish are quite hardy and provide colour and movement in the upper aquarium. They are best suited to a tank containing medium-sized, peaceful fish and have no special requirements, accepting a variety of foods. They can be kept singly or in male–female groups, and males do not bother each other too much.

Tank decor is unimportant because the fish dwell above any decoration. Floating plants or trailing plant stems can provide cover at the surface, but they are not shy fish. They are a recommended species because of their relative ease of keeping, but they should not be housed with small fish.

There is a natural form of the Golden Wonder, which is much plainer and may sometimes be imported in shipments from India. These fish are much less popular than the golden form, which is bred commercially in the Far East for fishkeepers around the world.

Rachow's Nothobranch

stunning • colourful • small • antisocial

SCIENTIFIC NAME: *Nothobranchius rachovii* • FAMILY: Aplocheilidae • ORIGIN: Mozambique • NATURAL HABITAT: Marshland • AVERAGE ADULT SIZE: 5 cm (2 in) • COLOURS: Bright red body covered in a bright blue pattern
SEXUAL DIFFERENCES: Males are more colourful and larger • REPRODUCTION: Egg-scatterer • BREEDING POTENTIAL: Moderate • TANK LEVEL: Middle • FOOD: Frozen and live foods • PLANT FRIENDLY: Yes • SPECIAL NEEDS: Carnivorous diet • EASE OF KEEPING: Difficult

Aquarium needs

MINIMUM TANK SIZE: 60 cm (24 in)
TEMPERATURE: 20–24°C (68–75°F)
PH: 6–7
WATER HARDNESS: Soft and acidic
COMPATIBILITY WITH OTHER FISH: Low

This species is stunningly coloured and perhaps one of the most beautiful of all tropical fish. The disadvantages are that it is not one of the easiest fish to keep, and it is not really suitable for the community tank. They are annual fish, which means that in the wild the adults die every year after spawning.

The male fish is the colourful one and much larger than the female. Males will fight if kept together, so have just one male with several females in a tank on their own.

The tank set-up can be simple; if you wish to breed the fish, the tank has only to be functional. These are substrate spawners, and many keepers of substrate-spawning killifish sprinkle a layer of peat on the bottom of the tank in which the fish can lay their eggs. Peat also has the effect of acidifying the water.

Some reference books suggest that killifish do not need filtration. This is not necessarily true, and aquariums without filtration will quickly become polluted. Use an air-powered sponge filter and a heater-thermostat set on low. Add some live plants to provide refuges.

Killifish

Florida Flag Fish

unusual • peaceful • slow swimmers • plant eaters

SCIENTIFIC NAME: *Jordanella floridae* • FAMILY: Cyprinodontidae • ORIGIN: USA (Florida) • NATURAL HABITAT: Weedy ponds and ditches • AVERAGE ADULT SIZE: 5 cm (2 in) • COLOURS: Olive green with rows of iridescent spots • SEXUAL DIFFERENCES: Males are larger and develop red coloration; females have a black spot on the dorsal fin • REPRODUCTION: Egg-depositor • BREEDING POTENTIAL: Moderate • TANK LEVEL: Middle • FOOD: Flake, frozen and live foods • PLANT FRIENDLY: No • SPECIAL NEEDS: Cool water; herbivorous diet • EASE OF KEEPING: Moderate

Killifish

Aquarium needs

MINIMUM TANK SIZE: 60 cm (24 in)

TEMPERATURE: 20°C (68°F)

PH: 7–7.5

WATER HARDNESS: Neutral to hard and alkaline

COMPATIBILITY WITH OTHER FISH: Moderate

Florida Flag Fish would be hard to identify as killifish because they look like a mixture of several fish families.

They have deep bodies with a thick base to the tail, and males are subtly coloured. They cannot be described as pretty, but they have their admirers and aren't too demanding to keep. The plainer females are smaller and can be recognized by the black blotch on the dorsal fin.

They are a slow-swimming, peaceful species that will do best in a tank with slow, air-powered filtration. They

don't do very well when fed on tropical foods alone, and, because they are plant eaters, it is a good idea to place some floating duckweed (*Lemna minor*) in the tank. If indoor temperatures are warm, the tank will not need a heater-thermostat and can be set up with bogwood and a sandy bottom as decoration. Tough plants, such as Java Fern (*Microsorium pteropus*), can be added and will contribute to the weedy backwater effect that suits the species.

They do best when a group is kept on its own, with two females to every male.

Tanganyika Lamp Eye

colourful • slender • large • sought after

SCIENTIFIC NAME: *Lamprichthys tanganicanus* • FAMILY: Poeciliidae • ORIGIN: Africa (Lake Tanganyika) • NATURAL HABITAT: Rocky surfaces and caves • AVERAGE ADULT SIZE: 15 cm (6 in) • COLOURS: Blue iridescent dots on an opaque, reflective body • SEXUAL DIFFERENCES: Males are larger and more colourful • REPRODUCTION: Egg-depositor • BREEDING POTENTIAL: Moderate • TANK LEVEL: Top • FOOD: Flake, frozen and live foods • PLANT FRIENDLY: Yes • SPECIAL NEEDS: Regular feeding; excellent water quality • EASE OF KEEPING: Moderate

Aquarium needs

MINIMUM TANK SIZE: 1.2 m (4 ft)
TEMPERATURE: 23–25°C (73–77°F)
PH: 8–8.2
WATER HARDNESS: Hard and alkaline
COMPATIBILITY WITH OTHER FISH: Moderate

When people think of killifish they think of small, vividly coloured fish from semi-permanent pools in tropical forests. The Tanganyika Lamp Eye comes not from an acidic pool, but from Lake Tanganyika, one of the largest freshwater lakes in the world, which has very alkaline, very permanent waters.

This species grows larger than most killifish, with male fish reaching 15 cm (6 in) long when fully grown. Adult specimens are difficult to find and expensive.

The tank should be mature, with power filtration to provide excellent water quality. The pH and hardness of the water should be like that found in the natural habitat, and the decor should be predominantly rocks with a sandy bottom.

A group of fish should be added to the aquarium, with males out-numbered by the smaller, less colourful females. The tank must be large enough for the killifish to swim without encroaching on the territories of any rock-dwelling Tanganyikan cichlids also in the tank.

Feed the killifish little and often to maintain their ideal weight. They can be susceptible to bacterial infection when they are first imported. It is possible to breed these fish in the tank; the parents squirt the eggs into cracks in the rockwork.

Killifish

Miscellaneous fish

This group encompasses a number of freshwater and marine species, sometimes known as oddballs by fishkeepers. These fish include several different-looking, rare and non-community species. A fish can be termed non-community for a number of reasons: it may be territorial, predatory, grow large or behave aggressively, or have all these characteristics. On the other hand, it could be sensitive and need specialist care.

Specialist care

The species described in this section all hail from the major tropical river systems of the world, and represent three continents: Africa, South America and Asia. Even the smallest species, Peter's Elephant-nose (*Gnathonemus petersii*; page 191), will need a large tank to accommodate a group and mature, efficient filtration to keep them thriving. The Red Snakehead (*Channa micropeltes*; page 188) and Silver Arowana (*Osteoglossum bicirrhosum*; page 192) top 1 m (3 ft) long when fully grown and will need huge aquariums or large, tropical indoor ponds to live in the long term. Both could deliver a nasty bite and are not recommended if you have small children. The Ocellated Stingray (*Potamotrygon motoro*; page 189) grows large, is sensitive to all but perfect water conditions and carries a potentially lethal sting in its tail.

The appeal

So what do the keepers of these fish get in return for their commitment and spending? The answer is a chance to keep a species of fish from a genus that is like no other. These species are highly adapted to their environments, and predatory fish have to be more intelligent than prey fish in order to be able to

catch them. A solitary fish will form a bond with its owner, and become a pet and addition to the family.

A fish like a stingray represents the extreme diversity of the freshwater hobby, and taming and successfully keeping a fish from a part of the world thousands of miles away is almost as good as going on safari for

A strange-looking fish, Peter's Elephant-nose is not for beginners.

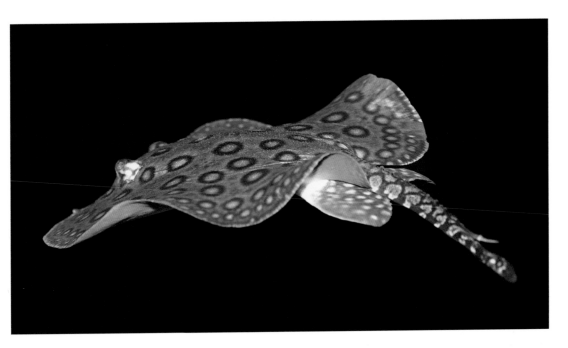

Stingrays glide through the water before burying themselves in the sand.

owners, who can sit and watch these magnificent fish in the comfort of their own living rooms. Such specimens are now being bred in captivity, too.

Prehistoric fish

The stingray is descended from ocean-going rays that adapted to freshwater millions of years ago. It is evolution encapsulated, as all life began in the sea and evolved to conquer new habitats far inside the land mass. The Amazon basin, with its thousands of miles of waterways and soft sand, proved to be a tempting permanent home for the freshwater stingrays and they have remained there unchanged ever since.

The Ornate Bichir (*Polypterus ornatipinnis*; page 193) is another modern link with the past. Its stiff pectoral and ventral fins enable it to 'walk' across the bottom, and even leave the water and travel over land for short distances. It also has a developed swim bladder that allows it to breathe air – a massive evolutionary feat and one that made it possible for water-based organisms to penetrate the land.

Bichirs are hardy fish that tolerate a wide range of water conditions. Because of their mobility, a lid should be fitted on their aquarium.

TIP

Lots of thinking and preparation must be done before you take on any of these species, as their long-term care and the initial purchase of the right aquarium equipment can be expensive.

Red Snakehead

large • aggressive • predatory • fast growing

SCIENTIFIC NAME: *Channa micropeltes* • FAMILY: Channidae • ORIGIN: India • NATURAL HABITAT: Rivers, canals and lakes • AVERAGE ADULT SIZE: 1 m (3 ft 3 in) • COLOURS: Juveniles have white and black stripes with a red tail; adults are duller • SEXUAL DIFFERENCES: Females have fuller bodies • REPRODUCTION: Egg-depositor • BREEDING POTENTIAL: Low • TANK LEVEL: Middle • FOOD: Fish, shellfish • PLANT FRIENDLY: Yes • SPECIAL NEEDS: A huge tank EASE OF KEEPING: Moderate

Miscellaneous fish

Aquarium needs

MINIMUM TANK SIZE: 2.4 m (8 ft)

TEMPERATURE: 24–28°C (75–82°F)

PH: 6–7.5

WATER HARDNESS: Soft and acidic to hard and alkaline

COMPATIBILITY WITH OTHER FISH: Low

The Red Snakehead is an effective predator that shows off its skills well in the aquarium. The juveniles are brightly coloured, with white and black horizontal stripes on a red body, but they turn into dully coloured, aggressive monsters as they grow.

The youngsters are highly predatory of small fish and of each other, and will examine tank mates to see if they will fit in their mouths. They should be kept alone or with large, armoured catfish that cannot be swallowed. There are tales of Red Snakeheads in the wild attacking swimmers who went too close to their brood. Adult fish could inflict nasty bites on your hand so feed with tongs, and all snakeheads are expert escapees, so use a tight-fitting lid.

The suitability of this fish for domestic aquariums is questionable. They need large tanks and ample

filtration. They are also long lived and costly to feed as they grow. And they become more aggressive and less colourful as they mature, making them difficult to re-home.

There are many other better behaved dwarf snakeheads more suitable for captivity – the Rainbow Snakehead (*Channa bleheri*), for example – and the Red Snakehead should be taken on only by aquarists who can offer it ample space and serious long-term commitment.

Warning!

This species grows large.

Ocellated Stingray

large • bizarre looking • prehistoric • sensitive

SCIENTIFIC NAME: *Potamotrygon motoro* • FAMILY: Dasyatidae • ORIGIN: South America (Amazon River)
NATURAL HABITAT: Soft, acidic waters over fine sand and mud • AVERAGE ADULT SIZE: 30 cm (12 in) • COLOURS:
Brown with large circular patterns over the body • SEXUAL DIFFERENCES: Males have claspers • REPRODUCTION:
Livebearer • BREEDING POTENTIAL: Low • TANK LEVEL: Bottom • FOOD: Fish, shellfish, earthworms • PLANT FRIENDLY:
Yes • SPECIAL NEEDS: Excellent water quality; the right foods • EASE OF KEEPING: Difficult

Aquarium needs

MINIMUM TANK SIZE: 1.8 m (6 ft)
TEMPERATURE: 24–26°C (75–79°F)
PH: 6–7
WATER HARDNESS: Soft and acidic
COMPATIBILITY WITH OTHER FISH: Moderate

Part of the appeal of stingrays is their unusual and beautiful appearance. The Ocellated Stingray is from South America and has adapted to live in the freshwaters of the River Amazon. They need lots of space to swim in and a substrate of fine sand. Water quality has to be excellent at all times if they are to thrive, and they are sensitive to medications, such as malachite green, in the water.

They are often reluctant to feed when first imported, and it is wise to see one feed in the store before you purchase it. The larger the fish, the stronger it will be and if it has been captive for some time it should be active and full bodied. Unhealthy stingrays have visible bones under the skin by the base of the tail, and can suffer from deathcurl, which is a fatal loss of control of the disc and constant upward curling.

Care should be taken when handling stingrays, as they all have a poisonous sting in the tail that will cause serious pain. These are certainly fish for experts only.

Warning!
This species is not for beginners.

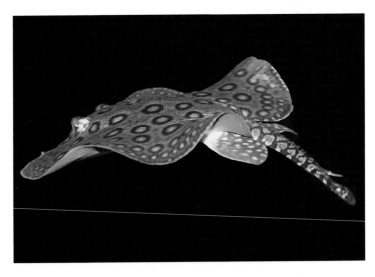

Miscellaneous fish

Fire Eel

large • colourful • attractive • secretive

SCIENTIFIC NAME: *Mastacembelus erythrotaenia* • FAMILY: Mastacembelidae • ORIGIN: Borneo, Burma (Myanmar), Sumatra, Thailand • NATURAL HABITAT: Marshland and rice paddies • AVERAGE ADULT SIZE: 1 m (3 ft 3 in) • COLOURS: Brown and black with vivid red horizontal stripes • SEXUAL DIFFERENCES: Females develop fuller bodies • REPRODUCTION: Egg-scatterer • BREEDING POTENTIAL: Low • TANK LEVEL: Bottom • FOOD: Flake, frozen and live foods • PLANT FRIENDLY: Yes • SPECIAL NEEDS: Retreats; a tight-fitting lid • EASE OF KEEPING: Moderate

Miscellaneous fish

Aquarium needs

MINIMUM TANK SIZE: 1.2 m (4 ft)
TEMPERATURE: 24–28°C (75–82°F)
PH: 7–7.5
WATER HARDNESS: Soft and acidic to medium hard
COMPATIBILITY WITH OTHER FISH: Moderate

The Fire Eel has outstanding markings, and large examples look particularly impressive. It belongs to the spiny eel family, so called because of their serrated dorsal fin which is quite sharp and jagged to the touch. The Fire Eel is the biggest and most colourful of the spiny eels, but it can still be accommodated in aquariums of 1.2 m (4 ft) and over in length.

These fish are adapted to squeeze themselves between vegetation and rocks, and they love to burrow. The aquarium should be heavily decorated with rocks, bogwood and live plants to provide the maximum number of hiding places. The fish will also appreciate a substrate of soft sand. They are equally

at home in a piece of plastic or pipe, cut to length to fit their whole body snugly.

When they are first purchased feeding can be a problem, and many will accept either red mosquito larvae or nothing at all. They should be offered a variety of foods, including frozen shrimps and earthworms, and over time they can be hand fed on presoaked flake. They will eat small fish, so should be kept with larger, peaceful fish. A tight-fitting lid should always be used to prevent them escaping from the tank.

Peter's Elephant-nose

bizarre looking • unusual • sensitive • large

SCIENTIFIC NAME: *Gnathonemus petersii* • FAMILY: Mormyridae • ORIGIN: Togo, Nigeria, Cameroon, Democratic Republic of Congo • NATURAL HABITAT: Muddy river bottoms • AVERAGE ADULT SIZE: 20 cm (8 in) • COLOURS: Black with white markings between the dorsal and anal fins • SEXUAL DIFFERENCES: Males have concave anal fins • REPRODUCTION: Egg-scatterer • BREEDING POTENTIAL: Low • TANK LEVEL: Bottom • FOOD: Live and frozen foods • PLANT FRIENDLY: Yes • SPECIAL NEEDS: Excellent water quality; the right foods • EASE OF KEEPING: Difficult

Aquarium needs

MINIMUM TANK SIZE: 1.2 m (4 ft)

TEMPERATURE: 22–28°C (72–82°F)

PH: 6–7

WATER HARDNESS: Soft and acidic to hard and alkaline

COMPATIBILITY WITH OTHER FISH: Moderate

Elephant-noses are popular because of their long 'noses', which are actually adaptations enabling them to find invertebrates in the mud and silt of the rivers of their natural habitat. In the aquarium they will appreciate a deep bed of fine sand so they can continue that natural behaviour.

Other decoration can consist of pieces of bogwood and some tough plants, such as ferns. Lighting should be subdued, and the water quality should be high and well maintained.

These fish should be kept in groups, but they do tend to squabble, and that trait, combined with their medium to large adult size, necessitates a large tank 1.2 m (4 ft) or more long. Any tank mates should be medium sized and peaceful, or these fish can be kept in a group on their own. Offer a variety of live and frozen foods.

They have not been bred in captivity so all fish will be wild caught. A period of quarantine is advised.

Miscellaneous fish

Silver Arowana

huge • unusual looking • surface swimming • predatory

SCIENTIFIC NAME: *Osteoglossum bicirrhosum* • FAMILY: Osteoglossidae • ORIGIN: South America (Amazon River basin) • NATURAL HABITAT: Rivers that flood forests seasonally • AVERAGE ADULT SIZE: 105 cm (42 in) • COLOURS: Silver with some red in the fins • SEXUAL DIFFERENCES: Mature males have a longer anal fin • REPRODUCTION: Mouth-brooder • BREEDING POTENTIAL: Low • TANK LEVEL: Top • FOOD: Fish, shellfish, insects, food sticks • PLANT FRIENDLY: Yes • SPECIAL NEEDS: A huge tank • EASE OF KEEPING: Difficult

Miscellaneous fish

Aquarium needs

MINIMUM TANK SIZE: 2.4 m (8 ft)
TEMPERATURE: 24–28°C (75–82°F)
PH: 6–7
WATER HARDNESS: Soft and acidic
COMPATIBILITY WITH OTHER FISH: Moderate

Silver Arowana are huge, surface-gliding predators from the Amazon. When the forests flood, arowanas swim into them and jump up out of the water to take insects and birds that are resting on branches above.

They are appealing as juveniles but there is no disguising the huge, trapdoor mouth that engulfs its prey.

They are totally unsuitable for most aquariums because of their eventual size, but if you wish to keep them the ideal conditions would be a massive tank, half-filled with water and with branches and terrestrial plants hanging above. Fish that look to the bottom to take sinking foods can develop drop eye, a condition in which the fish's eyes start to face downwards. Overhanging decoration will help to prevent it.

The water quality should be consistently good. These are active swimmers, so provide the maximum possible swimming space. Two arowanas may fight if kept together in the same tank, but a single specimen can be mixed with other large fish. A tank set up as an Amazon biotope is the ideal. Few fishkeepers will be able to provide properly for this species for its whole life.

Warning!
This species grows large.

Ornate Bichir

patterned • snake like • predatory • hardy

SCIENTIFIC NAME: *Polypterus ornatipinnis* • FAMILY: Polypteridae • ORIGIN: Democratic Republic of Congo
NATURAL HABITAT: Rivers, streams and lake tributaries • AVERAGE ADULT SIZE: 60 cm (24 in) • COLOURS: Black and
gold patterning • SEXUAL DIFFERENCES: Males have a longer anal fin • REPRODUCTION: Egg-depositor • BREEDING
POTENTIAL: Low • TANK LEVEL: Bottom • FOOD: Fish, shellfish, worms • PLANT FRIENDLY: Yes • SPECIAL NEEDS: Air
gap above the surface; lid on the aquarium • EASE OF KEEPING: Easy

Aquarium needs

MINIMUM TANK SIZE: 1.2 m (4 ft)
TEMPERATURE: 26–28°C (79–82°F)
PH: 6–7
WATER HARDNESS: Soft and acidic to hard and alkaline
COMPATIBILITY WITH OTHER FISH: Moderate

Polypterus species or bichirs are ancient-looking predatory fish from Africa. They have adapted to breathe atmospheric air, and almost seem to walk on their fins. Their attraction lies in the fact that they are quite different from other fish. The Ornate Bichir is one of the largest species, and more colourful than the other species in the genus. It epitomizes the odd looks and behaviour that make this group of fish appealing.

To create a suitable habitat for Ornate Bichirs, decorate the tank with different materials to form hiding places. Live plants can be included, but the lighting should be subdued, so use tough ferns or floating plants to dapple the light. The water quality should be good. The fish are tolerant when it comes to pH and temperature, although the filtration should be adequate to deal with the rich waste they produce.

Tank mates should be large enough not to be eaten but also not too quick at taking foods, as a fish like an Oscar would always get to the food first. Adult fish can be sexed: males have a longer, more fleshy anal fin.

Miscellaneous fish

Brackish-water fish

The fish in this group have adapted to life in the estuaries where freshwater rivers meet the oceans. It is an extreme environment, and the fish have to cope with changes in water level, temperature and salinity. The salt in the oceans is a major barrier to most freshwater fish, and vice versa for marine fish, but brackish-water fish can live in both environments and feed off the rich pickings in the river mouths. The mangrove tree is found in this type of environment, and its large, exposed roots provide shelter and breeding grounds for these fish.

The brackish aquarium

In order to keep brackish-water fish you will need to recreate their natural environment in the aquarium. Brackish tanks can look unique when they are aquascaped with a combination of marine and freshwater decoration. Shells and coral chips can be used together with plants and bogwood to create an estuarine scene. For authenticity, use live mangrove plants under bright lighting or dead mangrove roots over fine sand. For Archer Fish (*Toxotes jaculatrix*; page 201) and Mudskippers (*Periophthalmus vulgaris*; page 197) reduce the water level to create a terrestrial area and another dimension to the layout.

Species selection

The species you choose to keep will largely depend on compatibility, as it is possible to keep a community of larger brackish fish. Scats, Monos and Archer Fish may be combined in large aquariums, but Bumblebee Gobies (*Hypogymnogobius xanthozona*; page 196) would be lost in anything over 60 cm (24 in) long. Mudskippers are bordering on amphibian, spending much of their time out of water instead of in it, so the tank should really be decorated to suit their specialist needs, to the exclusion of other species.

Smaller brackish aquariums can be successful and hold interesting species. Bumblebee Gobies can be combined with two estuarine, livebearing species, the Celebes Halfbeak (*Nomorhampus liemi liemi*; page 51) and the Black Molly (*Poecilia sphenops*; page 56), if just enough salt is added to keep the three fish species happy. Tough, live plants, such as the Java Fern (*Microsorium pteropus*), can also be added to great effect into the aquascape.

Mudskippers are strange fish that crawl out on to the sand for long periods.

Archer Fish are great fun to keep as they shoot water at prey above the surface.

Single-species aquariums

Brackish-water fish do have much presence and character, and a fish such as the Mudskipper would be better in an aquarium set up to meet its special needs – with a large expanse of wet sand instead of lots of water and swimming space. Its predatory nature and boisterous ways would also be better catered for in a single-species aquarium.

The Green Spotted Pufferfish (*Tetraodon nigriviridis*; page 200) is also a suitable choice for the single-species aquarium. It is a deep-bodied species that is active at all levels and easily entertaining enough to deserve its own aquarium. Its sharp beak will not be able to harm less robust tank mates, and when there are several specimens they will create a lively, colourful display that would catch anyone's eye yet be specialized enough to keep the more avid fishkeepers among us satisfied.

Finally, the behaviour and feeding specialization of the Archer Fish is so engrained that spitting for insects and food morsels can be easily provoked if the fish are kept in the right environment. A corner of the room would have to be dedicated to a mock mangrove swamp, with shallow water below and lots of branches and leaves above the surface. The spectacle of a group of Archer Fish shooting jets of water into the leafy canopy is possible within your own home, and would be quite a sight.

Bumblebee Goby

tiny • striking • colourful • shy

SCIENTIFIC NAME: *Hypogymnogobius xanthozona* • FAMILY: Gobiidae • ORIGIN: Indonesia • NATURAL HABITAT:
Sandy, freshwater streams with fresh and brackish water • AVERAGE ADULT SIZE: 4 cm (1½ in) • COLOURS: Yellow
body divided by four broad black bands • SEXUAL DIFFERENCES: Males are more colourful • REPRODUCTION:
Egg-depositor • BREEDING POTENTIAL: Moderate • TANK LEVEL: Bottom • FOOD: Small live and frozen foods
PLANT FRIENDLY: Yes • SPECIAL NEEDS: Retreats • EASE OF KEEPING: Moderate

Aquarium needs

MINIMUM TANK SIZE: 30 cm (12 in)
TEMPERATURE: 24–28°C (75–82°F)
PH: 7.5–8.2
WATER HARDNESS: Hard and alkaline
COMPATIBILITY WITH OTHER FISH: Moderate

Bumblebee Gobies are popular small
fish, but they are not suitable for
everyone's tank. First, they are a
brackish-water species, so the fish
appreciate some marine salt in the
water. Second, they are tiny fish and
they do not do well when kept in a
large tank with boisterous fish.

These fish will do best in a small,
gently filtered tank with some salt
added. The decoration should consist
of sand on the tank bottom, together
with bogwood and pebbles to form
caves. Salt-tolerant plants, such as
Java Fern (*Microsorium pteropus*), or

plastic plants can be included, and
cut bamboo canes look effective.

They are difficult feeders as they
will be reluctant to eat flake and dry
foods, preferring frozen foods such
as *Daphnia* and *Cyclops* instead. If
they are healthy and settled into the
tank they may spawn, with the male
protecting the brood in a cave.

A small tank allows the aquarist to
observe the fish and to look at the
vivid coloration that makes them so
popular in the first place. They have
fused pelvic fins that enable them to
stick to surfaces such as plant leaves
or the aquarium glass.

Mudskipper

bizarre looking • amphibious • greedy • boisterous

SCIENTIFIC NAME: *Periophthalmus vulgaris* • FAMILY: Gobidae • ORIGIN: Eastern Africa, Madagascar and across the Indian Ocean • NATURAL HABITAT: Tidal mud and sand areas where they bask on land • AVERAGE ADULT SIZE: 25 cm (10 in) • COLOURS: Brown and grey with colour in the dorsal fins • SEXUAL DIFFERENCES: Unknown
REPRODUCTION: Unknown • BREEDING POTENTIAL: Low • TANK LEVEL: Bottom • FOOD: Fish, frozen foods, shellfish
PLANT FRIENDLY: No • SPECIAL NEEDS: A land area; saltwater • EASE OF KEEPING: Moderate

Aquarium needs

MINIMUM TANK SIZE: 1.2 m (4 ft)
TEMPERATURE: 26–30°C (79–86°F)
PH: 7.5–8.2
WATER HARDNESS: Hard and alkaline
COMPATIBILITY WITH OTHER FISH: Low

Mudskippers are completely different from other fish because they seek out and hop on to dry land. They survive by being able to breathe atmospheric air and return to water occasionally to wet their skin. They have evolved to take advantage of the food that is exposed by the tropical, tidal mud-flats. These huge expanses of mud are taken over by the Mudskippers at low tide, and they form territories, feeding and displaying to each other. Their top-mounted eyes are positioned to spot any approaching danger, and if something threatens they will dash for cover underwater.

A suitable aquarium should be predominantly sand with an area of water in one corner. The water should be filtered and heated, and marine salt should be added.

These fish are predators and will try to eat anything that is placed in the tank with them, so they are best kept as a group of adults. They are easy to feed, and will entertain as they splash sand on to the front glass as they hop and jump. The water should be changed regularly together with the sand, as it can turn anaerobic because it is so shallow. Mudskippers are incredibly salt tolerant and will go from fresh to full marine salt values, but a

brackish salinity of 10–15 grams of salt per 10 litres (1–2 tablespoons per 2 gallons) will suffice.

Mono

shoaling • metallic • active • large

SCIENTIFIC NAME: *Monodactylus argenteus* • FAMILY: Monodactylidae • ORIGIN: The coastlines of the Indian and western Pacific Oceans • NATURAL HABITAT: Mangrove swamps and river estuaries • AVERAGE ADULT SIZE: 25 cm (10 in) • COLOURS: Silver body with yellow dorsal and anal fins and tail • SEXUAL DIFFERENCES: Indistinguishable • REPRODUCTION: Egg-scatterer • BREEDING POTENTIAL: Low • TANK LEVEL: Middle • FOOD: Frozen and live foods • PLANT FRIENDLY: No • SPECIAL NEEDS: A shoal; brackish water • EASE OF KEEPING: Moderate

Brackish-water fish

Aquarium needs
MINIMUM TANK SIZE: 1.5 m (5 ft)
TEMPERATURE: 22–28°C (72–82°F)
PH: 7.5–8.2
WATER HARDNESS: Hard and alkaline
COMPATIBILITY WITH OTHER FISH: Moderate

Monos are sometimes mistaken for freshwater Angelfish because of their deep, striped bodies. They are quite different, however, because they naturally inhabit marine and estuarine waters that are hard and alkaline, not soft and acidic. They look effective in shoals and are often used in public aquariums to provide movement in the midwater levels.

They are often in freshwater aquariums when they are purchased, but will need to be kept in brackish or full saltwater conditions in the long term. The tank should be large enough to accommodate a shoal, and the set-up should provide them with free swimming space. The decor can range from a mock mangrove swamp with resin to a barren rocky aquascape. The fish will not be bothered by your choice, but they must have excellent water quality, some water movement and regular feeds of frozen and live foods, such as krill. If you can also get them to eat dry foods, such as flake, it will benefit them.

They are compatible with many other sorts of fish but avoid keeping them with very tiny or very large fish. They have not been bred in captivity.

Scat

deep bodied • gregarious • active • omnivorous

SCIENTIFIC NAME: *Scatophagus argus argus* • FAMILY: Scatophagidae • ORIGIN: The coastlines of the Indian and western Pacific Oceans • NATURAL HABITAT: River estuaries, lagoons and harbours, and wherever saltwater meets fresh • AVERAGE ADULT SIZE: 30 cm (12 in) • COLOURS: Bronze body with large, black spots • SEXUAL DIFFERENCES: Unknown • REPRODUCTION: Unknown • BREEDING POTENTIAL: Low • TANK LEVEL: Middle • FOOD: Flake, frozen and live foods • PLANT FRIENDLY: No • SPECIAL NEEDS: A large tank; good water quality • EASE OF KEEPING: Moderate

Aquarium needs

MINIMUM TANK SIZE: 1.5 m (5 ft)
TEMPERATURE: 20–28°C (68–82°F)
PH: 7.5–8.2
WATER HARDNESS: Hard and alkaline
COMPATIBILITY WITH OTHER FISH: Moderate

Scats look quite different from anything else, and they do appeal to some people. Along with Monos and Archer Fish, Scats are typical brackish-water species, and the three are often mixed together to simulate a brackish biotope.

Juvenile Scats are quite appealing; adults are less so but are nevertheless impressive fish. You will need a large tank with adequate power filtration and regular maintenance. Decoration should be minimal, and any live plants will quickly be eaten.

These are definitely gregarious fish. They can never be fed too much as they are driven by their stomachs, and it will take a special effort by the owner just to keep weight on them, let alone get them to thrive and grow. Feed regularly

throughout the day on frozen foods, such as brine shrimp, *Mysis* and krill, along with flake, food sticks and tablet foods.

They will need to be kept in brackish water in the long term and can be acclimatized to live in full seawater, but a fish-only aquarium would be necessary as a reef tank is not be appropriate. They have not been bred in aquariums.

Brackish-water fish

Green Spotted Pufferfish

cute • colourful • active • unusual

SCIENTIFIC NAME: *Tetraodon nigriviridis* • FAMILY: Tetraodontidae • ORIGIN: Borneo, Sumatra • NATURAL HABITAT: Shallow streams and rivers • AVERAGE ADULT SIZE: 15 cm (6 in) • COLOURS: Yellow back and white underside; the back is also covered in black spots • SEXUAL DIFFERENCES: Unknown • REPRODUCTION: Egg-depositor
BREEDING POTENTIAL: Low • TANK LEVEL: Middle • FOOD: Molluscs, shellfish • PLANT FRIENDLY: No • SPECIAL NEEDS: Meaty foods • EASE OF KEEPING: Moderate

Brackish-water fish

Aquarium needs
MINIMUM TANK SIZE: 1.2 m (4 ft)
TEMPERATURE: 24–28°C (75–82°F)
PH: 7.5–8.2
WATER HARDNESS: Hard and alkaline
COMPATIBILITY WITH OTHER FISH: Low

Pufferfish are mainly marine species, and those that are tolerant of brackish and freshwater conditions are snapped up by fishkeepers who want to keep something different. The Green Spotted Pufferfish is certainly different, with its egg-shaped body, yellow patterned back and large, mobile eyes.

Their appealing appearance disguises an adapted mouth which contains a sharp 'beak' that is capable of crushing snails and crustaceans. This well-equipped fish can cause havoc if it is not put in the right sort of set-up, and some people find that it can prove difficult to keep.

The tank should include robust furnishings, such as rocks and pieces of bogwood, and the tank

bottom should be covered by fine sand. Filtration should be mature and adequate to cope with the rich waste produced by a meaty diet. The water should contain some marine salt.

Delicate fish will be nipped and harassed, so keep pufferfish as a group of their own species or mix them with other robust brackish-water fish, like Monos and Scats. They will eat cockles, mussels, prawns and whitebait, and snails and cockles in their shells will help to keep their teeth ground down. They are rarely bred in captivity.

Archer Fish

surface swimmer • predator • jumper • interesting

SCIENTIFIC NAME: *Toxotes jaculatrix* • FAMILY: Toxotidae • ORIGIN: India, Malaysia, Burma (Myanmar), Thailand, Philipines • NATURAL HABITAT: Mangroves and lagoons with overhanging vegetation • AVERAGE ADULT SIZE: 25 cm (10 in) • COLOURS: Silver with large black blotches on the flanks and a black-edged anal fin • SEXUAL DIFFERENCES: Unknown • REPRODUCTION: Unknown • BREEDING POTENTIAL: Low • TANK LEVEL: Top • FOOD: Insects, frozen foods, fish • PLANT FRIENDLY: Yes • SPECIAL NEEDS: The right foods; brackish water; a tank with a lid • EASE OF KEEPING: Moderate

Aquarium needs

MINIMUM TANK SIZE: 1.5 m (5 ft)
TEMPERATURE: 24–30°C (75–86°F)
PH: 7.5–8.2
WATER HARDNESS: Hard and alkaline
COMPATIBILITY WITH OTHER FISH: Moderate

Archer Fish are one of the wonders of the natural world, and they are often seen on wildlife programmes shooting insects from overhanging vegetation. They are very good at this, being able to shoot at a distance of over 1 metre (3 feet) and taking into account the refraction of the water surface. If the prey is close enough, they can also jump from the water to capture it.

The ideal aquarium is half-filled with water, with plenty of overhanging vegetation so that the fish can show off their skills. The water should be brackish and well filtered. Decoration below the water line can simply be some pieces of bogwood or fake mangrove roots for authenticity.

Keep these fish in groups of similarly sized individuals to prevent them becoming aggressive with each other. They can be combined with other large brackish-water fish, such as Monos and Scats. However, small gobies and mollies should be avoided, as they may be eaten.

Lots of different foods can be offered, but they will enjoy live insects most. They will also eat chopped shellfish and fish.

Archer Fish can be kept in full marine conditions, but the brackish mangrove tank will look stunning and provide the conditions that suit them best. They have not yet been bred in aquariums.

Brackish-water fish

Marine fish

Tropical saltwater fish are the most colourful and varied of all fish, and we are lucky enough to be able to keep them for our viewing pleasure. Fishkeepers who have previously kept freshwater fish will find that marine fish are a step up in terms of both budget and the knowledge they will need of the fish's requirements. For those who have not kept any fish before, these fish will be a real challenge, and much research and learning must be undertaken before the first purchase is made.

What you should know

Marine fish are more difficult to keep than freshwater fish, having specialized in the stable marine environment to such a degree that they may die if their particular requirements are not met. Most marine fish are caught in the wild, and shipping alone will inflict stress before they reach your aquarium. Providing optimum conditions and proper care and attention to these fish may at times feel like a lot to take on.

The good news is that the technology has improved and there are now many experienced aquarists who have been keeping and even breeding marine fish for decades. While the collection of wild fish is closely monitored and has a low environmental impact, more and more species are being bred in commercial hatcheries. About 20 species are regularly bred in captivity, meaning that a tank can be set up with the intention of keeping only fish that have been raised in captivity, along with farmed corals and other invertebrates.

Recommended species

The number one recommended species must be the Common Clownfish (*Amphiprion ocellaris*; page 238), which scores in terms of adaptability, sociability, colour and size. They can be kept in the minimum recommended size of marine aquarium, mix with nearly all smaller species and readily accept a wide range of food.

The Green Chromis (*Chromis viridis*; page 239) runs the Common Clownfish a close second for most suitable marine species. A small fish, it is not aggressive and territorial, and can be kept in groups even in smaller aquariums without harming corals or invertebrates. The Yellow Tang (*Zebrasoma flavescens*; page 207) and Coral Beauty (*Centropyge bispinosa*; page 235) are more difficult to keep, but bring colour and presence to the aquarium and like to graze algae from live rock.

Attractive and adaptable, Clownfish are the ideal marine fish for beginners.

The right environment

The stable environment of coral reefs and the exacting requirements of the fish mean that the recommended temperature for all tropical marine fish is 25°C (77°F), which can be maintained by a heater-thermostat. This information applies to all species, so has not been listed under individual profiles; similarly, the water pH, hardness and alkalinity should always be the same. In all cases, the pH level should not fall below 8.2. Higher pH values are appreciated by corals and can be achieved by adding a range of supplements to the water, but a pH of 8.2 will normally be achieved as soon as the salt mix is added to freshwater, because synthetic salts contain buffering agents to set the pH at that value.

Sexual differences

Sexual differences appear to be minimal in the vast majority of marine fish species. For this reason, information about sexual differences has been left out of the profiles of most of the marine fish covered in this book.

Reproduction

Information about the reproduction of marine fish has been omitted simply because there is insufficient data about the breeding habits of the majority of species.

Add with caution

Specialized feeders, such as the Moorish Idol (*Zanclus cornutus*; page 253), seahorses (*Hippocampus reidi*; page 252), Pakistani Butterfly Fish (*Chaetodon collare*; page 215) and the Cleaner Wrasse (*Labroides dimidiatus*; page 227), will struggle to survive in the aquarium.

Powder Blue Tang

colourful • active • territorial • aggressive

SCIENTIFIC NAME: *Acanthurus leucosternon* • FAMILY: Acanthuridae • ORIGIN: Indian Ocean • NATURAL HABITAT: Sunlit waters with a strong current over rocks • AVERAGE ADULT SIZE: 20 cm (8 in) • COLOURS: Bright blue body with a yellow dorsal fin, white anal fin and black face • TANK LEVEL: Middle • FOOD: Frozen food; some dry food • CORAL FRIENDLY: Yes • INVERTEBRATE FRIENDLY: Yes • SPECIAL NEEDS: A large tank • EASE OF KEEPING: Difficult

Marine fish

Aquarium needs

MINIMUM TANK SIZE: 1.2 m (4 ft)

COMPATIBILITY WITH OTHER FISH: Moderate

Powder Blue Tangs are beautiful fish, but they can be a bit fiery at times. They are more territorial than other species of tang, with which they can be mixed only in huge aquariums, and they will not readily mix with their own kind at all.

They are good algae grazers, and need to feed regularly to keep their body weight up. Bright lighting is preferable as it will encourage algae to grow on the rocks and so simulate their natural environment. They are safe to be kept with all corals, and stony and branching hard corals suit the biotope. Reef aquariums are preferable because of the grazing opportunities they offer this species,

but they could also be kept in fish-only aquariums with robust fish species and some live rock.

Their coloration is variable, but the bluer the better, and there are special dietary supplements available to try to keep the colour of fish like Powder Blue Tangs at its best.

These fish are susceptible to whitespot, so quarantine new purchases and fit an ultraviolet sterilizer to the system.

Always keep them in as large a tank as possible, which may lessen their aggression, and provide plenty of swimming space and water flow.

Lipstick Tang

large • majestic • territorial • expensive

SCIENTIFIC NAME: *Naso lituratus* • FAMILY: Acanthuridae • OTHER NAMES: Smooth-headed Unicorn Fish, Naso Tang • ORIGIN: Indo-Pacific • NATURAL HABITAT: Coral reefs • AVERAGE ADULT SIZE: 45 cm (18 in) • COLOURS: Grey with intricate facial markings and a yellow forehead • TANK LEVEL: Middle • FOOD: Flake, frozen foods, algae CORAL FRIENDLY: Yes • INVERTEBRATE FRIENDLY: Yes • SPECIAL NEEDS: A large tank • EASE OF KEEPING: Moderate

Aquarium needs

MINIMUM TANK SIZE: 1.5 m (5 ft)
COMPATIBILITY WITH OTHER FISH: Good

Lipstick Tangs are large fish that need an aquarium which can offer them plenty of room for swimming. The tank will need to hold more than 500 litres (100 gallons) to house one of these fish in the long term, but they usually stay significantly smaller than their maximum wild size.

Although the body coloration is grey, this is a handsome, majestic fish with a face pattern that looks as if it has been painted and a lyre-shaped tail. They can be expensive but would be considered one of the main display fish in a reef aquarium.

It is safe with small fish and can be mixed with other tang species, such as Yellow Tangs (*Zebrasoma flavescens*; page 207), in a large aquarium. They are intolerant of their own kind, so have just one individual in a tank.

They are not too susceptible to whitespot, but fit an ultraviolet sterilizer just in case. The water quality must be excellent, and the aquarium should contain lots of live rock to aid biological filtration and provide the Lipstick Tang with areas to graze. Feed little and often with a variety of frozen foods, including brine shrimp, *Mysis*, krill and vegetable foods, such as macro-algae and seaweeds.

Marine fish

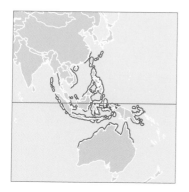

Regal Tang

colourful • vivid • active • shoaling

SCIENTIFIC NAME: *Paracanthurus hepatus* • FAMILY: Acanthuridae • ORIGIN: Indo-Pacific • NATURAL HABITAT: Reef edge with open water and open rock structure for grazing • AVERAGE ADULT SIZE: 20 cm (8 in) • COLOURS: Bright blue with black pattern along the back and a yellow tail • TANK LEVEL: Middle • FOOD: Flake, frozen foods, algae • CORAL FRIENDLY: Yes • INVERTEBRATE FRIENDLY: Yes • SPECIAL NEEDS: Algae-based diet • EASE OF KEEPING: Moderate

Marine fish

Aquarium needs

MINIMUM TANK SIZE: 1.2 m (4 ft)

COMPATIBILITY WITH OTHER FISH: Moderate

Regal Tangs are popular fish with stunning, blue coloration. They are available in several sizes, and small fish can be kept together and will grow up as a shoal. Large specimens may be less willing to do this.

They don't graze as much as some species of tang and will spend most of the day swimming the length of the tank. They will do better in reef aquariums than in fish-only tanks, because the live rock in the reef will produce food in the form of plankton and algae. Provide as large a tank as possible with some flow to exercise the fish. Feed them

little and often to keep weight on them, and the water quality should be excellent at all times.

They can be mixed with small fish with no difficulty, but should be put with other tangs only in large tanks. Similarly, a tank aimed at holding a shoal of Regal Tangs in the long term should contain more than 500 litres (100 gallons) of water.

They can be susceptible to whitespot and should be quarantined before placing them into the main display aquarium. In addition, fitting an ultraviolet sterilizer may help to combat this recurrent problem.

Yellow Tang

colourful • algae eater • active • shoaling

SCIENTIFIC NAME: *Zebrasoma flavescens* • FAMILY: Acanthuridae • ORIGIN: Southwestern Pacific Ocean • NATURAL HABITAT: Areas with strong current and rocky surfaces on the bottom for grazing • AVERAGE ADULT SIZE: 15 cm (6 in) • COLOURS: Bright yellow with a white spur near the base of the tail • TANK LEVEL: Middle • FOOD: Flake, frozen foods, marine algae • CORAL FRIENDLY: Yes • INVERTEBRATE FRIENDLY: Yes • SPECIAL NEEDS: Live rock for grazing • EASE OF KEEPING: Moderate

Aquarium needs

MINIMUM TANK SIZE: 1.2 m (4 ft)

COMPATIBILITY WITH OTHER FISH: Moderate

Yellow Tangs are very colourful and active, and one of the most popular marine fish among aquarists. They are predominantly algae grazers, and they use their specialized mouths to rasp away algae from rocks. Until recently they were kept singly with other species, but a shoal of similarly sized individuals can be added to a tank at the same time to great effect. The tank would need a capacity of more than 500 litres (100 gallons) and would benefit from the inclusion of a protein skimmer to remove the accumulation of waste products.

They graze constantly on rocks, and live rock is ideal as it produces plankton and macro-algae for grazing. They also feed greedily on frozen foods including *Mysis*, brine shrimp and krill. If your tank does not contain live rock add commercially grown seaweed as a supplement.

Adult Yellow Tangs may feel that the tank is their territory and may act aggressively towards new additions, especially other tangs and angelfish. The aggression should stop after a few days.

These fish are susceptible to whitespot, although not as much as Regal or Powder Blue Tangs; fitting an ultraviolet sterilizer would be a sensible precaution.

Marine fish

Frogfish

bizarre looking • camouflaged • predatory • interesting

SCIENTIFIC NAME: *Antennarius* spp. • FAMILY: Antennariidae • OTHER NAMES: Sponge Fish, Angler Fish • ORIGIN: Indo-Pacific • NATURAL HABITAT: Coral reefs around sponges for camouflage • AVERAGE ADULT SIZE: 30 cm (12 in) COLOURS: Yellow-green and other interchangeable colours • TANK LEVEL: Bottom • FOOD: Fish • CORAL FRIENDLY: Yes • INVERTEBRATE FRIENDLY: No • SPECIAL NEEDS: Perches • EASE OF KEEPING: Moderate

Marine fish

Aquarium needs

MINIMUM TANK SIZE: 90 cm (36 in)

COMPATIBILITY WITH OTHER FISH: Moderate

Frogfish are also known as Angler Fish because they possess a single antenna on the top of their heads that they wave around to attract fish, which are then devoured by their huge, upward-opening mouths.

To watch one of these fish fishing is a fascinating sight. First, they are masters of camouflage, and they can change colour and are shaped to mimic their surroundings. Second, when they move they don't swim but walk on their specially adapted pectoral fins until they are in position. Finally, the thin lure is exposed from its position on the head and waved in

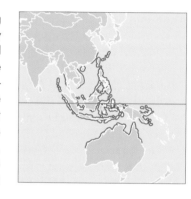

a motion that would make human lure anglers feel jealous.

Sadly, you won't see much of this behaviour in captivity because the Frogfish should be fed on dead fish, not live ones. For ethical reasons, this should always be the case. They are highly predatory fish and will eat tank mates and each other if a little bit smaller than themselves.

The tank can be simple, with live rock, a perch and a protein skimmer for filtration. It could be devoted just to Frogfish, as they are exciting enough on their own. The colourful species are more expensive to buy.

Bangaii Cardinal

attractive • elegant • shoaling • reef safe

SCIENTIFIC NAME: *Pterapogon kauderni* • FAMILY: Apogonidae • OTHER NAME: Highfin Cardinal Fish • ORIGIN: Indonesia • NATURAL HABITAT: Coral reefs among the spines of long-spined sea urchins and branching corals AVERAGE ADULT SIZE: 8 cm (3in) • COLOURS: White or brown body with black vertical bands running into the dorsal, anal and pelvic fins; luminescent white spots on the flanks and fins • TANK LEVEL: Middle • FOOD: Frozen foods • CORAL FRIENDLY: Yes • INVERTEBRATE FRIENDLY: Yes • SPECIAL NEEDS: Keep in groups • EASE OF KEEPING: Moderate

Aquarium needs

MINIMUM TANK SIZE: **90 cm (36 in)**

COMPATIBILITY WITH OTHER FISH: **Moderate**

The Bangaii Cardinal is a stunning, reef-friendly marine fish. They are black and white, the white seeming almost fluorescent under bright lighting. They have big eyes and a big mouth, but are not predatory of any small fish. Instead, the big mouth is used for holding their fry, because they are mouth-brooders.

This is a great advantage for the reef-keeper who wishes to breed fish, because the fry of mouth-brooders are born larger and will accept proprietary fry foods straight away. Most marine fish fry have a pelagic (deep-water) stage, which means that they float around the ocean as plankton and are hard to rear in captivity, but any owner of Bangaii Cardinals has a good chance of breeding and raising them. Yet they are endangered in the wild because of over-collection for marine fishkeepers!

These fish must be kept in groups so that a pair can form, because if two individuals are put together they may fight to the death. They are peaceful towards other fish and will readily accept most marine frozen foods.

Wild-caught Bangaii Cardinals – if there any left – may need to be quarantined because they often come with parasites.

Marine fish

Picasso Triggerfish

unusual looking • tough • active • predatory

SCIENTIFIC NAME: *Rhinecanthus aculeatus* • FAMILY: Balistidae • ORIGIN: Indo-Pacific • NATURAL HABITAT: Coral reefs • AVERAGE ADULT SIZE: 25 cm (10 in) • COLOURS: An intricate pattern of white, brown and yellow stripes on a white body with blue bands between the eyes • TANK LEVEL: Middle • FOOD: Cockles, mussels, whitebait, shrimp • CORAL FRIENDLY: No • INVERTEBRATE FRIENDLY: No • SPECIAL NEEDS: A large tank; robust tank mates EASE OF KEEPING: Moderate

Marine fish

Aquarium needs

MINIMUM TANK SIZE: 1.5 m (5 ft)

COMPATIBILITY WITH OTHER FISH: Moderate

Triggerfish are oddly shaped fish, with a huge snout, a small mouth and eyes set far back on the head. Their swimming action is odd too, as they are propelled by their dorsal and anal fins. They are called Triggerfish because they have erectile spurs on the top and bottom of their bodies that can be locked into place if a fish tries to eat them or if they sense danger. They are boisterous fish and are usually the ones causing the trouble.

The Picasso Triggerfish, however, is not too boisterous and one of the attractively marked species. It should not be kept with corals and may devour invertebrates, like crabs and

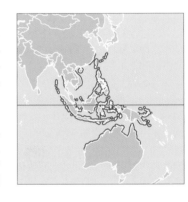

shrimps, which would make up part of their natural diet. The small mouth hides powerful jaws and sharp teeth, so feed them with tongs and be aware of their position in the tank when you carry out maintenance.

Juvenile Picasso Triggerfish are particularly attractive and endearing, but they will eventually need a large, fish-only tank. They can be mixed with other fish-only specimens, including pufferfish, groupers, lionfish and large angelfish. They are intelligent fish that make great pets, and they are reasonably priced, too.

Algae Blenny

comical • camouflaged • endearing • algae eater

SCIENTIFIC NAME: *Salarius fasciatus* • FAMILY: Blennidae • ORIGIN: Indo-Pacific • NATURAL HABITAT: Rocky areas around the coral reef • AVERAGE ADULT SIZE: 13 cm (5 in) • COLOURS: Changeable, depending on mood and surroundings; grey and white to green and white with fluorescent green dots around the face • TANK LEVEL: Middle • FOOD: Algae, flake and frozen foods • CORAL FRIENDLY: Yes • INVERTEBRATE FRIENDLY: Yes • SPECIAL NEEDS: Grazing sites • EASE OF KEEPING: Moderate

Aquarium needs

MINIMUM TANK SIZE: 1.2 m (4 ft)

COMPATIBILITY WITH OTHER FISH: Moderate

Algae Blennies are masters of disguise, and they have great personalities, too. The eyes placed high on the head, the wide mouth and the stalks on the head make the fish look more like one of the Muppets than a fish.

They are bought mainly because of their usefulness as algae eaters, but owners soon fall in love with them as they discover that they are one of the most endearing characters in the tank. They are quite shy fish and can change colour rapidly to match their surroundings. Remarkably, an Algae Blenny becomes aware of you watching it, even from a distance, and stops what it is doing. It will only resume its algae eating when you cease looking directly at it.

Before purchasing one make sure that you have enough algae and live rock for it to graze on. They often starve in clean aquariums or tanks with the wrong type of algae. They won't touch the slime algae that develop in all new tanks and that stop any other algae from growing underneath it. If algae is in short supply you must supplement their diet with algae-based marine flake. A small specimen is the best purchase as it needs to eat less each day.

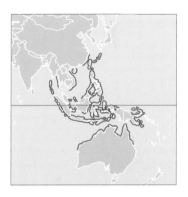

Marine fish

Mandarin

colourful • cute • bottom dwelling • popular

SCIENTIFIC NAME: *Synchiropus splendidus* • FAMILY: Callionymidae • ORIGIN: Southwestern Pacific Ocean
NATURAL HABITAT: Quieter areas of the reef, such as lagoons • AVERAGE ADULT SIZE: 8 cm (3 in) • COLOURS:
Paisley patterning in a mix of colours, including green-blue and orange, a red eye and gold cheeks
TANK LEVEL: Bottom • FOOD: Frozen and live foods • CORAL FRIENDLY: Yes • INVERTEBRATE FRIENDLY: Yes • SPECIAL
NEEDS: Live rock; a mature tank • EASE OF KEEPING: Difficult

Marine fish

Aquarium needs

MINIMUM TANK SIZE: 90 cm (36 in)
COMPATIBILITY WITH OTHER FISH: Moderate

Mandarins are much sought after because of their intricate coloration and interesting behaviour. They should not be added to tanks less than about six months old because they naturally feed on tiny shrimp, and a reef tank with live rock will also in time produce this food for them. Generally, avoid thin Mandarins in aquatic stores as they may already be starved. However, if you have a mature tank that is crawling with little bugs it will be the best place for them.

They don't appreciate excessive flow and would suit a tank that is set up to replicate the lagoon zones of the ocean, with lush macro-algae growth and a mature sand bed. They will take some frozen foods, such as brine shrimp and *Mysis*, but they always need that little bit extra from the rock. Modern systems with a refugium in the sump provide good conditions for Mandarins, because the refugium serves as a breeding ground for copepods (minute crustaceans), which are pumped into the main tank and serve as food.

Male Mandarins have a longer dorsal fin than females. They are largely intolerant of their own kind. Keep them with peaceful fish.

Long-nosed Butterfly Fish

colourful • endearing • unusual looking • sensitive

SCIENTIFIC NAME: *Forcipiger flavissimus* • FAMILY: Chaetodontidae • ORIGIN: Indo-Pacific • NATURAL HABITAT: Intricate coral reefs with tiny holes providing feeding opportunities • AVERAGE ADULT SIZE: 15 cm (6 in)
COLOURS: Bright yellow body, dorsal and anal fins, a white snout and black forehead with a black circle on the anal fin • TANK LEVEL: Middle • FOOD: Frozen foods • CORAL FRIENDLY: Yes • INVERTEBRATE FRIENDLY: No
SPECIAL NEEDS: The right foods • EASE OF KEEPING: Difficult

Aquarium needs

MINIMUM TANK SIZE: 1.2 m (4 ft)
COMPATIBILITY WITH OTHER FISH: Moderate

The Long-nosed Butterfly Fish is sought after because of its shape and strong coloration, but it is not a fish for beginners and requires specialist care. The difficulty in maintaining one is to get it feeding, and to keep it feeding and healthy in the long term. Make regular offerings of brine shrimp, *Mysis*, krill and chopped cockles and mussels. It will rarely accept flake. When buying, check that the specimen is already feeding in the store.

This fish needs a large tank with excellent water quality and lots of live rock to provide refuge and grazing areas. The tiny invertebrates that breed in the live rock will certainly be on the fish's menu, and its specialized mouth can delve into crevices in the rock to get at them. It may nibble corals occasionally, but is generally safe to be kept with them. It will pick at Feather-duster Tubeworms (*Sabellastarte magnifica*), so they are best left out.

There is another Long-nosed Butterfly Fish with an almost identical pattern and body shape. *Forcipiger longirostris* may be mistaken for *F. flavissimus*, but it has a smaller mouth and is harder to keep. Keep both species singly unless bought as a pair, and they are best as the only species of butterfly fish in a tank.

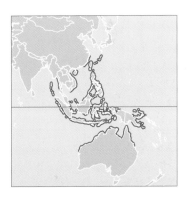

Marine fish

Wimple Fish

deep bodied • striking • active • shoaling

SCIENTIFIC NAME: *Heniochus acuminatus* • FAMILY: Chaetodontidae • OTHER NAMES: Longfin Bannerfish, Pennant Butterfly Fish, Heniochus Butterfly Fish, Poor Man's Moorish Idol • ORIGIN: Indo-Pacific • NATURAL HABITAT: Coral reefs • AVERAGE ADULT SIZE: 20 cm (8 in) • COLOURS: Broad black and white alternate banding on the body and a white, extended dorsal fin • TANK LEVEL: Middle • FOOD: Frozen foods • CORAL FRIENDLY: No INVERTEBRATE FRIENDLY: No • SPECIAL NEEDS: A group; the right foods • EASE OF KEEPING: Difficult

Marine fish

Aquarium needs

MINIMUM TANK SIZE: 1.5 m (5 ft)
COMPATIBILITY WITH OTHER FISH: Moderate

Wimple Fish have been kept by marine aquarists for decades. Their shape and markings are not only attractive but also indicative of the hugely varied designs of reef fish.

These are fish for the fish-only aquarium as they can harass corals in reef tanks. The fish-only aquarium will, however, benefit from the inclusion of live rock because the biological filtration and water quality should be very good.

Wimple Fish are a shoaling species and they are always active and out on display in midwater. They are sensitive fish, and to keep them full bodied and healthy you will have to provide them with

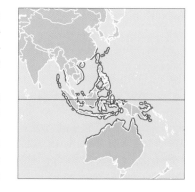

frequent feeds of meaty frozen foods throughout the day.

They are large enough to be kept with groupers and lionfish, but should not be kept with other butterfly fish. They will also mix with lots of other species, including damselfish, and they have been used in the past to form displays with Humbug Damselfish (*Dascyllus aruanus*), which have the same vertical black and white stripes. They are similar looking to the Moorish Idol (*Zanclus cornutus*; page 253), but are thankfully easier to keep.

Pakistani Butterfly Fish

patterned • majestic • graceful • sensitive

SCIENTIFIC NAME: *Chaetodon collare* • FAMILY: Chaetodontidae • OTHER NAME: Collare Butterfly Fish • ORIGIN: Indian Ocean, East African coast • NATURAL HABITAT: Coral reefs with stony corals and branching corals AVERAGE ADULT SIZE: 15 cm (6 in) • COLOURS: Grey body with a red tail and black and white marked face TANK LEVEL: Middle • FOOD: Frozen foods • CORAL FRIENDLY: No • INVERTEBRATE FRIENDLY: No • SPECIAL NEEDS: Regular feeding • EASE OF KEEPING: Difficult

Aquarium needs

MINIMUM TANK SIZE: 1.5 m (5 ft)

COMPATIBILITY WITH OTHER FISH: Moderate

Although predominantly grey in colour, Pakistani Butterfly Fish are stunningly beautiful. They are hard to keep alive and healthy in captivity, so think carefully about whether your aquarium can give them what they need. They must have excellent water quality, provided by lots of mature live rock and effective protein skimming. The tank must also be large enough to allow swimming space and grazing areas among the rocks.

In the wild they eat coral polyps, which makes their diet difficult to replicate in captivity. Growing corals to feed them is beyond the budget of most, so offer substitutes in the hope that they will accept them. Juveniles may be more willing to try other foods than adults that have spent many years in the ocean. Offer brine shrimp, *Mysis*, krill, cockles, mussels, octopus and reef gel, which is specially formulated for butterfly fish and similar species.

If, after a week or so, they come round to accepting the different foods they stand a good chance of surviving, but this is not a fish for beginners, and you should not attempt to keep one unless you can provide the highest standard of care.

Pakistani Butterly Fish are best kept alone or in pairs as the only butterfly fish in the tank.

Warning!

This species is not for beginners.

Marine fish

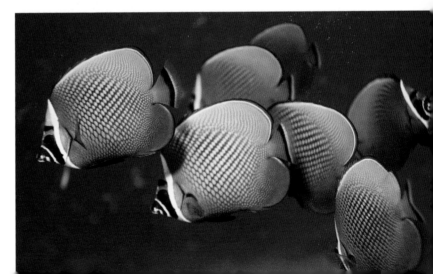

Copperband Butterfly Fish

unusual looking • popular • sensitive • demanding

SCIENTIFIC NAME: *Chelmon rostratus* • FAMILY: Chaetodontidae • ORIGIN: Indo-Pacific • NATURAL HABITAT: Intricate rock structures on coral reefs • AVERAGE ADULT SIZE: 20 cm (8 in) • COLOURS: Silver-white with broad, orange, vertical bands and a black circle in the rear of the dorsal fin • TANK LEVEL: Middle • FOOD: Frozen foods, special gels • CORAL FRIENDLY: No • INVERTEBRATE FRIENDLY: No • SPECIAL NEEDS: The right foods • EASE OF KEEPING: Difficult

Marine fish

Aquarium needs

MINIMUM TANK SIZE: 1.5 m (5 ft)

COMPATIBILITY WITH OTHER FISH: Moderate

The shape of Copperband Butterfly Fish is typical of fish in this group: they have a deep, compressed body and a long snout with a specialized mouth.

Most of this group are specialized coral polyp eaters. The Copperband Butterfly Fish are not quite that bad, but they may nip at some corals. On the plus side, they may eat rock anemones (*Aiptaisia* spp.), which can be a real problem if they become established in reef aquariums. They may also eat bristleworms; however, opinion has changed towards these in recent years, and they are now regarded as useful.

Copperband Butterfly Fish are sensitive and deserve perfect water conditions and a large tank. The main problem arises with feeding them, as they are not adapted to take food in open water. The aquarist should try stuffing some food into crevices in the rockwork. Special gels have been formulated for this type of fish, and may be the way to increase survival rates in captivity.

A reef tank is the best place for them, but they may cause trouble. Individuals behave differently, and some will be fine with all invertebrates. However, they do not get along with each other unless bought as a pair.

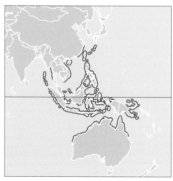

Emperor Angelfish

large • impressive • colourful • expensive

SCIENTIFIC NAME: *Pomacanthus imperator* • FAMILY: Chaetodontidae • ORIGIN: Indo-Pacific • NATURAL HABITAT: Coral reefs • AVERAGE ADULT SIZE: 30 cm (12 in) • COLOURS: Juveniles are dark blue with white and blue lines; adults are yellow with blue diagonal lines, dark eye patches and gill covers and a white snout • TANK LEVEL: Middle • FOOD: Frozen foods • CORAL FRIENDLY: No • INVERTEBRATE FRIENDLY: No • SPECIAL NEEDS: A large tank; excellent water quality • EASE OF KEEPING: Difficult

Aquarium needs

MINIMUM TANK SIZE: 1.5 m (5 ft)

COMPATIBILITY WITH OTHER FISH: Moderate

The Emperor Angelfish is an impressive fish that commands a high price. It would be more popular among aquarists, despite its price, if it were reef friendly.

It is typical of larger angelfish in that it will nip at, eat and harass corals and invertebrates. However, live rock in the aquarium is still recommended, as it will aid filtration, make a realistic aquascape and provide this fish with areas to graze on.

It feeds on meaty marine foods, such as krill, octopus, cockles and mussels, together with some marine algae.

An adult Emperor Angelfish is a deep-bodied, thick-set fish that is more than capable of looking after itself. It can be quite dominant in a tank and may pick on and bully other species of angelfish, but it can be kept with other large fish, including groupers, lionfish and butterfly fish.

Juvenile fish have a distinct colour pattern and look very different from their adult appearance. Juveniles that change colour in the aquarium are often not as colourful as an adult that has been collected from the ocean.

Marine fish

Scarlet Hawkfish

colourful • intelligent • predatory • interesting

SCIENTIFIC NAME: *Neocirrhites armatus* • FAMILY: Cirrhitidae • ORIGIN: Western and Indo-Pacific Ocean
NATURAL HABITAT: Coral reefs • AVERAGE ADULT SIZE: 10 cm (4 in) • COLOURS: Bright red body with a black line in the dorsal fin and a black ring around the eyes • TANK LEVEL: Middle • FOOD: Frozen foods • CORAL FRIENDLY: Yes • INVERTEBRATE FRIENDLY: No • SPECIAL NEEDS: None • EASE OF KEEPING: Moderate

Marine fish

Aquarium needs

MINIMUM TANK SIZE: 90 cm (36 in)
COMPATIBILITY WITH OTHER FISH: Moderate

Scarlet Hawkfish are colourful and likeable fish that move around the aquarium with a sense of purpose. The rich red coloration makes them a sought-after species, and they are better behaved than some of their larger cousins.

A favourite antic is to perch on a rock and watch what is happening in and outside the aquarium. The fish will hop from rock to rock, perching on its pectoral fins as it goes. It is a micro-predator and will prey on snails, crabs, shrimp and even small fish, such as juvenile damselfish. Don't mix this species with Firefish and most gobies, as it may attack them. It is coral friendly

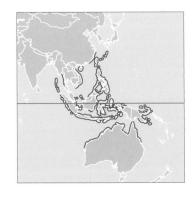

but may occasionally perch on them, a trait exhibited in the wild that causes corals to retract.

The fish will accept a range of larger foods, including krill and *Mysis*, along with chopped cockle, mussel and whitebait. The aquarium set-up should ideally be a reef aquarium with larger fish and few invertebrates. It should contain lots of mature live rock, which will provide hiding places and also aid biological filtration.

They are expensive fish, and they can be prone to parasitic infection, so quarantine newly purchased fish.

Porcupine Pufferfish

active • bizarre looking • intelligent • pet fish

SCIENTIFIC NAME: *Diodon holocanthus* • FAMILY: Diodontidae • ORIGIN: Nearly all tropical seas • NATURAL HABITAT: Coral reefs and rocky areas; also found in open water • AVERAGE ADULT SIZE: 30 cm (12 in) • COLOURS: Brown with some black spotting and light brown or yellow spines • TANK LEVEL: Middle • FOOD: Cockles, mussels, prawns • CORAL FRIENDLY: No • INVERTEBRATE FRIENDLY: No • SPECIAL NEEDS: None • EASE OF KEEPING: Easy

Aquarium needs

MINIMUM TANK SIZE: 1.5 m (5 ft)

COMPATIBILITY WITH OTHER FISH: Moderate

Porcupine Pufferfish are incredibly active, intelligent fish, and they make great pets. They could even be kept on their own, and the owner would seldom tire of them. They are not colourful but have a kind of cartoon body shape with a big head and large, forward-facing eyes. They are covered in spines, which stick out all over the body when the fish is inflated with water. Inflation is a defence mechanism, and they will puff up when they feel they are in danger. A pufferfish that keeps inflating in the aquarium is probably stressed, and the water quality should be checked and the fish inspected for signs of marine whitespot.

They swim the whole length of the tank and go into a frenzy at feeding time. They will even spit water and swim backwards in order to get your attention when hungry. Don't be tempted to hand feed them as they have a nasty bite.

They are generally hardy and easy to keep, but the tank should be a fish-only tank and does not have to contain live rock. Instead, filter the tank with an external canister filter filled with ceramic, biological media, and use an oversized protein skimmer.

Marine fish

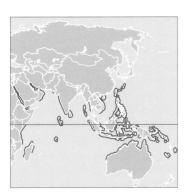

Round Batfish

large • long lived • peaceful • dither fish

SCIENTIFIC NAME: *Platax orbicularis* • FAMILY: Ephippidae • ORIGIN: Indo-Pacific • NATURAL HABITAT: Open water around coral reefs • AVERAGE ADULT SIZE: 50 cm (20 in) • COLOURS: Brown with a black stripe running vertically through the eye • TANK LEVEL: Middle • FOOD: Frozen foods • CORAL FRIENDLY: No • INVERTEBRATE FRIENDLY: No SPECIAL NEEDS: A large tank • EASE OF KEEPING: Moderate

Marine fish

Aquarium needs

MINIMUM TANK SIZE: **2.4 m (8 ft)**
COMPATIBILITY WITH OTHER FISH: **Moderate**

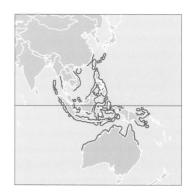

Batfish are incredibly tall fish, taller than they are long. If you consider that these fish grow to 50 cm (20 in) long, you will realize that a fully grown adult is huge and totally unsuitable for most aquariums.

Juveniles could be mistaken for freshwater angelfish, but the stripes on batfish fade as they get older.

They need to be kept in groups in fish-only aquariums because they are not reef safe. They are peaceful and can be housed with a large selection of fish, and they make good dither fish in large fish-only display aquariums as they are far too large to be considered as a meal, even by big moray eels and groupers.

They need to be fed on chopped cockles and mussels along with other meaty fare, and the filtration system should be sufficiently large to cope. There should also be substantial water changes.

The tank must be very tall as well as long and wide, because if they feel confined they can become stressed. Because of their eventual size and longevity they are not recommended even though they will be seen for sale in most marine stores. They are better suited to public aquariums.

Several species of batfish are available. All have a similar outline, but some are deeper-bodied than others. Their profile from the front is very slim and they would appear to be fragile fish, but they are robust and strong swimmers.

Warning!

This species grows large.

Yellow Goby

small • colourful • reef safe • shy

SCIENTIFIC NAME: *Gobiodon okinawae* • FAMILY: Gobiidae • ORIGIN: Indo-Pacific • NATURAL HABITAT: Branching corals • AVERAGE ADULT SIZE: 3 cm (1¼ in) • COLOURS: Bright yellow all over the body • TANK LEVEL: Middle FOOD: Frozen foods • CORAL FRIENDLY: Yes • INVERTEBRATE FRIENDLY: Yes • SPECIAL NEEDS: Retreats • EASE OF KEEPING: Moderate

Aquarium needs

MINIMUM TANK SIZE: 90 cm (36 in)

COMPATIBILITY WITH OTHER FISH: Moderate

Yellow Gobies are ideal for reef aquariums, and although they are small fish, they will be seen from a distance as they perch on the rock face.

In the wild they live among branching hard corals, such as *Acropora* spp. Corals are not necessary in the aquarium, but if you have thriving branching corals a group of these bright yellow fish could further enhance the tank.

If you add a group a pair may form and they may spawn, but the fry would need to be reared away from the main tank. They squabble among themselves, and do not do well if picked on by larger species, such as wrasses or dwarf angelfish, which may take offence at them sitting on their reef. They have some protection against predation in the form of bad-tasting body slime, but it may be of no use if they get mouthed by a hawkfish or something similar.

They also need regular feeds of small foods such as *Cyclops* so that they do not become thin. A tank could be set up specially for this species, and it could be smaller than usual although it should have plenty of live rock. Small reef aquariums – under 90 cm (36 in) long – are referred to as nano reefs.

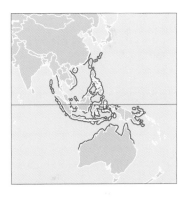

Marine fish

Neon Goby

tiny • peaceful • colourful • active

SCIENTIFIC NAME: *Elactinus oceanops* • FAMILY: Gobiidae • ORIGIN: East Atlantic Ocean • NATURAL HABITAT: Coral heads • AVERAGE ADULT SIZE: 5 cm (2 in) • COLOURS: Black with a neon blue stripe running from the tip of the snout to the base of the tail • TANK LEVEL: Middle • FOOD: Frozen foods • CORAL FRIENDLY: Yes • INVERTEBRATE FRIENDLY: Yes • SPECIAL NEEDS: Retreats • EASE OF KEEPING: Moderate

Marine fish

Aquarium needs

MINIMUM TANK SIZE: 90 cm (36 in)

COMPATIBILITY WITH OTHER FISH: Moderate

Neon Gobies are great little fish for the reef aquarium, and they exhibit interesting behaviour as they some-times clean fish of parasites (like a Cleaner Wrasse, *Labroides dimidiatus*; page 227). They have also been bred in captivity and may spawn in your tank. The advantage of little reef fish is that your mini-reef can seem like a whole natural reef to them, and they will go about their business as if they were in the wild.

The aquarium should be mature with no large or boisterous fish, and nothing that may eat them. Add a pair or large group and they should take up residence about halfway up the tank, among the rocks.

They should be fed on brine shrimp and *Cyclops*, and they may soon spawn. The ideal spawning site is a piece of PVC pipe. The young will need to be removed and fed on zooplankton if they are to survive. Alternatively, you could set up a 60-cm (24-in) aquarium with just a pair of Neon Gobies in the first place, then remove the parents to the main tank when they spawn. These fish are available tank-bred from commercial hatcheries, a practice that should be encouraged. A similar species is the Sharknose Goby (*Gobiosoma evelynae*).

Blue-cheeked Goby

substrate sifter • bottom dwelling • peaceful • active

SCIENTIFIC NAME: *Valencienna strigata* • FAMILY: Gobiidae • ORIGIN: Indo-Pacific • NATURAL HABITAT: Sandy areas adjacent to coral reefs • AVERAGE ADULT SIZE: 15 cm (6 in) • COLOURS: White or pale grey with a yellow face and blue cheek stripes • TANK LEVEL: Bottom • FOOD: Frozen foods • CORAL FRIENDLY: Yes • INVERTEBRATE FRIENDLY: Yes • SPECIAL NEEDS: A large expanse of sand • EASE OF KEEPING: Moderate

Aquarium needs

MINIMUM TANK SIZE: 1.2 m (4 ft)

COMPATIBILITY WITH OTHER FISH: Good

Blue-cheeked Gobies provide movement in the lower water levels and a useful service to the fishkeeper. They are tireless sand sifters, meaning that their constant turning over of the sand keeps it clean and prevents it from turning anaerobic. The one disadvantage of this practice is that the fish are prone to swimming high into the upper water layers with mouthfuls of sand and then dumping it over any corals below. Spreading some fine food particles into the water can be an advantage, but repeatedly dropping sand on to a coral or anemone will impair it in the long term.

They are peaceful fish and can be kept in pairs in a mixed community of smaller or larger fish. They should be fed frequently to keep their body weight high, because the substrate is less nutritious in the aquarium than in the ocean, and they can get thin quite quickly. Live rock can be used to 'seed' any sand beds with tiny burrowing invertebrates that will help to keep the gobies well fed. Refugiums attached to the main tank and live sand will also help.

Marine fish

Royal Gramma

colourful • small • reef safe • easy to keep

SCIENTIFIC NAME: *Gramma loreto* • FAMILY: Grammidae • ORIGIN: West Atlantic Ocean, Caribbean Sea
NATURAL HABITAT: Caves and overhanging rocks on coral reefs • AVERAGE ADULT SIZE: 8 cm (3 in) • COLOURS:
Bright pink or purple upper body and a bright yellow lower body and tail • TANK LEVEL: Middle • FOOD:
Frozen foods • CORAL FRIENDLY: Yes • INVERTEBRATE FRIENDLY: Yes • SPECIAL NEEDS: Retreats • EASE OF KEEPING:
Moderate

Aquarium needs

MINIMUM TANK SIZE: 90 cm (36 in)
COMPATIBILITY WITH OTHER FISH: Moderate

Royal Grammas are a popular choice for the reef aquarium because they are colourful, reef friendly and undemanding. Their coloration is stunning: their bodies have a bright pink or purple front half and a bright yellow rear half.

They can be kept singly or in pairs, and in the wild live in large groups, so this could also be possible in a large aquarium. They will be shy at first, until they find a suitable retreat. They will then stay close to the rocks but on view and will defend their cave from other small fish by opening their mouths wide and displaying. They are easy to feed and will accept brine shrimp, *Mysis* and krill.

A pair of Royal Grammas may spawn in the aquarium, and they have been commercially bred, but the fry will need special care if you are to raise them.

There is a similar-looking species known as the False Gramma or Royal Dottyback (*Pseudochromis paccagnellae*). The two species should not be confused as the latter is an extremely aggressive little fish. The Royal Gramma has rich coloration on its fins, while the False Gramma has none. The False Gramma will not mix with other small fish.

Marine fish

Harlequin Tusk Fish

large • impressive • sought after • expensive

SCIENTIFIC NAME: *Choerodon fasciatus* • FAMILY: Labridae • ORIGIN: Western and Indo-Pacific Ocean • NATURAL HABITAT: Coral reefs • AVERAGE ADULT SIZE: 30 cm (12 in) • COLOURS: Orange and white vertical bands edged in bright blue and red-edged fins • TANK LEVEL: Bottom • FOOD: Shellfish • CORAL FRIENDLY: No • INVERTEBRATE FRIENDLY: No • SPECIAL NEEDS: A large tank • EASE OF KEEPING: Moderate

Aquarium needs

MINIMUM TANK SIZE: 1.8 m (6 ft)

COMPATIBILITY WITH OTHER FISH: Moderate

The Harlequin Tusk Fish has a very striking and somewhat menacing appearance. This species grows large, and other members of the genus can grow to a huge 90 cm (3 ft) long. It is actually a wrasse, and the sharp, protruding teeth are used for grabbing and crunching invertebrates.

It is not as menacing towards other fish as it looks, however, and it can be combined with most other large species in a fish-only aquarium. The tank should be large and well filtered, with efficient protein skimming. Decor can be real live rock or the fake type, and there should be a layer of sand on the bottom of the tank.

They should be fed on a diet of mainly shellfish, including cockles, mussels and prawns. The cockles can be offered in their shells to provide more of a challenge and to give the fish something to sink its teeth into.

Juvenile coloration changes, to become bluer with red fins. Adult fish are expensive to ship, as it should be the only one of the species in the tank. They are sensitive to copper-based medications so be careful when you are treating sick fish.

Marine fish

Scott's Fairy Wrasse

beautiful • colourful • active • expensive

SCIENTIFIC NAME: *Cirrhilabrus scottorum* • FAMILY: Labridae • ORIGIN: Pacific Ocean • NATURAL HABITAT: Areas of stony corals on coral reefs • AVERAGE ADULT SIZE: 13 cm (5 in) • COLOURS: Green-blue and yellow pattern with a red blotch on the flanks • TANK LEVEL: Middle • FOOD: Frozen foods • CORAL FRIENDLY: Yes • INVERTEBRATE FRIENDLY: Yes • SPECIAL NEEDS: Excellent water quality • EASE OF KEEPING: Moderate

Marine fish

Aquarium needs

MINIMUM TANK SIZE: 1.5 m (5 ft)

COMPATIBILITY WITH OTHER FISH: Moderate

Scott's Fairy Wrasse is a superbly coloured reef fish that is very fashionable at the moment and very expensive. The fish are often displayed as the pride of the world's top reef aquariums, swimming constantly through shoals of Yellow Tangs, anthias and Green Chromis, over a careful selection of colourful hard corals and branching corals.

The males are the larger and more colourful, and they need to be kept with a group of females. They are well behaved and don't show any of the invertebrate-murdering behaviour that some wrasses can display.

They suit a hard coral aquarium, with bright lighting, lots of flow and

pristine, calcium-rich water. They will accept a wide range of frozen foods, including brine shrimp, *Mysis* and krill, and should be fed several times a day as they are planktivores and in nature swim through a rich soup of food that is available all day long.

These fish are not suitable for beginners, and they are, in any case, prohibitively expensive. They serve to signify to those in the know that their owner is a devoted reef keeper with the experience and expertise to keep them and a tank full of difficult corals.

Cleaner Wrasse

cleaner • active • colourful • demanding

SCIENTIFIC NAME: *Labroides dimidiatus* • FAMILY: Labridae • ORIGIN: Indo-Pacific • NATURAL HABITAT: Coral reefs and coral heads at the top of the reef • AVERAGE ADULT SIZE: 10 cm (4 in) • COLOURS: Black and white horizontal stripes and a blue tail • TANK LEVEL: Middle • FOOD: Parasites, fish mucus, some frozen foods
CORAL FRIENDLY: Yes • INVERTEBRATE FRIENDLY: Yes • SPECIAL NEEDS: Large host fish • EASE OF KEEPING: Difficult

Aquarium needs

MINIMUM TANK SIZE: 1.8 m (6 ft)
COMPATIBILITY WITH OTHER FISH: Good

Cleaner Wrasse are famous for their symbiosis with other, larger fish. In the wild they hang around on outcrops on the reef and set up cleaning stations for the local inhabitants. They are only small, but their cryptic coloration as well as years of experience and evolution has taught other fish that Cleaner Wrasse can be of use to them. Instead of eating them when they come near, the host fish submit and allow the wrasse to pick at parasites and dead skin all over their bodies, including in their mouths and under their gill covers.

In the aquarium fish numbers are obviously much smaller, as are parasite numbers and Cleaner Wrasse, because of their specialization, can quickly starve. Even a reef tank full of live rock is not enough and no substitute for other fish's flanks. The only way to keep them successfully would be to add one to a huge tank full of large angelfish, butterfly fish and groupers and hope that between them they would have enough surface area of skin for the wrasse to survive on. To add two wrasse would halve the available amount for each, so would not be a good idea.

Warning!
This species is not for beginners.

Marine fish

Dragon Wrasse

large • tough • active • unusual looking

SCIENTIFIC NAME: *Novaculichthys taeniourus* • FAMILY: Labridae • OTHER NAME • Rockchucker Wrasse • ORIGIN: Indo-Pacific • NATURAL HABITAT: Areas of coral and reef rubble • AVERAGE ADULT SIZE: 30 cm (12 in) • COLOURS: Green and white mottled body, face and fins • TANK LEVEL: Bottom • FOOD: Frozen foods • CORAL FRIENDLY: No INVERTEBRATE FRIENDLY: No • SPECIAL NEEDS: Rocks and sand • EASE OF KEEPING: Moderate

Marine fish

Aquarium needs

MINIMUM TANK SIZE: 1.5 m (5 ft)

COMPATIBILITY WITH OTHER FISH: Moderate

The alternative common name, Rockchucker Wrasse, derives from the habit these fish have of lifting up and moving small rocks and pieces of rubble to find invertebrates underneath them.

In the aquarium the tireless behaviour of these fish can be quite endearing, but they do grow large and they are certainly not for the reef aquarium as they will devour snails, crabs, shrimp and starfish, and will harass corals by trying to dig under them. They require a large tank with efficient filtration and heavy protein skimming.

A fish-only tank is necessary but with live rock, not for aesthetic purposes – nothing desirable will have a chance to grow on it – but to provide the wrasse with something to do. Give them several inches (centimetres) of coral sand or coral gravel to dig around in as well.

They can be kept with robust tank mates, such as triggerfish, pufferfish, large angelfish and groupers, but they are best as the only wrasse in the tank. They need to be fed several times a day so that they don't get thin, on cockles, mussels, krill and whole shrimp.

Usually for sale at 5–8 cm (2–3 in) long, they can reach 30 cm (12 in) in length and can be quite pugnacious when they are adults. Their patterning changes dramatically when they mature.

Pajama Wrasse

small • active • hardy • easy to keep

SCIENTIFIC NAME: *Pseudocheilinus hexataenia* • FAMILY: Labridae • ORIGIN: Indo-Pacific • NATURAL HABITAT: Retreats in and around coral reefs • AVERAGE ADULT SIZE: 8 cm (3 in) • COLOURS: Purple body with six blue, horizontal lines edged in orange and red and white striped eyes • TANK LEVEL: Middle • FOOD: Frozen foods CORAL FRIENDLY: Yes • INVERTEBRATE FRIENDLY: Yes • SPECIAL NEEDS: Retreats • EASE OF KEEPING: Easy

Aquarium needs

MINIMUM TANK SIZE: 90 cm (36 in)
COMPATIBILITY WITH OTHER FISH: Moderate

Pajama Wrasse are great fish for beginners to marine fishkeeping. They have an unusual appearance, and are hardy and quite disease resistant. They are best suited to reef aquariums with plenty of live rock and are even happy in quite small reef tanks. They will be secretive at first, but they are active behind the scenes, eating tiny invertebrates that have colonized the undersides of the live rock. They are good at eating bristleworms and flatworms and can help to keep the reef free of pests.

Adult wrasse are small and have attractively coloured and patterned bodies, and their eyes are always on anything that moves. They are quick to find the food when offered, and will eat all marine fare, including brine shrimp, *Mysis* and krill.

They are intolerant of other wrasses but may be kept as a pair if both are introduced simultaneously, and a pair may spawn in the aquarium. They can change sex so any two can be added.

Once they settle in, you will see more and more of them as they get used to their surroundings and to you. They are reef safe, but may occasionally nip at larger shrimp that are moulting and vulnerable. They leave corals alone.

Marine fish

Firefish

small • colourful • slender • nervous

SCIENTIFIC NAME: *Nemateleotris magnifica* • FAMILY: Microdesmidae • ORIGIN: Indo-Pacific • NATURAL HABITAT: Holes and rockwork on coral reefs • AVERAGE ADULT SIZE: 8 cm (3 in) • COLOURS: A yellow face with a white upper body, merging into orange and a red tail • TANK LEVEL: Middle • FOOD: Frozen foods • CORAL FRIENDLY: Yes • INVERTEBRATE FRIENDLY: Yes • SPECIAL NEEDS: None • EASE OF KEEPING: Moderate

Marine fish

Aquarium needs

MINIMUM TANK SIZE: 90 cm (36 in)

COMPATIBILITY WITH OTHER FISH: Moderate

Firefish are completely reef friendly and are one of the most popular choices for the reef aquarium. They are best kept singly, or in a small group in a large tank, as they will otherwise kill each other. They mix with any other small reef fish.

They like to have retreats and will usually hover over their favourite bolthole, in case of any disturbance. In aquatic stores, when they are being fished out of the aquarium, they will often dash to some piece of live rock in their tank and then refuse to come out, even when the rock is removed from the water. This can also happen in a domestic aquarium, so if you have a change around in the tank remember that your Firefish may well be stuck in the piece of rock that you have just removed.

They are generally easy to feed and will accept a wide range of frozen foods, including brine shrimp, *Mysis*, krill and *Cyclops*. They will also often snap up any copepods that may emerge from live rock.

Firefish are prone to jumping, so be careful if you have an open-topped aquarium, although they tend to be less likely to jump once they have settled in.

Snowflake Moray Eel

unusual looking • predatory • hardy • shy

SCIENTIFIC NAME: *Echidna nebulosa* • FAMILY: Muraenidae • ORIGIN: Indo-Pacific • NATURAL HABITAT: Hideouts and caves in coral reefs • AVERAGE ADULT SIZE: 75 cm (30 in) • COLOURS: Black vertical bands on a white body with gold spots running the length of the body • TANK LEVEL: Bottom • FOOD: Meaty frozen foods • CORAL FRIENDLY: Yes • INVERTEBRATE FRIENDLY: No • SPECIAL NEEDS: Hiding places • EASE OF KEEPING: Moderate

Aquarium needs

MINIMUM TANK SIZE: 1.2 m (4 ft)

COMPATIBILITY WITH OTHER FISH: Moderate

Snowflake Moray Eels are liked by some aquarists and loathed by others. Their snakelike bodies and sharp jaws scare some people – and rightly so. Moray eels are large marine predators. Their narrow bodies enable them to squeeze through cracks in rocks to seize their prey. Their teeth are backward pointing so that anything they bite will not get away easily, and they commonly throw themselves into a death roll as well. The Snowflake Moray Eel is one of the smaller morays and can be kept in captivity relatively easily. It must not be fed by hand because of its teeth, and it will devour small fish, shrimps and crabs. It can be kept with larger fish, including angelfish, groupers, lionfish and pufferfish, and even adults will not tackle any fish larger than about 15 cm (6 in) long.

It needs hiding places in order to feel secure, and anything from a piece of plastic pipe to a pile of rocks will be fine. If a hiding place is not offered it may well try to escape.

Fish-only aquariums are the best accommodation for them, with or without live rock, and they are often seen lurking in sunken urns in display aquariums.

Marine fish

Yellow-headed Jawfish

small • interesting • sensitive • burrower

SCIENTIFIC NAME: *Opistognathus aurifrons* • FAMILY: Opistognathidae • ORIGIN: Caribbean Sea • NATURAL HABITAT: Burrows made from coral sand and coral fragments at the base of the reef • AVERAGE ADULT SIZE: 10 cm (4 in) • COLOURS: White body with a blue sheen and a yellow face • TANK LEVEL: Bottom • FOOD: Frozen foods • CORAL FRIENDLY: Yes • INVERTEBRATE FRIENDLY: Yes • SPECIAL NEEDS: Deep substrate • EASE OF KEEPING: Difficult

Marine fish

Aquarium needs

MINIMUM TANK SIZE: 90 cm (36 in)
COMPATIBILITY WITH OTHER FISH: Moderate

Jawfish make interesting aquarium inhabitants because they build and live in burrows. In the wild they construct burrows in the sand by gathering bits of shell and broken coral to reinforce the sand walls. You can encourage this behaviour in the aquarium by providing a bed of sand about 10 cm (4 in) deep. Sprinkle some broken shells and coral gravel over the substrate and then add some live rock, bedding it down before the sand goes in so that the fish's digging activities do not cause a rockfall. When the burrow is constructed the fish will hover over it and dash inside if it sees danger.

Add a group of jawfish to the tank and a pair may form. They are mouth-brooders, the male carrying eggs and fry in his mouth. The male develops black spots on his throat when spawning. They should be kept only with small, peaceful tank mates or with no other fish at all.

Newly purchased specimens may not take to captivity very well and may be difficult to feed, and they may try to jump out of the aquarium. At first you should keep them singly or as a group, because two fish together might fight if they are not a pair.

Cube Boxfish

bizarre looking • colourful • sensitive • demanding

SCIENTIFIC NAME: *Ostracion cubicus* • FAMILY: Ostraciidae • ORIGIN: Indo-Pacific • NATURAL HABITAT: Coral reefs
AVERAGE ADULT SIZE: 45 cm (18 in) • COLOURS: Bright yellow with small black and white spots • TANK LEVEL:
Middle • FOOD: Frozen foods • CORAL FRIENDLY: No • INVERTEBRATE FRIENDLY: No • SPECIAL NEEDS: Good water
quality; frequent feeding • EASE OF KEEPING: Difficult

Aquarium needs

MINIMUM TANK SIZE: 1.5 m (5 ft)
COMPATIBILITY WITH OTHER FISH: Moderate

The Cube Boxfish is unmistakable: the body shape of small specimens is almost a cube. The odd shape and interesting coloration make them look appealing, and they would be popular with marine fish-keepers were it not for three things. First, if they are stressed they can release a toxin that will poison everything in the tank, including themselves. That should be enough to put anyone off. Second, in the

wild these fish can attain a length of 45 cm (18 in) and become less cube-shaped and more elongated and aggressive. Third, they are not reef safe, which means that they must be kept in a fish-only aquarium.

Larger specimens of Cube Boxfish can be hard to feed, and smaller specimens will feed but usually cannot get the nutrition that they require and die. Specimens

are available as small as just a few millimetres across, but at this size their suitability for aquarists is questionable.

If you still want to keep this odd-looking fish, setting up a tank especially for them would be a good idea. This will allow you to monitor the feeding closely and avoid the elimination of other live-stock in the tank.

Marine fish

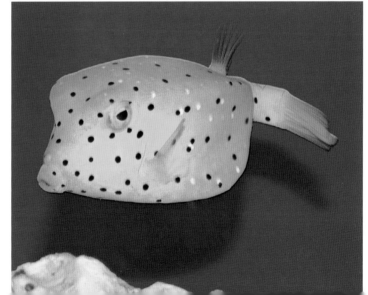

Bicolor Angelfish

striking • colourful • small • rock dwelling

SCIENTIFIC NAME: *Centropyge bicolor* • FAMILY: Pomacanthidae • ORIGIN: Indo-Pacific • NATURAL HABITAT: Coral reef structures with retreats • AVERAGE ADULT SIZE: 10 cm (4 in) • COLOURS: Bright yellow at the front, dark blue at the rear and a yellow tail • TANK LEVEL: Middle • FOOD: Frozen foods, algae • CORAL FRIENDLY: Yes INVERTEBRATE FRIENDLY: Yes • SPECIAL NEEDS: Retreats; live rock • EASE OF KEEPING: Moderate

Marine fish

Aquarium needs

MINIMUM TANK SIZE: 1 m (3 ft 3 in)
COMPATIBILITY WITH OTHER FISH: Moderate

Bicolor Angelfish are one of the larger dwarf angelfish, and with a maximum length of 15 cm (6 in) in the wild they are right on the margin of being classified as a dwarf angelfish. They also behave rather more like a large angelfish species in that they are likely to nibble clam mantles and will certainly have a go at Featherduster Tubeworms (*Sabellastarte magnifica*). They may also nip at coral polyps. If clams and tubeworms are not added to the tank and hardy, soft corals are included instead, the Bicolor Angelfish can be classed as reef safe and will not harm any shrimp or crabs.

There should be only one dwarf angelfish in the tank as the species is intolerant of its own kind. These fish will squabble with Yellow Tangs when they are first introduced because of their colour pattern and the competition for grazing sites, but they should calm down within days. They are quite secretive and will spend a lot of time among the rockwork, feeding on copepods. They should accept a wide range of frozen foods and will certainly come out at feeding time. They are slow-growing fish and rarely attain their maximum size in captivity.

Coral Beauty

small • colourful • peaceful • rock dwelling

SCIENTIFIC NAME: *Centropyge bispinosa* • FAMILY: Pomacanthidae • ORIGIN: Indo-Pacific • NATURAL HABITAT: Caves and retreats on coral reefs • AVERAGE ADULT SIZE: 10 cm (4 in) • COLOURS: Deep purple with an orange patch on the flanks • TANK LEVEL: Middle • FOOD: Frozen foods, algae, some flake • CORAL FRIENDLY: Yes INVERTEBRATE FRIENDLY: Yes • SPECIAL NEEDS: Live rock for grazing • EASE OF KEEPING: Moderate

Aquarium needs

MINIMUM TANK SIZE: 1 m (3 ft 3 in)
COMPATIBILITY WITH OTHER FISH: Good

The Coral Beauty is a dwarf angelfish, which means that it will remain small. In general, dwarf angelfish are reef safe, while large angelfish species are not. The Coral Beauty is one of the hardiest and best behaved of the dwarf angelfish, making it one of the most suitable for a reef aquarium. They may occasionally nip clam mantles and Featherduster Tubeworms (*Sabellastarte magnifica*), but some aquarists have had no trouble at all.

The ideal set-up for this species is a mature reef aquarium with no boisterous fish. Coral Beauties will be shy at first and will disappear into the rockwork for days, but there is food among live rocks in the form of amphipods and copepods, and they usually reappear well fed. They spend their lives close to the rockwork and will also eat any macro-algae that start to grow.

In general, there should be only one dwarf angelfish species in all but the largest tanks, but occasionally a pair can be purchased and will live together happily.

There are two colour variants: one tends towards purple all over, and the other is more rusty coloured on the flanks. They will be happy in quite small reef tanks as long as there is sufficient rockwork.

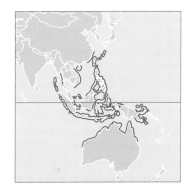

Marine fish

Flame Angelfish

vivid • small • active • expensive

SCIENTIFIC NAME: *Centropyge loricula* • FAMILY: Pomacanthidae • ORIGIN: Pacific Ocean • NATURAL HABITAT: Coral reef structures • AVERAGE ADULT SIZE: 10 cm (4 in) • COLOURS: Vivid red with blue-edged dorsal and anal fins TANK LEVEL: Middle • FOOD: Frozen foods, algae • CORAL FRIENDLY: Yes • INVERTEBRATE FRIENDLY: Yes • SPECIAL NEEDS: Live rock • EASE OF KEEPING: Moderate

Marine fish

Aquarium needs

MINIMUM TANK SIZE: 1 m (3 ft 3 in)

COMPATIBILITY WITH OTHER FISH: Moderate

Flame Angelfish really stand out in an aquarium because of their vivid red coloration. They are reef-safe dwarf angelfish, which command a high price. They are generally well behaved but individuals may occasionally nip at the mantles of clams and Featherduster Tube-worms (*Sabellastarte magnifica*). They can be kept in quite small reef aquariums as long as these are mature and contain plenty of live rock. The water quality should be consistently good with a proportion changed frequently.

This species should not be mixed with other dwarf angelfish as they may fight for territory. In general, a

Flame Angelfish should be the only dwarf angelfish kept in an aquarium, but sometimes a pair will live happily together.

Live rock provides these fish with refuges and with food in the form of tiny invertebrates and algae. They will be shy when first introduced and may not appear for days. They may also attract the attention of grazers such as tangs, which may intimidate them initially. They should be fed on a variety of foods, including frozen *Mysis*, brine shrimp and krill, and they may accept some flake once they have settled. Feed them little and often.

Majestic Angelfish

large • beautiful • sometimes aggressive • expensive

SCIENTIFIC NAME: *Pomacanthus navarchus* • FAMILY: Pomacanthidae • ORIGIN: Western Pacific Ocean • NATURAL HABITAT: Coral reefs • AVERAGE ADULT SIZE: 30 cm (12 in) • COLOURS: Bright orange dorsal fin and flanks and a bright orange tail; dark blue across the head and on the base of the tail and anal and pelvic fins • TANK LEVEL: Middle • FOOD: Frozen foods, algae • CORAL FRIENDLY: No • INVERTEBRATE FRIENDLY: No • SPECIAL NEEDS: Retreats EASE OF KEEPING: Moderate

Aquarium needs

MINIMUM TANK SIZE: 1.5 m (5 ft)
COMPATIBILITY WITH OTHER FISH: Moderate

Majestic Angelfish are large angelfish, and they are not compatible with corals or invertebrates, such as clams and Featherduster Tubeworms (*Sabellastarte magnifica*), because they will nip them.

They should be kept in fish-only aquariums, but live rock can be used to aid filtration and provide refuges and grazing areas. They may squabble with other angelfish species, so make them the only angelfish in the tank or combine them with others in huge aquariums where there is space for the fish to get out of each others' way. They are also intolerant of their own species, but are compatible with a large range of different-looking species, from smaller wrasses to large groupers and lionfish.

The water quality should be kept consistently good. The fish should be offered a variety of frozen foods, including *Mysis*, krill, cockles, mussels, octopus and marine algae. Live rock may provide some food in the form of tiny invertebrates and algae.

Juveniles look quite different, with blue vertical lines covering an almost black body. Juveniles that have grown up in captivity will be hardier but may not exhibit the rich coloration of the wild adults. Adult Majestic Angelfish are expensive.

Marine fish

Common Clownfish

peaceful • colourful • comical • easy to keep

SCIENTIFIC NAME: *Amphiprion ocellaris* • FAMILY: Pomacentridae • ORIGIN: Indo-Pacific Ocean • NATURAL HABITAT: Coral reefs, in association with sea anemones • AVERAGE ADULT SIZE: 10 cm (4 in) • COLOURS: Orange body with three broad white bands and black-edged fins and bands • TANK LEVEL: Middle • FOOD: Flake and frozen foods CORAL FRIENDLY: Yes • INVERTEBRATE FRIENDLY: Yes • SPECIAL NEEDS: Another clownfish • EASE OF KEEPING: Easy

Marine fish

Aquarium needs

MINIMUM TANK SIZE: 90 cm (36 in)
COMPATIBILITY WITH OTHER FISH: Good

Clownfish are instantly recognizable by their markings, and Common Clownfish and the similar Percula Clownfish (*Amphiprion percula*) will be forever known by young children as Nemo, from the animated movie *Finding Nemo*.

The good news is that these are perhaps the most suitable marine fish species for aquariums, and they are bred in captivity in huge numbers across the world. In the wild Common Clownfish live in pairs among sea anemones, and they develop an immunity to their stinging tentacles. In exchange for protection, the fish give the anemone food and help to keep it clean.

In captivity, tank-reared clownfish do not need to be kept with anemones and indeed may never have seen one before. If you have

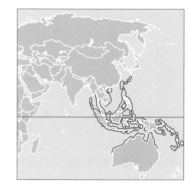

bright lighting, an anemone can be added to the tank, and a pair of clownfish may eventually take up residence within its tentacles and will look very happy with the arrangement.

A pair of clownfish can be formed simply by placing two individuals of the same species together. One will grow larger and become female and dominant; the other will remain smaller and change sex to be a submissive male. They are rarely bred in the home aquarium because the fry are difficult to rear.

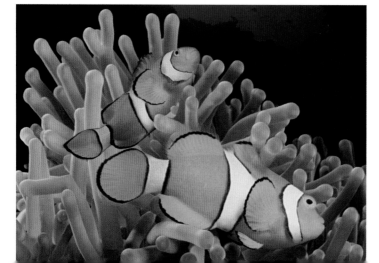

Green Chromis

small • peaceful • shoaling • reef safe

SCIENTIFIC NAME: *Chromis viridis* • FAMILY: Pomacentridae • ORIGIN: Indo-Pacific • NATURAL HABITAT: Reef crests around coral clusters and in strong currents • AVERAGE ADULT SIZE: 8 cm (3 in) • COLOURS: Blue-green with a metallic sheen • TANK LEVEL: Top • FOOD: Flake and frozen foods • CORAL FRIENDLY: Yes • INVERTEBRATE FRIENDLY: Yes • SPECIAL NEEDS: A shoal of five or more • EASE OF KEEPING: Easy

Aquarium needs

MINIMUM TANK SIZE: 90 cm (36 in)
COMPATIBILITY WITH OTHER FISH: Good

Green Chromis are perfect reef fish: they do not touch corals or any other surface and they swim around the tank all day.

These damselfish are small fish and should not be kept with large specimens, such as lionfish, which may eat them. They should also not be kept with territorial species, such as other damselfish, which may attack them. They are often used in groups for effect and are even added to tanks containing difficult, hard corals because they are tolerant of a strong flow and are guaranteed not to harm the coral.

They can be added to fish-only tanks, but look best in reef aquariums, and a group can be accommodated in even a small tank. Bright lighting makes their colours look even better. If two or three individuals are kept together to maturity they may lose their shoaling instinct over time, so keep numbers high.

This species is suitable for beginners, and Green Chromis can be the first fish added to a new tank. When they are seen in the store they may not be the exotic-looking species that new fishkeepers want to acquire, but they are by far the most suitable and will grace even the most complex reef aquariums.

Marine fish

Domino Damselfish

hardy • active • aggressive • antisocial

SCIENTIFIC NAME: *Dascyllus trimaculatus* • FAMILY: Pomacentridae • ORIGIN: Indo-Pacific • NATURAL HABITAT: Anemones and coral heads on coral reefs • AVERAGE ADULT SIZE: 13 cm (5 in) • COLOURS: Jet black with a white spot under the dorsal fin and on the forehead • TANK LEVEL: Middle • FOOD: Flake and frozen foods CORAL FRIENDLY: Yes • INVERTEBRATE FRIENDLY: Yes • SPECIAL NEEDS: None • EASE OF KEEPING: Moderate

Marine fish

Aquarium needs

MINIMUM TANK SIZE: 90 cm (36 in)

COMPATIBILITY WITH OTHER FISH: Moderate

Domino Damselfish have a high survival rate in captivity and are generally hardy and easy to keep. They used to be recommended to beginners because of these qualities, but many people found them difficult to keep.

Juvenile fish shoal together and look very appealing as they swim around the tank. As the fish mature, however, the shoal splits up and fighting breaks out. A dominant pair will form and annihilate the others, continuing to grow in size. The pair become more formidable and territorial as they grow. They may even spawn, but they will make life very difficult for other fish

in the tank. They are only doing what damselfish in the wild do, but they are not suitable for most reef aquariums because of their intolerance of other fish in the vicinity.

Their potential adult size of 13 cm (5 in) means that they are much better suited to large, fish-only aquariums. They should be mixed with fish that are larger than themselves and with species that can give as good as they get. Adult pairs of Domino Damselfish have little monetary value to aquarists because of their anti-social behaviour.

Blue Damselfish

hardy • colourful • active • aggressive

SCIENTIFIC NAME: *Pomacentrus caeruleus* • FAMILY: Pomacentridae • ORIGIN: Indo-Pacific • NATURAL HABITAT: Reef crest in currents and strong light, and around corals • AVERAGE ADULT SIZE: 10 cm (4 in) • COLOURS: Bright blue TANK LEVEL: Middle • FOOD: Flake and frozen foods • CORAL FRIENDLY: Yes • INVERTEBRATE FRIENDLY: Yes • SPECIAL NEEDS: None • EASE OF KEEPING: Easy

Aquarium needs

MINIMUM TANK SIZE: **90 cm (36 in)**
COMPATIBILITY WITH OTHER FISH: **Moderate**

Blue Damselfish are stocked in most marine stores and are inexpensive fish. They can be aggressive, however, and may pick on each other and other species, especially newcomers to the tank.

They are small, colourful and hardy. A single individual should be kept with other robust species and should be added after the other species have become established. Blue Damselfish can be mixed with angelfish, tangs, butterfly fish, triggerfish and wrasses, but they may be eaten by lionfish and groupers. They may be too aggressive for small gobies as they defend their territories and may out-compete them for food. They are safe with corals and invertebrates and could be kept as the only species in reef tanks where corals predominate and fish are used just to provide a bit of movement.

Although they can be added to fish-only aquariums, they are best kept in reef aquariums, where the live rock will provide them with food in the form of tiny invertebrates and algae. They are easy to feed and will readily accept flake and frozen foods, including brine shrimp, *Mysis* and krill.

A pair will form if a large group is added to a tank and the others are removed once it has formed, but a pair of Blue Damselfish will be even more trouble than a single fish, so this is not recommended.

Marine fish

Maroon Clownfish

large • aggressive • colourful • active

SCIENTIFIC NAME: *Premnas biaculeatus* • FAMILY: Pomacentridae • ORIGIN: Western and Indo-Pacific Ocean
NATURAL HABITAT: Coral reefs, in association with sea anemones • AVERAGE ADULT SIZE: 15 cm (6 in) • COLOURS:
Red body with three white vertical bands • TANK LEVEL: Middle • FOOD: Flake and frozen foods • CORAL
FRIENDLY: Yes • INVERTEBRATE FRIENDLY: Yes • SPECIAL NEEDS: Anemones • EASE OF KEEPING: Moderate

Marine fish

Aquarium needs

MINIMUM TANK SIZE: 1.2 m (4 ft)
COMPATIBILITY WITH OTHER FISH: Moderate

The Maroon Clownfish, the largest of the clownfish species, is in a different genus from all the other clownfish species. They are beautiful fish and can be kept singly or in pairs. If you want to form a pair, adding a very small fish to a very large one should work, but bear in mind that these fish are more prone to initial fighting than other species. They are also best as the only clownfish species in the tank, as they will try to kill any others when they mature. The female gets much larger than the male, which seems to stop growing.

Maroon Clownfish are happiest with a host anemone to live in. The Bubble Anemone (*Entacmaea quadricolor*) is their favourite species. Once inside, the fish will clean and feed it and defend it against all comers, including you. Water quality should be consistently good to house an anemone, and lighting should be very bright.

Maroon Clownfish are bold fish and will readily accept most foods, including frozen brine shrimp, *Mysis*, krill and some flake.

The Yellow-banded Maroon Clownfish is similar, but has yellow bands instead of white ones on its body. It should be treated in exactly the same way.

Orchid Dottyback

small • colourful • reef safe • easy to keep

SCIENTIFIC NAME: *Pseudochromis fridmani* • FAMILY: Pseudochromidae • ORIGIN: Red Sea • NATURAL HABITAT: Vertical coral reefs • AVERAGE ADULT SIZE: **8 cm (3 in)** • COLOURS: Deep purple with a black line running from the snout to the eye • TANK LEVEL: Middle • FOOD: Frozen foods • CORAL FRIENDLY: Yes • INVERTEBRATE FRIENDLY: Yes • SPECIAL NEEDS: Retreats • EASE OF KEEPING: Moderate

Aquarium needs

MINIMUM TANK SIZE: **90 cm (36 in)**
COMPATIBILITY WITH OTHER FISH: Moderate

The Orchid Dottyback is a small, colourful fish from the Red Sea. It can be kept singly, in pairs or in groups, and it has been bred in captivity by commercial breeders on a number of occasions. They may well spawn in the home aquarium, but the fry would need extra care as they are pelagic (see page 209) and need special foods.

Adult fish make great additions to the reef aquarium and can be mixed with other small reef fish and non-boisterous larger fish, such as Yellow Tangs (*Zebrasoma flavescens*; page 207). They accept a range of frozen foods, including brine shrimp, *Mysis* and *Cyclops*, and will also find live foods among live rock in the form of copepods. The tank set-up should be mature and include plenty of live rock. These fish are completely safe with corals and invertebrates.

The Magenta Dottyback (*Pseudochromis porphyreus*) looks similar to the Orchid Dottyback, but it is a bit more pink in colour and does not have a black line running through the eye. It is a much more aggressive fish and territorial, and is therefore less desirable. The Orchid Dottyback is more expensive and may be twice the price of the Magenta Dottyback.

Marine fish

Dwarf Fuzzy Lionfish

predatory • shy • camouflaged • venomous

SCIENTIFIC NAME: *Dendrochirus brachypterus* • FAMILY: Scorpaenidae • ORIGIN: Indo-Pacific • NATURAL HABITAT: Coral reefs, in close association with corals, sponges and algae for camouflage • AVERAGE ADULT SIZE: 15 cm (6 in) • COLOURS: Brown patches with red flecks all over the body and fins • TANK LEVEL: Middle • FOOD: Frozen foods, fish • CORAL FRIENDLY: Yes • INVERTEBRATE FRIENDLY: No • SPECIAL NEEDS: Retreats • EASE OF KEEPING: Moderate

Marine fish

Aquarium needs

MINIMUM TANK SIZE: 90 cm (36 in)

COMPATIBILITY WITH OTHER FISH: Moderate

The Dwarf Fuzzy Lionfish may look more endearing than its relatives, but it is equipped with a large mouth and venomous spines on its back. These fish are fully grown at about 15 cm (6 in) in length, by which time they will be capable of swallowing most reef-friendly fish, including clownfish.

When they are small, feed Dwarf Fuzzy Lionfish on krill and *Mysis* and hold the food in front of a power head until the flow pushes it off and around the tank. This will make the fish think that it is live. Larger fish will appreciate thawed whole whitebait and smelt, which should be held in tongs and waggled around in the water to encourage feeding. If a newly imported fish will not feed, some live river shrimp will do the

trick, but always try frozen alternatives first. Never feed them on live freshwater fish because these are not good for them.

When you are carrying out tank maintenance always make sure that you know where the fish is. Lionfish can lurk in holes in the rockwork and will not be seen until it is too late. The venom should break down in hot water, so if you get stung immerse the affected area in water that is as hot as you can stand.

Warning!

This species is venomous.

Volitans Lionfish

large • predatory • venomous • impressive

SCIENTIFIC NAME: *Pterois volitans* • FAMILY: Scorpaenidae • ORIGIN: Indo-Pacific • NATURAL HABITAT: Coral reefs
AVERAGE ADULT SIZE: 35 cm (14 in) • COLOURS: Brown and white vertical stripes and striations all over the body
TANK LEVEL: Middle • FOOD: Frozen foods, fish • CORAL FRIENDLY: Yes • INVERTEBRATE FRIENDLY: No • SPECIAL NEEDS:
Space • EASE OF KEEPING: Moderate

Aquarium needs

MINIMUM TANK SIZE: 1.8 m (6 ft)
COMPATIBILITY WITH OTHER FISH: Moderate

The Volitans Lionfish is a larger lionfish that needs a spacious aquarium with lots of open water for swimming. Its fin spread is as wide as its body is long, an adaptation for herding small fish into a corner before devouring them at lightning speed.

These fish have been kept by marine aquarists for decades and present few problems. However, you may have difficulty in persuading a new fish to feed. Try offering krill and *Mysis* if they are small or whitebait, smelt or thawed whole shrimp if they are larger. Never feed them live freshwater fish. Not only is this cruel, but freshwater fish are not good for them as they are not a natural food. If you are giving them whole fish, feed them every other day as this is a large meal.

A healthy Volitans Lionfish should grow quickly, and it swims in midwater away from decor.

Take care when you put your hands in the tank because a lionfish that feels threatened will swim with its poisonous spines towards you. If you do get stung, immerse the affected area in very hot water. People do react differently to the venom, however, so if you are in any doubt seek medical advice immediately.

Warning!
This species is venomous.

Marine fish

Leaf Fish

sedate • predatory • camouflaged • venomous

SCIENTIFIC NAME: *Taenianotus triacanthus* • FAMILY: Scorpaenidae • ORIGIN: Indo-Pacific • NATURAL HABITAT: Coral reefs, next to sponges and macro-algae • AVERAGE ADULT SIZE: 10 cm (4 in) • COLOURS: Bright pink, bright green or yellow • TANK LEVEL: Bottom • FOOD: Fish • CORAL FRIENDLY: Yes • INVERTEBRATE FRIENDLY: No • SPECIAL NEEDS: Perches • EASE OF KEEPING: Moderate

Marine fish

Aquarium needs
MINIMUM TANK SIZE: 90 cm (36 in)
COMPATIBILITY WITH OTHER FISH: Low

Leaf Fish are slow-moving, predatory fish, which use camouflage to help them catch their prey. They are available in pink, green and yellow colours, their natural camouflage against a backdrop of colourful algae and sponges on rockwork.

They can be kept in reef aquariums and will eat small fish and shrimp, but should not be kept with boisterous fish that may steal their food. They will be reluctant feeders at first and may have to be fed on live river shrimp before they learn to take frozen whitebait. Feed every other day. They are very thin fish and even after a large meal appear very compressed.

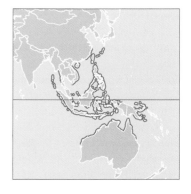

The tank can simply include live rock and a protein skimmer; it does not have to be large as the fish do not move around much.

Perching in full view with dorsal fin erect, Leaf Fish make a conversation piece. They appeal to aquarists who like the weird and wonderful Frogfish (*Antennarius* spp.; page 208), and the two combined make an interesting display. Unlike Frogfish, however, Leaf Fish are venomous and should not be handled.

Warning!
This species is venomous.

Panther Grouper

large • predatory • hardy • graceful

SCIENTIFIC NAME: *Cromileptes altivelis* • FAMILY: Serranidae • ORIGIN: Indo-Pacific • NATURAL HABITAT: Coral reefs
AVERAGE ADULT SIZE: 50 cm (20 in) • COLOURS: White body and fins with large black spots all over • TANK LEVEL:
Middle • FOOD: Meaty frozen foods, fish • CORAL FRIENDLY: Yes • INVERTEBRATE FRIENDLY: No • SPECIAL NEEDS: A
large tank • EASE OF KEEPING: Moderate

Aquarium needs

MINIMUM TANK SIZE: 1.8 m (6 ft)
COMPATIBILITY WITH OTHER FISH: Moderate

The Panther Grouper is the arche-typal large, fish-only marine fish. It has been kept by aquarists for decades and is a hardy and long-lived fish. Its narrow head disguises a large mouth, and its appetite grows as it does. This fish can reach 50 cm (20 in) in length, making it unsuitable for most tanks, and it will need a long-term commitment and substantial investment in equipment and tanks to keep it properly.

Fit a big protein skimmer and carry out large water changes, because it produces rich waste.

This is a slow, graceful mover that can make an impressive display fish in the right tank. It should be fed on cockles, mussels, prawns and white-bait and needs feeding only every other day when it is mature.

It can be mixed with any other large fish, including angelfish, bat-fish, lionfish, moray eels, pufferfish and even small sharks. It does not like its own kind, however, and prefers a solitary existence.

The Panther Grouper is easy to keep and undemanding, but rehous-ing a very large specimen will be difficult. Think long and hard about whether or not you can meet its long-term needs.

Warning!

This species grows large.

Lyretail Anthias

active • colourful • shoaling • demanding

SCIENTIFIC NAME: *Pseudanthias squamipinnis* • FAMILY: Serranidae • OTHER NAME: Wreckfish • ORIGIN: Indo-Pacific • NATURAL HABITAT: Reef edge, over branching corals and coral heads in strong currents • AVERAGE ADULT SIZE: 10 cm (4 in) • COLOURS: Females are amber-coloured; males are red and develop a pink patch on the flanks • TANK LEVEL: Top • FOOD: Frozen foods • CORAL FRIENDLY: Yes • INVERTEBRATE FRIENDLY: Yes • SPECIAL NEEDS: A group • EASE OF KEEPING: Difficult

Marine fish

Aquarium needs

MINIMUM TANK SIZE: 1.5 m (5 ft)
COMPATIBILITY WITH OTHER FISH: Good

Anthias, sometimes known as wreckfish, are beautiful shoaling species that grace the coral reefs of the Indo-Pacific. They shoal in their thousands, swimming tirelessly against the currents that surge up the reef, bringing planktonic food.

The Lyretail Anthias is the most widespread species in the wild. Sadly, they are not easy to keep, although the best marine fishkeepers have had some success. The major difficulty is food. In the wild they feed constantly on floating microscopic life. In the aquarium they need to be fed four or more times a day on a mix of brine shrimp, *Mysis*, *Cyclops* and krill. The mixture should be liquidized

for a few seconds then added to the tank by one of the power heads. The fish will then feed naturally.

They like lots of flow in the tank and are best suited to high-tech, hard-coral systems, in which the parameters are constantly monitored and controlled by computer.

The males are larger and more colourful than the females. This fish should be stocked in groups of one male to several females, and looks stunning in a shoal.

Warning!
This species is not for beginners.

Chalk Bass

peaceful • colourful • shoaling • reef safe

SCIENTIFIC NAME: *Serranus tortugarum* • FAMILY: Serranidae • ORIGIN: West Atlantic Ocean • NATURAL HABITAT:
Top of reefs • AVERAGE ADULT SIZE: 8 cm (3 in) • COLOURS: Light blue and red vertical bands with a powder blue
belly • TANK LEVEL: Middle • FOOD: Frozen foods • CORAL FRIENDLY: Yes • INVERTEBRATE FRIENDLY: Yes SPECIAL
NEEDS: None • EASE OF KEEPING: Moderate

Aquarium needs

MINIMUM TANK SIZE: 90 cm (36 in)
COMPATIBILITY WITH OTHER FISH: Good

Chalk Bass are good reef-friendly fish that will fit into most tanks. They are handsome, shoaling fish and subtly coloured, with blue and red bands on a blue body. A shoal of them makes a good alternative to chromis or damselfish.

When they are introduced to a tank they may hide for the first few days, but when they have settled they should be out in the midwater all the time. They are prone to jumping when frightened, so don't make any sudden movements in front of the tank, especially if you have an open-topped aquarium.

They should be fed on frozen *Mysis* and krill and will predate small ornamental shrimps, but on the whole they are well behaved. They can be prone to the disorder known as popeye, so keep water conditions as good as possible and, ideally, quarantine them when they are first purchased.

Don't combine Chalk Bass with boisterous fish, but they are compatible with almost everything else. They will suit a reef aquarium with lots of live rock better than a fish-only aquarium that is sparsely decorated. They are safe with all corals and will not touch any rockwork to graze it, preferring to take food in midwater.

Marine fish

Foxface

large • algae eater • nervous • venomous

SCIENTIFIC NAME: *Siganus vulpinus* • FAMILY: Siganidae • ORIGIN: Southwestern Pacific Ocean • NATURAL HABITAT: Rocks on coral reefs • AVERAGE ADULT SIZE: 25 cm (10 in) • COLOURS: Bright yellow body with a black and white striped face • TANK LEVEL: Middle • FOOD: Algae, frozen foods • CORAL FRIENDLY: Yes • INVERTEBRATE FRIENDLY: Yes • SPECIAL NEEDS: Algae for grazing • EASE OF KEEPING: Moderate

Marine fish

Aquarium needs

MINIMUM TANK SIZE: 1.5 m (5 ft)

COMPATIBILITY WITH OTHER FISH: Moderate

This fish belongs to the Siganidae family, the members of which are known as rabbitfish. They have been given this name because of their grazing capabilities, and the Foxface is often chosen for reef aquariums because of this skill.

New aquariums will invariably bloom with nuisance algae, and the aquarist will employ a number of fish and invertebrates to help to combat it. A Foxface is not only colourful but will graze constantly on algae.

These fish grow quite large, and an adult needs a spacious tank and plenty of live rock to graze if it is to stay healthy. They are best kept singly in a community of other fish, and should be fed frequently.

If a Foxface is scared it will fit, alarming everyone who sees this for the first time. The fish will appear to be dead, as its body colour changes to resemble that of a decaying fish and the fish lies at an angle with all fins erect. This behaviour is really a warning; rabbitfish have venomous spines in their dorsal fins, a defence that makes them safe even with sharks.

Warning!

This species is venomous.

Messmate Pipefish

unusual looking • active • interesting • sensitive

SCIENTIFIC NAME: *Corythoichthys intestinalis* • FAMILY: Syngnathidae • ORIGIN: Southwestern Pacific Ocean
NATURAL HABITAT: Coral rubble and broken branching corals at the reef floor • AVERAGE ADULT SIZE: 18 cm (7 in)
COLOURS: White and yellow body with green vertical banding • TANK LEVEL: Bottom • FOOD: Frozen and live
foods • CORAL FRIENDLY: Yes • INVERTEBRATE FRIENDLY: Yes • SPECIAL NEEDS: Their own tank • EASE OF KEEPING: Difficult

Aquarium needs

MINIMUM TANK SIZE: 90 cm (36 in)
COMPATIBILITY WITH OTHER FISH: Low

Pipefish are related to the seahorse, and there are many species to choose among. Messmate Pipefish may be seen occasionally in aquatic stores or can be ordered specially. They inhabit reef rubble and broken branching coral heads that have been deposited by storms. The dead coral branches form an intricate network in which the slim pipefish are perfectly adapted to live. Avoid very thin specimens.

To keep pipefish properly you should set up a 90-cm (36-in) tank along with a sump tank containing a refugium. Put pieces of storm-broken Pacific Ocean live rock in the tank, which will be just what the pipefish are used to. Place the rocks haphazardly across the tank bottom and mature the system until the refugium fills the tank with little bugs and creepy-crawlies. Add a pair or a group of pipefish with no other fish –

not even seahorses, which are too slow – and watch their intricate behaviour and courtship patterns. Male pipefish have a pouch into which fertilized eggs are placed and kept until the young are released.

The species is by no means easy to keep. If the fish are reluctant to feed, you might at first have to offer live food, such as *Mysis* and brine shrimp. Pipefish are very specialized marine fish, but they can be rewarding if a special effort is made by the aquarist.

Warning!
This species is not for beginners.

Marine fish

Long-snout Seahorse

unusual looking • slow swimmer • sensitive • demanding

SCIENTIFIC NAME: *Hippocampus reidi* • FAMILY: Syngnathidae • ORIGIN: West Indies • NATURAL HABITAT: Shallow water and quiet areas in lagoons with sea grasses • AVERAGE ADULT SIZE: 15 cm (6 in) • COLOURS: Yellow most of the time but can change depending on mood • TANK LEVEL: Bottom • FOOD: *Mysis* shrimp • CORAL FRIENDLY: Yes • INVERTEBRATE FRIENDLY: Yes • SPECIAL NEEDS: Their own tank • EASE OF KEEPING: Difficult

Marine fish

Aquarium needs

MINIMUM TANK SIZE: 90 cm (36 in)
COMPATIBILITY WITH OTHER FISH: Low

Seahorses are instantly recognizable by their shape and are high on the list of marine fish that people want in a marine aquarium. What many do not realize is that seahorses can be very difficult to keep.

First, they come from a different marine environment to that of most other tropical marine fish. Their natural habitat is quiet lagoons with rich macro-algae growth and less water flow than is found at the reefs. There are fewer rocks and more expanses of open sand with sea grasses. Seahorses hold on to the sea grasses with their prehensile tails and suck up the tiny shrimp that swim past. The aquarium should copy the lagoon environment, with less water flow and plenty of lush macro-algae growth.

Seahorses are best kept alone because they are slow to find and eat food, which would allow other

fish to steal it. They must be fed on a plentiful supply of *Mysis* shrimp (up to 60 a day for adults), and captive-raised specimens should take frozen shrimp as opposed to live food. Modern systems incorporating refugiums in sumps that produce live foods and so feed the main tank are beneficial.

Males carry their young in a pouch. Happy seahorses will be yellow in colour, while unhappy ones turn a darker shade.

Warning!

This species is not for beginners.

Moorish Idol

striking • sensitive • demanding • expensive

SCIENTIFIC NAME: *Zanclus cornutus* • FAMILY: Zanclidae • ORIGIN: Indo-Pacific • NATURAL HABITAT: Coral reefs
AVERAGE ADULT SIZE: 25 cm (10 in) • COLOURS: Black, white and yellow divided into vertical sections across the
body • FOOD: Frozen foods • TANK LEVEL: Middle • CORAL FRIENDLY: No • INVERTEBRATE FRIENDLY: Yes • SPECIAL
NEEDS: Excellent water quality; the right food • EASE OF KEEPING: Difficult

Aquarium needs

MINIMUM TANK SIZE: 1.5 m (5 ft)
COMPATIBILITY WITH OTHER FISH: Moderate

The Moorish Idol is a stunning fish, but unsuitable for all but a very tiny percentage of marine tanks. They are abundant in the ocean, but are one of the marine species that do not take well to life in captivity.

This species needs excellent water quality and a large tank, which many fishkeepers can provide. The problems arise because the fish are often reluctant to feed. In the wild they feed on sponges, but no aquarium with live rock can provide the amount of food they need. Some will take brine shrimp, *Mysis* and krill, but still seem to fall into decline. Most aquarists should steer well clear of the species if they see it in an aquarium store. The new reef gels may help them survive, as they are food made into a putty-like form that can be moulded and stuck into rock crevices for fish to feed on.

Purists may argue that a fish with such a low survival rate in captivity should not be imported in the first place. Marine fishkeeping is becoming incredibly advanced, however, and a better understanding of the species' requirements may lead to more success in the future.

Warning!

This species is not for beginners.

Acknowledgements

Natural Visions/Heather Angel 20, 64, 80, 91, 109, 121, 193, 227, 246, 250, Ian Took 219, Keith Sagar 207, 210, 213.
Aqua Press 10, 12, 27, 35, 44, 46, 47, 49, 51, 53, 54, 58, 65, 66, 67, 84, 94, 120, 123, 130, 137, 142, 148, 151, 159, 160, 165, 171, 172, 173, 174, 175, 176, 179 top right, 179 bottom, 182, 185, 187, 189, 195, 196, 200, 201, 223, 229, 234, 239, 241.
Ardea.com/Brian Bevan 126, Jean Michel Labat 56, 101, 145, 191, 225 186, Pat Morris 156, Ron & Valerie Taylor 214, 215, 251.
Getty Images/Darryl Torckler 202, 238.
Iggy Tavares 30 bottom right, 34, 41, 50, 52, 81, 100, 105, 147, 149, 150, 169, 170, 194, 197, 198, 205, 217, 218, 222, 231, 233, 237, 244.
Neil Hepworth 1, 8 bottom right, 9, 11, 14, 17 centre right, 17 bottom right, 19, 24, 25, 26, 39, 59, 68, 71, 73, 79, 83, 88, 89, 90, 92, 93, 96, 97, 102, 103, 110, 113, 115, 116, 117, 131, 138, 152, 161, 164, 204, 206, 209, 211, 230, 242.
N.H.P.A./Lutra 31, 42.

Oxford Scientific Films/Max Gibbs 3-4, 7, 8 centre right, 32, 33, 36, 37, 38, 40, 57, 60, 61, 62, 63, 69, 70, 72, 74, 75, 77, 86, 87, 95, 98, 99, 104, 106, 108, 111, 112, 114, 118, 119, 122, 125, 128, 129, 132, 133, 134, 135, 136, 139, 140, 141, 143, 144, 153, 154, 155, 157, 158, 162, 163, 167, 168, 177, 178, 180, 181, 184, 188, 192, 199, 203, 208, 216, 220, 221, 224, 226, 232, 235, 236, 240, 243, 247, 249, Peter Gathercole 48, 55, 76, 124, 146, 183, 245, Steffen Hauser 212, Zig Leszcynski 78, David Fleetham 2-3, 107, 248, 253.
www.photomax.org.uk 19, 82, 85, 45.
Science Photo Library/David Hall 252.
Zhou Hang 127.

Executive Editor: Trevor Davies
Project Editor: Kate Tuckett, Fiona Robertson
Design: OME Design
Production Controller: Nigel Reed
Picture Researcher: Aruna Mathur